AROUND THE WORLD IN 78 DAYS

AROUND THE WORLD IN 78 DAYS

Nicholas Coleridge

McGRAW-HILL BOOK COMPANY
New York   St. Louis   San Francisco
Hamburg   Mexico

First published in England in 1984 by William Heinemann Ltd.,
10 Upper Grosvenor Street, London W1X 9PA.

First U.S. publication in 1985 by McGraw-Hill Book Company.

1 2 3 4 5 6 7 8 9 DOC DOC 8 7 6 5

ISBN 0-07-011699-7

LIBRARY OF CONGRESS CATALOGING IN PUBLICATION DATA

Coleridge, Nicholas, 1957-
    Around the world in 78 days.
    1. Coleridge, Nicholas, 1957-   . 2. Voyages
around the world—1951-   . I. Title. II. Title:
Around the world in seventy-eight days.
G440.C734C65   1985   910.4′1   84-28891
ISBN 0-07-011699-7

Book design by Kathryn Parise

To my brothers
Timmy and Christopher

ACKNOWLEDGEMENTS

In addition to my publishers, I would like to thank the following people and institutions who aided and abetted my dash around the world. Louis Kirby, Editor of the *Standard*, who encouraged the expedition from the start and published dispatches. Also Keith Turner, Dick Garrett, Peter Jessup, Nigel Horne, David Johnson and Angus McGill of that newspaper.

Cunard Arabian Middle East Lines, especially Captain Womlgenuth and the crew of the *Aqaba Crown*.

Ben Line Steamers Company, especially Captain Donald Cowie and the crew of the *Benavon*, John Tan and Chan Yew Gin of their Singapore office, and their London Agents Killick Martin.

The Canada Line and Compagnie Maritime Belge, especially Captain Walter Marien and the crew of the *Dart Europe*.

Also Christopher Hodsoll, John St John, Napier Miles, Alistair Scott, Nicholas Allan, Sophie Hicks, Scott Crolla and Lloyds agents in London and Honolulu.

And finally Reginald Piggott who drew the maps.

CONTENTS

Acknowledgements   vii

Map 1   From London to Hong Kong   xii–xiii

Map 2   From Hong Kong to London   xiv–xv

Chapter

1 | *In which the author is inspired to embark upon a Great Adventure and sets about acquiring appropriate clothing for the journey.*   1

2 | *In which the author departs from the Reform Club on the stroke of noon and arrives in Paris by way of Folkestone and Calais.*   11

3 | *In which a large portion of Europe is covered by railway. And there are unforeseen delays in Brindisi and Piraeus.*   17

4 | *In which a painful visit is paid to an Egyptian dentist, and a new face joins the crew of the* Aqaba Crown.   31

5 | *In which the* Aqaba Crown *is further delayed while port-hopping down the Red Sea.*   45

6 | *In which nothing very significant happens in the Sudan. But all of it to the point.*   54

7 | *In which the length of Ethiopia's Red Sea coast is traversed by taxi. And mention is made of crocodiles and Cubans.*   61

8 | *In which a visit is paid to a house of small virtue. And a dhow is sought across the Arabian Sea.*   73

Chapter

9 | *In which the Arabian Sea is crossed by motorised dhow.*
      And time passes more sluggishly than elsewhere.   80

10 | *In which the whole width of India is traversed by rail-*
      way. And disparities emerge over the duration of the
      journey.   85

11 | *In which the Bay of Bengal is crossed by steamship.*
      And a visit is paid to a snake temple in Penang.   98

12 | *In which heels are kicked in the Republic of Singapore*
      while awaiting a cargo ship to Hong Kong.   113

13 | *In which the* Benavon *crosses the South China Sea.*
      And eyes are kept peeled for Vietnamese boat people.   124

14 | *In which an eventful stopover is made in Hong Kong.*
      And confusion is registered between China and Chel-
      tenham.   129

15 | *In which amnesia is experienced in a hotel bedroom.*
      And a hippy recherches à la contretemps perdu.   134

16 | *In which three and a half thousand miles of South*
      Pacific is crossed by freighter at the rate of five hundred
      calories per mile.   145

17 | *In which a yacht is sought in the marinas of Honolulu.*
      And a visit is paid to The South Pacific Man.   151

18 | *In which a voyage is undertaken from Honolulu to the*
      Golden Gate. And an insight gained into a particular
      state of matrimony.   161

19 | *In which an unexpected change of plan necessitates a*
      diversion. And mention is made of telephone sex and
      shoeshine boys.   167

20 | *In which certain incidents are related, only to be met*
      with on the San Francisco to Chicago railroad.   171

Chapter

21 | *In which the East Coast of the Americas is traversed with great haste and an excursion made into Canada.*   183

22 | *In which a voyage is undertaken in Arctic conditions. And the author expresses concern for his own sanity.*   188

23 | *In which a rescue is effected in the nick of time. And the Reform Club is at last revisited.*   195

24 | *In which it is proved that the author has gained nothing by this tour of the world, unless it be Contentment.*   198

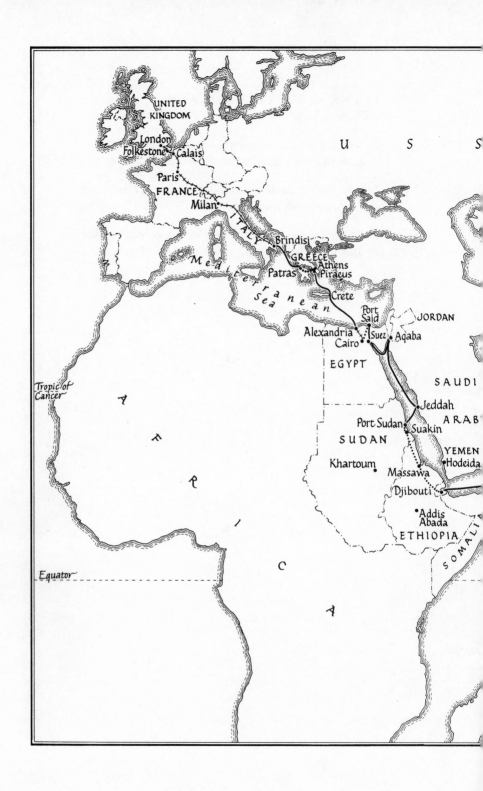

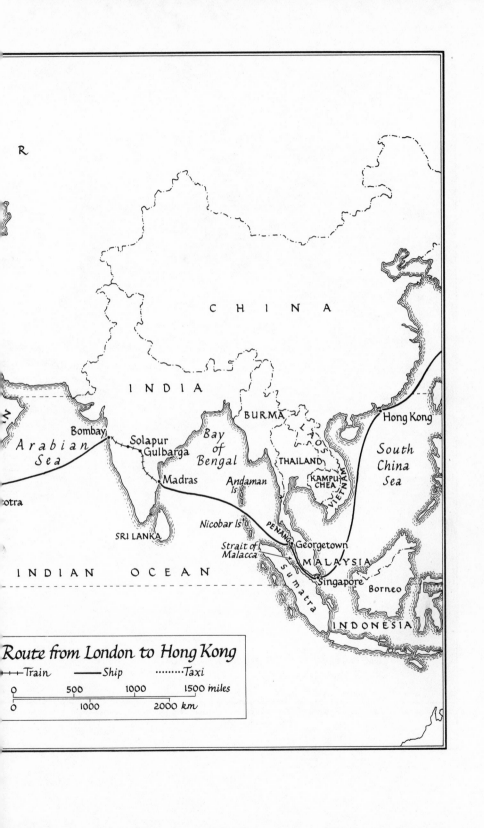

R

C H I N A

I N D I A

BURMA
LAOS

Arabian
Sea

Bombay
Solapur
Gulbarga
Madras

Bay
of
Bengal

THAILAND

KAMPU-
CHEA

VIETNAM

Hong Kong

South
China
Sea

otra

Andaman
Is.

Nicobar Is.

SRI LANKA

PENANG

Strait of
Malacca

Georgetown

MALAYSIA

I N D I A N   O C E A N

S u m a t r a

Singapore

Borneo

I N D O N E S I A

Route from London to Hong Kong

+++Train   ——Ship   ········Taxi

0   500   1000   1500 miles

0   1000   2000 km

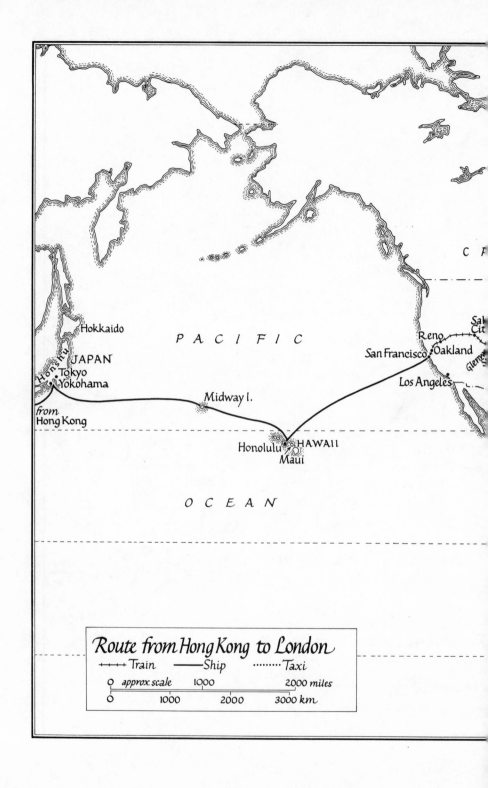

C

Sal
Cit

Reno

San Francisco · Oakland

Glenn

Los Angeles

Hokkaido

P A C I F I C

JAPAN

Honshu

Tokyo

Yokohama

from
Hong Kong

Midway I.

Honolulu · HAWAII
Maui

O C E A N

Route from Hong Kong to London
+++ Train ——Ship ········ Taxi

0   approx. scale   1000   2000 miles
0   1000   2000   3000 km

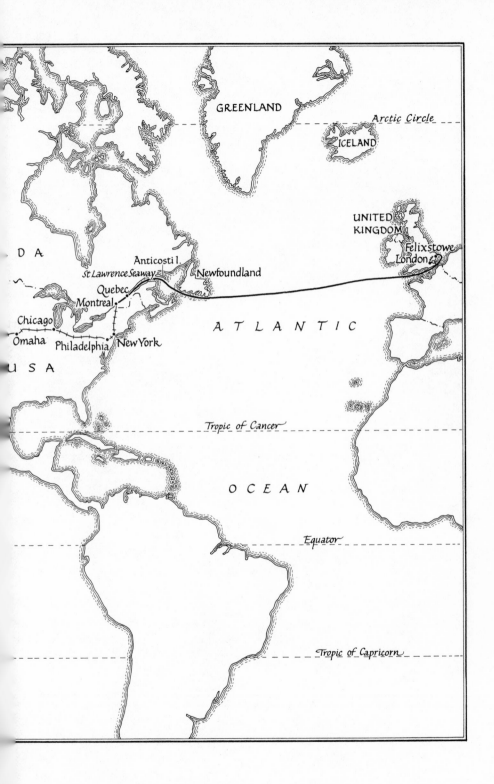

GREENLAND

Arctic Circle

ICELAND

UNITED
KINGDOM

Felixstowe
London

Anticosti I.
St Lawrence Seaway
Newfoundland

Quebec

Montreal

Chicago

Omaha
Philadelphia New York

U S A

D A

A T L A N T I C

Tropic of Cancer

O C E A N

Equator

Tropic of Capricorn

AROUND THE WORLD IN 78 DAYS

1 | *In which the author is inspired to embark upon a Great Adventure and sets about acquiring appropriate clothing for the journey.*

It is not known exactly how my prep school in Sussex came to own a copy of the film *Around the World in Eighty Days*; it was not a school with a vigorous cinema verité study group. But since the film was an item of school property, and furthermore cost nothing to show, it was consequently screened several times a term. I, for one, was never sorry when the opening frames returned us once again to Pall Mall and the Reform Club, where the phlegmatic Phileas Fogg was engaged in a gentle game of whist. For within a matter of seconds the celebrated wager was made: that it is possible to circumnavigate the globe, and return to the library of the Reform, in eighty days or less — that is, nineteen hundred and twenty hours, or 115,200 minutes.

Phileas Fogg made an improbable hero — the quintessential cool-blooded English gentleman who "did not give an idle look or allow himself a superfluous gesture." Even when he was formulating his portentous bet, he never made a wrong deal or played an injudicious card in his game of whist.

"But in order not to exceed the limit you must jump mathematically from trains into steamers, and steamers into trains," protested Fogg's partners at the card table. "You make no allowance for bad weather, contrary winds, shipwrecks, running off the track. What if Hindus tear up the rails! If they stop the trains, plunder the cars, scalp the passengers!"

"All included," replied Fogg, who, throwing down his cards added: "Two trumps."

Within an hour of formulating the wager, and pausing only to collect a small carpet bag and his French manservant Passepartout, Fogg was en route to Paris on a journey that took him halfway across Europe by sleeper to Brindisi, by steamer to Port Said and along the Suez Canal, down the Red Sea, via the Horn of Africa to Bombay, by rail across the subcontinent of India, by sea via Singapore to Hong Kong, steamer to Yokohama, across the Pacific to Honolulu and San Francisco, train from the West to the East Coast of America, cargo vessel across the Atlantic and then back to London and the Reform. To miss a single connection on the schedule meant certain failure, since every precarious leg of the journey was precisely timed to coincide with the next.

I have always found the story compelling, combining, as it does, a colourful and superficial adventure with a sense of purpose and the stimulus of deadlines; on every quay a rickshaw ticking over, primed to take a short cut through the spice market in hot pursuit of a departing train; "Catch the night mail to Madras and I'll triple the fare."

I have rarely been in a country without wishing I was in the next one. On holiday in Turkey I want to cross the border into Iran; once in Iran, Afghanistan suddenly seems feasible. I have a mania for maps, especially maps on which the ports sprout blue tentacles across the ocean connecting them with other, even more exotic marinas. And maps on which a tiny graphic of ferry is shown in the middle of the Arabian Sea, ploughing a course from Sharjah to Sarawak. Phileas Fogg, it seems to me, had made the ideal journey; gutting and filleting the globe with coolness and exactness, while employing every conceivable means of transport with the exception of aeroplanes — steamer, railway, dog cart, yacht, merchant vessel, taxi, elephant.

Except, of course, that he had made no such journey. *Around the World in Eighty Days* is Jules Verne's fiction, inspired by a contemporary fascination with the shrinking globe. A spate of newspaper articles was published throughout the middle of the last century, announcing how this or that number of days had lately been trimmed from the world schedule by the completion of the Rothal to Allahabad section of the Great Indian Peninsular Railway, or the San Francisco to New York Express. It was just such a calculation, in the *Morning Chronicle*, which provoked the impassable Fogg to quit the Reform Club for the back of beyond.

And so eighty days became the definitive ETA for a world tour by land and sea, though it remained entirely notional. The Jules Verne challenge had never successfully been completed, though two serious (and several half-hearted) attempts had been made. I found several journals of the battier shots in the basement of the London Library and their titles were not encouraging: *Once Was Enough — My Voyage Around the Tropic of Capricorn* by a spurious sounding ensign; and *Never Again,* being the tortuous travelogue of a ton-up teetotaller from Thurso with a hang-up about the Kurds.

But I was not dismayed. Because, by then, standing between the dingy bookstacks housing the detritus of failed expeditions, I had decided to make my own crack at the Jules Verne challenge. I would quit London in January 1984, that watershed year which seemed such a stimulus to leave town, and re-run the Phileas Fogg switchback around the Orwellian globe. Departing from the Reform Club at noon on Monday 9th January I would cut a swathe through three continents, zig-zagging the 33° latitude on a mission which could be compromised by a single sacred cow on the rails. If everything went well, however, without let or hindrance, I would endeavour to arrive back in Pall Mall by twelve o'clock sharp on Thursday 29th March.

One dull December afternoon I set off to buy a copy of Verne's book. It is temporarily out of print and the only edition I could find was a mock leather volume from the Harrods Childrens Department. A foreword from the series' editor proclaimed "Nobody today would undertake a tour of the world by land. They would choose to fly, which they might achieve in one tenth the time." When I got home I flicked through the chapter headings and transposed Fogg's route onto the useful little world map at the back of my pocket diary. It didn't look very long, being little more than five inches across, and I doubted whether I could spin the journey out for eighty days. I gaily divided the map into eighty fingernail size stretches, anticipating long halts for sightseeing and resting up. The Far East looked especially simple, being mostly lost down the spine of the diary where no cuticle could follow.

When I transferred to an atlas, however, I felt a creeping apprehension. Whole pages of ocean, coloured turquoise with barely an island to relieve the monotony, suddenly appeared between the Red Sea and Bombay. Entirely new countries, such as Malaysia and Djibouti, too insignificant to qualify for a pocket diary, jostled for space on the itinerary and demanded idiosyncratic visas. Fogg's route, it emerged, is not only of monstrous length but meanders through vir-

tually every no-go area on the map. Wherever there is now a terminal
visa problem, there went Fogg. And there, *ipso facto*, must go I.

It became clear quite early on that my progress would differ from
Fogg's in several respects. The balance of world travel has shifted so
thoroughly that some stretches of the route would be faster (Amtrak
from San Francisco to New York) and some would be considerably
slower. Where Fogg had been able to take a direct steamer from Brindisi
to Port Said, and then from Port Said to Bombay, I would be obliged
to deck-hop across the Mediterranean (Brindisi — Piraeus — Alexandria); then take a convoluted route down the Red Sea by ship and
overland (Port Said — Aqaba — Jeddah — Port Sudan — Ethiopia — Djibouti — Bombay). Passenger ships which used to run once
or twice a week, carrying tea planters and civil servants from South-
ampton to Bombay, Penang, Singapore and Hong Kong, have been
laid up for years or turned into floating casinos. Those ships which
still run do so once every three or four weeks, or whenever they have
a full hold of cargo, whichever comes sooner. There were obviously
going to be days of relentless travelling to achieve a particular connection, followed by days of enforced inactivity waiting for a delayed
ship. I needed, in fact, to devise an itinerary at least as fast as Phileas
Fogg's, but with rather fewer cards (apart from credit cards) to play
with.

When is Fogg's route not Fogg's route? A ruling was obviously called
for, and I seemed ideally placed to make it, being the *sine qua non*
of the expedition. Just because Phileas Fogg did not call at Port Sudan,
since he was able to cruise straight past it on the MV *Mongolia*,
sunbathing on the poop deck, should I be disqualified for disembarking
there? Not, I resolved, so long as I was always moving forwards, sticking
to his route as closely as possible and leaving my card in the key Fogg
pitstops: Brindisi, Port Said, the Horn of Africa, Bombay, Singapore,
Hong Kong, Yokohama, San Francisco and New York.

The political map has also changed colour. Phileas Fogg was able
to make two-thirds of his journey on British territory. I would pass
through nineteen countries of which only one, Hong Kong, still has
a British Governor-General. Some of the countries, furthermore, are
not known for their hospitality. Southern Sudan has been waging a
small-time guerrilla war for so long against the government in Khartoum that its causes and objectives, the relative strengths of the two
sides, even the names of the leaders, are obscure. In Ethiopia, the

north part of the country, where I would need to enter, is so thoroughly controlled by Eritrean rebels that the Ethiopian Embassy in London cannot issue visas. It seemed unlikely, too, that any good thing would come out of Djibouti — unless, *inshallah*, it was the crucial ship to Bombay. I had been told that some kind of trade still continued across the Arabian Sea on an *ad hoc* basis, providing you approached the right person with an appropriate mound of cash, but it is a tenuous link in the world chain. Apart from its shipping, Djibouti is famous as the biggest hole in the world, formerly French Somaliland, only kept in business as a truck park for overland containers and as an end-of-bin brothel for the French Foreign Legion.

I read the two previous serious cracks at the Verne challenge. Jean Cocteau had tried it in 1958, sponsored by the French evening newspaper *Paris Soir*, for whom he wrote an eccentric series of reports on the pleasures of opium dens in Malaya. By the time he reached the Far East he was suffering badly from hallucinations, sea-sickness and exhaustion and did a bunk to Hollywood to interview Charlie Chaplin.

The American humorist, S J Perelman, who was also an adviser on Michael Todd's *Around the World in Eighty Days* film, made two separate attempts; his first, with the caricaturist Al Hirschfeld in 1947, took them eighteen months, mostly spent dawdling over high-balls on hotel terraces. His second try, as quite an old man, and undertaken in stages with long rests in between with the clock turned off, was notionally more rapid but did not follow Fogg's route.

Both challenges, I realized, had made the same crucial mistakes. They had begun at too leisurely a pace, wasting precious days which could never be made up; they chose unsuitable Passepartouts as companions, who preferred a comfortable night's rest to catching a midnight connection; and they took too much luggage.

I would travel light. Following a tiresome accident in Iran, when I toppled off the Palace of Darius at Persepolis and was crushed beneath a loaded rucksack, I am now incapable of lifting anything much heavier than the heart of a globe artichoke. Although I was assured by friends that you need never carry anything yourself, and there is always a porter within tipping distance, they were manifestly wrong: porters are like policemen, petrol stations, pissoirs, and prostitutes, you can never find one when you need one. If a bearer became a necessity I would hire one, several if need be: Passepartout, Passeparthree and Passeparfour. But I would not take a trunk.

Instead I was loaned an Edwardian carpet bag by the Pimlico antique dealer Christopher Hodsoll, which I later supplemented with a small Lark overnight case from Harvey Nichols. They seemed a good choice of luggage since, when lifted, they balanced each other quite well; an equal weight in each hand. For people who like precise inventories of kit, this is a comprehensive list of everything in my two bags when I set off round the world, not counting the clothes I stood up in: five cotton shirts (all of them from Sam's of Burlington Arcade, Nathan Road, Kowloon, Hong Kong), four pairs of socks, four pairs of underpants, one long-sleeved cardigan, one spare pair of trousers, a pair of cotton pyjamas, swimming trunks, a Braun quartz travelling alarm clock, a Hitachi waterproof Walkman, eight cassettes, a Konica camera and some film, a hip flask, thirty passport photographs for visas, several maps from Edward Stanfords' in Long Acre, including a street plan of Bombay, a spare cartridge for my pen, Fodor's *Egypt*, a battery razor, an international plug with attachments for five continents, a Swiss army penknife, a compass, a bag of washing tackle including sea-sickness and malaria pills and a traveller's toothbrush, a bathroom plug, a collapsible Panama hat, Agatha Christie's *At Bertram's Hotel* and an inflatable globe.

As an insurance against attack I also took with me an excellent maplewood swordstick, hand-made by James Smith & Sons of New Oxford Street, which can be whisked from its scabbard in a matter of minutes after a great deal of huffing and puffing. The important thing with a swordstick is to remember to replace the blade in the correct way: swivel it back to front and it is jammed. Already, in the fortnight between buying the stick and setting off, I twice had to return to the shop, with its range of bespoke umbrellas and school canes, to have it released. James Smith & Sons had offered me a choice of two models: their short twelve inch blade, which I chose since it might conceivably come in useful for flambéing emergency kebabs over a cigarette lighter; or the more traditional thirty-six inch for spearing dropped railway tickets. The day after I made my purchase I read that a Glaswegian hod carrier in white tie and tails had been arrested in a St Vincent Street nightclub for wielding a similar device on the dance floor, but I felt sure that customs officials in Saudi Arabia, Ethiopia, Singapore and Honolulu would find nothing suspicious about my arrival at immigration with an offensive weapon.

Finding a tropical suit was less simple. There is, I learnt, little demand for this garment any more. The splendid travel shop, Alkit in Cambridge Circus, said to be the model for General Crutwell's emporium in Evelyn Waugh's *Scoop* where William Boot purchased his inflatable canoe, sterilising plant and portable humidor, closed down two years ago and is now a Wendy's hamburger haven. John Hatt, the tropical travel expert, said he'd heard good reports of a store called Tropicadilly in Piccadilly and suggested I try there. So one afternoon in the week before Christmas I made an inspection.

Tropicadilly appears to specialise in fine evening wear for site construction engineers in Accra, and an assistant commented on how distinguished I looked in a white waisted tuxedo. I thought I looked like a referee in a wrestling bout at Croydon's Fairfield Hall, and said so.

"The jacket is one hundred percent polyester," chided the assistant, inviting me to examine the material. If I stood underneath a shower, he said, wearing this jacket, I could lather it with soap and it would still keep its shape. This seemed to be the cue to have something made. Crolla, the awesomely trendy tailor in Dover Street, thought they could run me up a tropical suit in less than a week, but not a white one. "Stone," said Scott Crolla. "Stone is the hip tropical colour this year."

Five days later I was fitted out for a travelling suit of exceptional ingenuity. The lining is cunningly slotted with zipped compartments, exactly the right size to carry passport and visas, and there is a small reinforced breast pocket for trifling coins to distribute as baksheesh.

A sturdy pair of walking shoes seemed a good idea. In the past I have always travelled in flip-flops or whatever I happened to have on my feet at the time, being slightly contemptuous of sensibly-shod tourists perambulating the Acropolis and the Boboli Gardens; but in the circumstances there was a definite case for prudence. I went to New & Lingwood in Jermyn Street, where, that week at least, a display of long-necked swan spurs together with the more elaborate spur of the Queen's Royal Irish Hussars, had ousted the Eton slipper from their front window.

I sat down on a leather stool and awaited my turn. On the next bench a crotchety-looking customer with a face like a toasted teacake was being fitted for a pair of hand-made riding boots. The trouble was, he explained, his feet were so crippled with gout that he was in constant pain. The boots only made matters worse.

The problem seemed insurmountable. "The wider we make Sir's

last, the more Sir's toes spread," said the assistant. Then he had a brainwave. "I know, Sir. We'll place a small piece of felt, about the size of a penny piece, between Sir's uppers and his leathers. That should provide a little padding."

The crotchety customer with a face like a toasted tea-cake was not impressed. "I've never heard of such a thing in my life before," he said, as though he had just been commended a pair of moleskin moccasins or in-flight slippers.

"Don't worry, Sir," said the assistant, quickly scanning the fitting room for concealed microphones. "The pad will be quite invisible. It will be a secret between Sir and I alone." On that strict understanding the crotchety customer looked happier, though hardly convinced, and hobbled painfully away until his next fitting, leaving me to buy my pair of brown Church's walking shoes without the impertinence of eavesdroppers.

On Christmas Eve I rolled up my sleeve and braced myself for inoculations. My family doctor in Sloane Avenue produced a small three-colour map of the world and traced my route through vibrant epidemic zones: cholera yellow, polio pink and a luminous green malaria.

"I'm sorry to tell you," he said, disappearing behind his rattan screen with a selection of syringes, "that you need the lot: cholera, typhoid, tetanus, polio booster, gamma globulin, smallpox and yellow fever."

Yellow fever, he explained, as he expertly acupunctured my arm, was beyond his professional jurisdiction and required a visit to the London Vaccination Centre in Great Cumberland Place.

The London Vaccination Centre has an imposing hall around which, like a Christian Aid breadline, winds a queue of businessmen each clutching a five pound note and nervously flexing a bicep to help relax it. I joined the end of the queue for long enough to learn that these men were en route to the Gambia, to attend a conference on cold storage. Then, for some reason, I was diverted by a nurse into a distant waiting room, pending, she said, further instructions. And there, I am sorry to say, I was forgotten: abandoned with only a dog-eared tower of old *Apollo* magazines for distraction, each copy of which might have harboured any number of tropical diseases within its antique covers.

By the time I was retrieved, the Centre had emptied for lunch and I was given my cursory jab full of angst about the foolhardiness of my impending adventure.

Thomas Cook, who surfaced from time to time in Fogg's expedition, were helpful. Their travel mastermind, Edmund Swinglehurst, now in semi-retirement, examined my itinerary over lunch in Browns Hotel. He is a natural travel pundit, being a quarter Welsh, a quarter Yorkshire, a quarter Chilean and a quarter Japanese. Over the pudding I produced my pocket map and asked how long he predicted the journey would take. He thought for a long time. "Allowing a small margin for illness and delays — a hundred and twenty days."

I contacted Ladbrokes for reassurance and sent them my route. Phileas Fogg, of course, wagered twenty thousand pounds on the outcome of his trip, but then he wasn't subject to currency regulations. It took Ladbrokes' special risk broker, Ron Pollard, a week of deliberation over an atlas to compute the odds. In the end he gave me two to one against: a one in three chance of success, providing I travelled non-stop and luck was with me all the way.

Luck, I kept being told, is of the essence. "You could spend eight weeks in the Pacific alone, watching the sun go up and watching it go down again," said Paul Theroux cheerfully.

In the week before my departure I selectively settled my debts. I sent cheques in advance to the gas, electricity and telephone boards to forestall disconnection, and tipped a festering heap of parking tickets into the pedal bin. Christmastime in London always fills me with goodwill to all menus, so I made a succession of nostalgic farewell visits to favourite restaurants, many of them ethnic, sceptical whether their expensive repertoires would be available in their countries of origin.

Every time I turned on the radio it broadcast a tinsel medley of bad taste Christmas releases: "Grandma was run over by a reindeer" and "My turkey died of fright on Christmas eve". No doubt, by the time I reached Hong Kong, the same song would be freshly re-released in Kowloon for the Chinese New Year. The television stations meanwhile were busy unveiling their identical spring programmes: epic series about India in the hey-day of the Raj. "It looks like India's all the raj right now," chortled every channel's anchorman, pretending the pun was off the cuff. It would be strange missing so much television. For the first time since leaving school I became conscious of "the last *Top of the Pops*" and "the last *South Bank Show*" and then "the last supper" before setting off.

Never had my small, comfortable flat with its shuddering fridge and portable television at the foot of the bed seemed more alluring. My bathroom, with its range of exotic pine essences and hot tap that can be activated by the flick of a big toe, was unlikely to be matched from Addis Ababa to Bangalore. But it was too late for U-turns. While my contemporaries in London moved up in the world, I would move only sideways: faster, perhaps, but always in a circle.

2 | *In which the author departs from the Reform Club on the stroke of noon and arrives in Paris by way of Folkestone and Calais.*

Empires and dictatorships have risen and fallen, monarchs and dynasties been deposed, men have walked on the crust of the moon, dogs have played banjos on television, modern printing presses have almost been installed in Fleet Street, but none of these milestones have made much impact on the routine of the Reform Club. Its dignified Barry facade, less flashy than the stuccoed Athenaeum to the left of it, more elegant than the Travellers to the right, is identified only by a brass number plate, designed to deter passers-by from loitering on the club steps and petitioning their betters. Just inside the door, in their little lobby, sit the Reform's inscrutable porters, some of whom were bell boys at the Club when Phileas Fogg made his famous journey, then only beginning their century-long training which includes a decade in the services, a spell as a floor walker at Fortnum & Masons, a degree in psychology and an attachment to Interpol. None of the Reform's porters holds a rank below that of full colonel in the Secret Service.

The Reform Club possesses the most striking hall in Pall Mall; a cavernous room with a mosaic floor and circular gallery supported by twenty Ionic columns of red porphyry, above which a blue-painted rotunda. It was here that Phileas Fogg took his only exercise, wearing down the mosaic with measured step while a club servant cut the pages of *The Times*. Arriving at his Club each morning at exactly twenty minutes to twelve, he immediately repaired to the dining-room with its nine windows overlooking the garden, and took his seat at his regular table where a plate was awaiting him. His breakfast was always the same: "a boiled fish with Reading sauce, a scarlet slice of roast beef garnished with mushrooms, a rhubarb and gooseberry tart, and a piece of Cheshire cheese, the whole washed down with that excellent tea, especially gathered for the stores of the Reform Club." At forty-seven minutes past noon, Fogg would embark upon his marathon read of *The Times*, which lasted him until a quarter to four, when he would immediately move on to the *Standard*, which occupied him until dinner. Exactly how he killed seven and a half hours with only two newspapers is not known, unless he found some bizarre satisfaction in scanning classified advertisements. By general consent, he was the most punctilious and sedentary man in London.

Nothing of substance has altered at the Reform since Fogg's day. The Club's ice, formerly "brought at great expense from the American lakes to keep the drinks at a satisfactory condition of freshness", is now made in a fridge. The Club's sherry "served in decanters of a lost mould" is occasionally poured straight from the bottle. The two libraries, "one devoted to literature, the other to law and politics", have Cona coffee percolators on side tables and collecting tins in which to pay for each cup. A telex machine in the hall advises members about the latest cricket scores and the state of the weather, thus saving them the bother of looking out of the window. But otherwise it is unchanged. An open fire flickers reassuringly in the library, the cloakroom smells of bay rum hair lotion, and members are reminded, in politely worded notices, that combs and pumice stone are the property of the Club and should not be taken away.

A fire was flickering in the grate the morning I left the Reform. The library jostled with well-wishers who had converged from the four corners of London to see the back of me: editors, publishers, merchant bankers, fashion models, mannequins, stringers from the society journals, brilliant men of letters, several of whom were known to me by sight. All, no doubt, had their own motives for attending the reception and ensuring I left town. Some, I expect, coveted my desk at the office; others, perhaps, saw this as an opportunity to penetrate the smart set and forge new friendships. Most, having nothing better to do with their mid-morning, simply liked the idea of a free glass of dry sherry. In this they were not disappointed. The Reform Club sherry is of an aridity I would not find again until I reached the wilderness of Sinai.

A procession of Club servants moved like genies through the throng, delivering telegrams of bon voyage. Guests slunk off into corners to make private bets about whether or not I would return — and looked shame-faced when spotted because the odds were in double figures to one against. And all the while the Ormolu clock above the fireplace ticked relentlessly onwards, waiting for no man.

At five to twelve I rolled out my carpet bag. An old schoolfriend made a gracious speech in which he hoped I would never be more than two days' camel ride from a Bloody Mary. There were murmurs of agreement. And then the clock chimed twelve. It was time to leave. I was heading East and I might be some time.

The pagination of the British Rail Sealink timetable to the Continent meant that, although I quit the Reform Club on the stroke of noon, my train from Victoria to Folkestone did not depart until 1.58 p.m. I asked to be driven as slowly as possible to the station, to have a last cool look at London. The English Tourist Board had risen to the occasion and seemed to be staging a special pageant for my benefit: they switched the sun on as we drove along the Mall, a fierce January glare, and a platoon of guards in bearskins hung a right from Buckingham Palace. Ranks of gleaming black taxis were ticking over outside the Grosvenor Hotel, without a dent or a scratch between them, and the tariff clearly displayed on their glass partitions. Victoria Station, on the other hand, was a shambles. The British have spoilt all their main line stations and none more than Victoria. An ugly squat snack bar called "The Downs" has been slotted beneath the high Victorian Arch, ruining the proportions. Inside, it is a twenty-four hour flop house for all manner of wretches: Bengali women accidentally separated from their husbands in the station crush, without money or forwarding address; students attempting to pay for coffee with Deutschmarks, winos sheltering from the cold. Presumably the cafe's name, The Downs, is a tribute to the North Downs, which can be reached by train from Victoria Station; it might just as easily be a reference to the customers.

I found my seat on the train. The carriage was deserted: it looked like I was the only first-class passenger to Folkestone that day. And yet all the seats had "reserved" cards on them. One had my name on it; the other ninety-nine reserved travellers were nowhere to be seen. Just as the train was about to leave, a man carrying a harpoon bumped his way along the corridor.

"All these goddam chairs are reserved. I've bought a goddam first-class ticket and there's nowhere to sit."

He came into my compartment to examine the sticker on the window, which also said "reserved". He ripped it off the glass leaving a torn gummed strip, and held the notice up to the light. "Looks ancient," he said. "Could have been there for weeks." He turned it over and tilted it, perhaps hoping to find an incriminating watermark: the Caxton Press.

I suggested he either sit down anywhere or consult the guard. He looked at me as though I were mad. "The goddam guard? He's the last person who'll know." Then he bumped his way back along the corridor with his harpoon.

Everybody describes the scenery from Victoria to Folkestone, the mock Tudor mansions, Norman spires, allotments and hop fields: all the corny bric-a-brac of merrie England. They must have been visible from the other side of the train. From my window the weald of Kent was one huge school lacrosse field: goal posts and club houses, goal posts and pavilions, all the way to the white cliffs. But at least we were moving — not fast nor smoothly, but in the right direction and perfectly on time.

The ferry detailed to make the mid-afternoon Channel crossing was the *Horsa*, registered in London but demonstrably a French vessel: the purser's many incoherent announcements were given only in fluent Basque. In every other respect this was a thoroughly modern ship. None of the passengers did anything so old-fashioned as to stand up on deck watching the last of England melt into the fog. For one thing it was dark before we left port. Instead they jostled around a one-armed bandit — The Lucky Strike — and argued over who should next be allowed to feed it pound coins. As the voyage progressed, and the machine had still paid nothing out, the tension rose dramatically and with it the clamour to play next.

"There must be five hundred quid in there now," marvelled one voice.

"Yeah. The forty pound jackpot is bursting. There you are, you see, two out of three bells. Nudge, go on, you wally, nudge it."

I took my passport to the walk-in walk-out visa booth. It was manned by a brace of French immigration officers in belted raincoats who greeted me with a barrage of questions in their own language. I answered them as best I could: politely, firmly, monosyllabically and in

English. It seemed rather early in the journey to start speaking in tongues. Then they examined my passport and at once their attitude changed. For here were visas of a quality not often seen on the Folkestone to Calais ferry: Egyptian, Saudi and Jordanian, visas with postage stamps of palm trees stuck down on the page, visas in the shape of the Sphinx. The two officers turned the pages in wonder, marvelling at the calligraphy, though this was quite beyond their professional jurisdiction, then sheepishly applied their own modest seal.

I went to the bar and ordered a Cinzano.

"Going far?" asked the English barman.

"Only round the world," I replied.

"Good for you, squire," said the barman. "Ice and slice?"

In Calais I transferred to the French train waiting at the foot of the companionway. This was the "400 Express"; eighteen sleek chrome carriages recently brought into service by the International Company Wagons-Lits. The rolling stock was much taller than British Rail, and upholstered in day-glo orange. Through the glass door of my compartment I had already spotted a buffet car, the Super-grill, with a delicious display of hors d'oeuvres: pots of pâté de foie, crusty rolls and wooden bowls of crudités, composed of walnuts, gherkins, raddicio and cubes of fresh avocado.

The 400 Express has such good suspension that I did not notice when we started to move; I thought it was the train on the next platform that was leaving. Outside it was pitch black and impossible to see anything until we reached Calais Ville, a mile up the line, where the polychrome clock tower of the town hall looms behind the ticket office. Somewhere close by was the statue of the cringing burghers with the key to the city dangling around their necks, but this was no time for historical digression — the train was back on the move.

It didn't stop again until we reached Amiens. "Amiens, this is Amiens. Amiens, ici Amiens. Amiens, this is Amiens," announced a gloomy voice over the loudspeaker. "Amiens, ici Amiens." It sounded like some weird multilingual toastmaster introducing guests at an Amiens-only cocktail party.

Amiens, it transpired, was the only stop between Calais and the Gare du Nord. We arrived at 10.28 p.m., local time, and the next fast train to Milan with a connection to Brindisi didn't leave until 7.46

the next morning. I had a free night in Paris and had been invited to dinner by an English friend who works for British *Vogue*. She was in Paris to help style some photographs of the couture, and had booked me into the same hotel in the Rue de l'Université as their photographer, hairdresser and models, the Hotel Lenox. I took a cab downtown. Since I was last in Paris the whole city had somehow been turned into a single sprawling advertisement for Stella Artois; every awning, every hoarding, every pavement umbrella was plugging the lite lager. It was very rum.

The Hotel Lenox had fortunately been spared the Stella promotion. It is the very essence of a small chic Parisian hotel. The bedroom shutters were covered by ruched herringbone curtains, hot water gushed from porcelain taps and the barman instinctively knew that a Bloody Mary without the juice of a whole lemon is hardly worth the vodka it's shaken on. Over by the reception desk a jejune model was sacking her distraught German boyfriend over the telephone, then consoling herself with the hairdresser. People were passing around Polaroids and assessing the merits of the American Bruce Weber as a photographer of Olympic athletes. Girls in the restaurant sold posies of red roses and copies of Andy Warhol's *Interview* from table to table. For dinner that night I had a dozen raw mussels, delivered on a bed of crushed ice, followed by queue et oreilles de cochon grilles avec un confit de canard garnee choucroute — the tail and ears of a pig with a piece of preserved duck and cabbage. It seemed quite likely that I was going to approve of the big wide world.

3 | In which a large portion of Europe is covered by railway. And there are unforeseen delays in Brindisi and Piraeus.

I had arrived in Paris in the dark and it was still dark when I left. The 7.46 Express from Gare de Lyon to Milan is a commuter train, packed with brisk chartered accountants en route to the provinces to perform annual audits. They rifled through their briefcases and chortled over strip cartoons in *Le Figaro*, while I stared out of the window at the thick fog; it was impossible to see further than ten yards either side of the track. The train was wide and bourgeois — grey, paunchy, burghermaster carriages painted grey with sealed windows. At Dijon all the businessmen left the train so I had the compartment to myself. At Frasne we passed through a recent snowfall and a spray of white powder was thrown up behind the engine like the wash behind a speedboat. We were whistling through an alpine forest, every pine of which was taller than the Christmas tree in Trafalgar Square, when we reached the Swiss border. This was a surprise. I hadn't realised we were going anywhere near Switzerland, and yet here we were at Vallorbe with Swiss immigration officials fumigating the hand baggage and frisking the plumbing. Two Swiss nationals joined the train at Vallorbe: a sinister man in black leather gloves who refused to catch my eye and was self-evidently a lunatic, and a vendor in charge of a food trolley. In due course the vendor wheeled his trolley into my compartment offering drinks, Emmenthal sandwiches and chocolate, and I bought a bottle of Valaisanne bier, paying in French francs. Later in the afternoon the vendor made a second circuit. This time I chose a bar of Tobler-O-Rum chocolate and again offered French francs. The vendor held the ten-franc note at some distance from his nose as though he had never seen one before and wasn't sure what it was. Then he waved it contemptuously away. "Swiss franc or Italian lira only. You have no Swiss franc?"

I said of course I hadn't. We had only spent forty minutes in Switzerland and I hadn't left the train. As for Italy, we had crossed the border ten minutes before so I was unlikely to have accumulated a supply of inflationary lire. I referred him once again to my ten-franc note. Finally, and with great sighs of reluctance, he accepted it and produced a calculator. The exchange rate was so derogatory that I might have fared better with the Mexican peso.

We had crossed into Italy at Brig and I was pleased to be there. Domodossola station had orange trees growing on the end of the platform and there were ruined farmhouses ripe for Tuscanyfication on every hilltop. I was within a few chapters of finishing Agatha Christie's *At Bertram's Hotel* when we approached Stresa, with its forty-six tunnels; with each new clue a new tunnel appeared, so I sat on the edge of my seat in pitch darkness through the longest denouement in the history of detective fiction. And then, at precisely 5.31 p.m., we pulled into Milan Central Station, on time to the very minute after our ten-hour journey from Paris.

I had five hours to kill in Milan until the nightrider left for Brindisi so I hailed a taxi and headed uptown. What diversions, I wondered, could this renaissance capital of Italy's fashion industry offer the transit visitor at six o'clock in the evening? One thing it could not offer was warmth. The city was bitterly cold, its inhabitants shuffling about in fur boots and thick overcoats buttoned up to the neck. Some passersby, I am sorry to say, stopped to point and jeer at this English traveller, dressed only in a white tropical suit and Panama hat, vigorously swaggering his swordstick to raise his body-heat a few degrees.

I was pausing a moment over the pavement hot-air vents outside the Milan Hilton, allowing blasts of kitchen steam to defrost my ankles, when my attention was drawn by a display of fairy lights and what sounded like the maniacal laugh of a caged hyena. The Moira Degli circus was in town, recently returned, according to their playbills, from an acclaimed season in Buenos Aires. I wandered into the big top, glad to escape from the permafrost, and took a ring-side seat. An exotic ring mistress in top hat and fishnet stockings, who I took to be Miss Moira Degli herself, was choreographing a giant polar bear on a tiny see-saw. Until last year, my neighbour on the front bench told me, this circus had also boasted a pride of leopards. Then, during a matinee performance, the polar bear had suddenly been disturbed by something, gone berserk, turned on the leopards and killed them with a flick of its massive paw. It had been million lire publicity for the circus, my neighbour added in all seriousness.

Coaxing the bears back into their cage without further loss of life, the ring mistress introduced her grand finale — a full grown Indian elephant with a howdah strapped on its back. Would any bambini in the audience like to come forward for a ride? No one moved. The children had, perhaps, witnessed the circus' million lire publicity stunt. Would anybody else, then, hazard a ride? Circus personnel patrolled the front few rows, appealing for volunteers. Suddenly I felt myself being led forward, hoisted onto the great beast's back and, despite my protestations, paraded around the sawdust to a jaunty Latin cover version of Boy George's *Karma Chameleon*. And so, in less than forty-eight hours after leaving London, I had made an elephant ride: not, like Phileas Fogg, from the Indian village of Kholby to Allahabad, but merely around the ring at Milan's premier circus.

After the excitement of the big top, I realised there was only half an hour to go until the train left. I summoned a taxi. "To the station, per favore." The driver set off at impressive speed, wheelie-ing over the central reservation with much crunching of gears. I sat in the back hanging onto my carpet bag. Only when we reached the suburbs of Milan and the new ribbon development did I become anxious. Which station were we heading for?

"Stazione di S. Cristoforo," said the driver, accelerating towards Milan's answer to Burnt Oak or Ongar. I don't know why he imagined I wanted this obscure branch line rather than Milan's massive neo-Fascist terminal in the centrum, but it was too late for an autopsy. There was barely ten minutes left to catch the train. We turned on a gettone and burned back towards Milan Central, cocking a snook at the Carabinieri and ignoring red lights.

"You see, for you I am colour blind," noted my driver through clenched gold teeth. With two minutes to spare we pulled up outside the correct station. Propelling a bundle of clammy lire into the front seat, I sprinted to the platform. Really, it seemed altogether too early in the adventure for so much excitement. I caught the train as it began to move; the sleeping car attendant whisked my bags out of my hand and winched me aboard.

Inside all was calm. The sleeper was only half full and I had a first-class couchette to myself. The sheets on the bed looked crisp and fresh, and a basin in a cupboard pumped scalding hot water out of both taps. I hung up my jacket, changed into pyjamas and lay on the bed. Outside in the corridor my fellow passengers seemed to be holding a Chianti bottle party but I did not feel inclined to join in; I needed a clear head to make a tight ferry connection the following morning. The sleeping car attendant tapped politely on the door, passed me a bottle of bor-granco acqua fonte gajum and wished me a good night.

I had kept the blind open and the industrial outskirts of Milan were flying past outside. So I read *Life* magazine with one eye while estimating the speed of the train with the other: a complicated calculation based on the distance between telegraph poles multiplied by the exchange rate. It soon emerged we were going so fast that, on current progress, I would be back in London in less than a fortnight. With this cheering thought, I fell asleep.

In the morning, however, I opened my blind to an unwelcome surprise. The train was running along the Adriatic coast just south of Polignano a Mare and monstrous waves were breaking over the sea walls. The sky was as black as the economy and storm clouds were congregating. It did not seem an auspicious moment to be embarking on a long boat journey.

At ten o'clock we arrived at Brindisi, the last stop on the line before Lecce. It had taken Phileas Fogg sixty-seven and a quarter hours to get this far; I had done it in forty-six. Fogg, on the other hand, had had an easy leg ahead of him; a direct packet from Brindisi to Port Said. It is over a quarter of a century since this route was discontinued; I was obliged to make a criss-cross detour along the Mediterranean: Brindisi to Patras, Patras to Piraeus, Piraeus to Alexandria and then overland across Egypt to Port Said.

Directly opposite Brindisi station is the Libra Maritime Port Office and they were advertising, in their capacity as agents for Hellenic Mediterranean and the Limassol Line, an afternoon sailing to Patras. Inside, the office was decorated with posters of the Acropolis and a selection of chained biro pens, apparently pilfered from a bank since none of them worked. An unreliable-looking young man was in sole charge of the booking counter and I enquired about the storm. He was reassuring. *Atlas IV*, he said, would sail on time come hell or even higher water; nothing would delay its regular shuttle voyage to

Patras. He produced a cache of tickets and said, "You are student?" I replied, "No, I am not a student," so he marked me down as "student."

"Student is twelve thousand lire discount," he explained. "We will split it — six thousand lire each. In Brindisi," he added owlishly, "everybody is student. If you travel, you experience. Experience is learning. Learning is study. So you are student."

No sooner had I paid for this ticket than there was the most dispiriting development. Into the booking office strode a crumpled port prefect dressed up as a freshly cashiered admiral, with unpicked braid trailing down his lapels, and called for a small espresso. You did not need to speak fluent Italian to gauge the drift of his conversation. No ship would be leaving Brindisi that afternoon, it was far too rough. All sailings had been postponed for four hours and he anticipated longer delays.

I don't believe I libel Brindisi when I say it is a port almost without interest. The tourist office are fighting a valiant rearguard action, promoting the Tancredi fountain "where the Crusaders used to water their horses before embarking for the Holy Land", and "the centuries-old terminal column at the end of the Appian Way", but it remains a non-place, a nautical truck park, neither wholly Italian nor Greek. Menus are printed in both languages, and even the postcard merchants can find nothing to merit a photograph, so they sell pictures of more alluring beach resorts further up the coast. I took a walk along the windswept quay to inspect the monument to Italian seamen killed in both wars, then holed up in the only warm trattoria in town. It was not a happy choice; the waiter was supercilious and intent only on inflating the bill. I ordered an hors d'oeuvre and a small bottle of mineral water; he brought a saucer of olives and a two-litre flagon. He seemed pleased by this trick, but it was his first tactical mistake: he would regret the two-litre bottle. It became colder outside and began to rain. Ferry passengers sought shelter and coffee but were obliged to order a full meal, and as soon as they had finished eating were brought a bill. The choice was ordering more and more food or braving the storm. I, on the other hand, had my two-litre acqua minerale. I read a book and eked out my water like a dying man in the Kalahari Desert, while the waiter prowled round and round the table in metal heels, swatting his hands with a napkin and rueing his avarice.

The *Atlas IV* left port at midnight, five hours late. She was not an elegant vessel; she looked like a floating deep-freeze with funnels like

thermostats. All afternoon the hold had been filling up with juggernauts, forty of them at least, which backed with difficulty up the
gangway. At ten o'clock passengers were allowed to proceed into a
dingy customs shed, where they were further disorientated by regular
announcements from the purser. For some reason all announcements
about the *Atlas IV*'s time of departure were given in Greek time, an
hour ahead, despite the fact we were still on Italian territory. So when
the purser said we would now be sailing at 2400 hours, he was at odds
with the clock in the waiting-room which said 2300 hours. It is a
ridiculous system, guaranteed to cause confusion. The British contingent, who had by now identified one another, saw opportunities for
even greater muddle if the system was applied to air travel: Qantas and
Malev taking off from Heathrow by the Australian and Hungarian
clock.

Between passport control and *Atlas IV*'s berth were five hundred
yards of perilous harbour wall. Most of the port lamps had dead bulbs,
so passengers were obliged to make their way from one pool of light
to the next across broken pavements, deep puddles and tram lines. I
had been assigned a double cabin, a large room with bunk beds and
an open port hole. My room-mate was already installed, wandering
about in his shirt tails and a pair of boxer shorts. He was an American
with a deep fringe of brown hair who retired early to bed, where he
said nothing but wrote furiously in a spiral notepad.

In the stern were two large rooms: a dining area already monopolised
by the truck drivers and a saloon full of upright seats. Several passengers
had elected to sit up all night to save the small cost of a bunk. One
was a raunchy American student travelling with his morose French
girlfriend; he said he had two thousand dollars in American Express
travellers cheques for three weeks in Greece but wouldn't waste two
thousand five hundred lire on a bed.

As soon as the *Atlas* left port she began to roll, lurching from side
to side and frisbee-ing plates all over the galley. I bought a small coffee
and studied the conditions of conveyance on the back of my ticket.
They were not designed to instil confidence in a passenger about to
chance his arm on a cruel sea: this was the most churlish liability
clause I had ever read.

"No liability is accepted for death or for any other personal injury
suffered by the passenger, his luggage or his property when the events
arise from:

1. Shipwreck, collision or stranding even caused by an error in navigation, the master, crew, pilots or other servants in the management of the vessel.
2. Fire.
3. Perils, danger or accidents of the sea or other navigable waters.
4. Act of God.
5. Act of war.
6. Act of public enemies.
7. Arrest or restraint of princes or rulers.
8. Quarantine restrictions.
9. Strikes, lock outs or stoppage of labour.
10. Riots and civil commotions.
11. Saving or attempting to save life.
12. Latent defects not discoverable by due diligence.
13. Suicide, drunkenness or disappearance of the passenger during transport."

As we reached open sea the listing intensified. Metal doors banged along the corridor, most of the passengers retired green-faced to their cabins, and the only constructive activity was a game of Old Maid being organised by the British contingent.

I became very anxious about our schedule. Two hours after leaving Brindisi we were still less than five miles from the heel of Italy, evidently making little headway. And yet it was crucial I reached Piraeus by eleven the following evening because that was when the *Expresso Egitto*, an Italian ship of the Adriatica line, left for Alexandria. To miss the crossing to Egypt would be fatal since it is, at best, a fortnightly service and the next boat not scheduled until February. I decided to consult the captain. I found him in his cabin with a litre bottle of Metaxa, having left the fate of the ship in the capable hands of his first lieutenant, and he poured me a measure into a tooth mug. I explained my problem in classical Greek and asked what steps he was taking to make up for lost time. He was most affable and enquired after the health of the Princess of Wales, but was not encouraging professionally. While the storm persisted he could only proceed at half speed. It was possible we would be six hours late by the time we reached Patras. I rejoined the British contingent at the card table in despondent mood. "Ha ha, *old maid!*" hooted the doctor from Marlow as his wife was left holding the Queen of Spades.

By dawn the storm had subsided a little. We were sailing about two miles off the Greek coast past the Island of Kerkira and the sky was very grey. Those passengers who had surfaced from their cabins were even greyer and few chose to join the British contingent for breakfast of boiled eggs, Ziyada coffee and feta cheese. By lunchtime we still seemed to be sailing along the Greek coast past the Island of Kerkira and the sky was still very grey. In fact it was now Lefkada Island we were passing with almost inconceivable lack of haste. From the dining-room window it wasn't possible to tell whether we were moving at all, or simply drifting with the current in the Adriatic. After lunch I paid a second visit to the captain whom I found on the bridge varnishing a pair of water skis. In the summer, he said, he drove a water-ski boat in Corfu. Had I visited the beautiful island of Corfu? I said I had but didn't want to make a detour now: I was jumpy about Patras.

"Oh Patras, Patras, Patras," said the captain. "Relax. Keep your hair on." (This was an expression he had picked up from English holidaymakers in the summer.) We would arrive when we arrived, not before, he philosophised orientally.

We arrived at 8 p.m., not before. The crossing had taken twenty-one hours. The *Expresso Egitto* was scheduled to leave Piraeus in three hours and Piraeus was two hundred and sixteen kilometers away. To make matters worse the Greek police had just carted off the ninety passengers' passports in a blue airways holdall. The passports took fifty minutes to process and a further fifty minutes to distribute. A police-man wearing dark glasses, though it was now pitch black outside, declaimed the surnames and countries of origins one by one for col-lection: "Espanol — Mr Domecq", "Japanese — Mr Kwai", "Ukay — Mr Coleridge". No passport could be returned until the one before had been claimed; most passengers had their names called several times before they recognised it as their own.

There was barely an hour left until the vital connection. I shared a taxi with an American marine biologist and his Japanese girlfriend and we burned into the night. The taxi driver had demanded enough drachma to put a deposit on a small house in Fulham, but this was no time for cheeseparing. It was conceivable, just conceivable, that the *Expresso Egitto* had also been delayed by the storm and postponed her sailing. The taxi driver was a huge man, his broad shoulders filled the entire front seat of the cab. And he drove very fast. He accelerated into corners and accelerated out of them: his strongest suit was the hairpin bend. The Japanese girl, Ritsu, was rather frightened and hung onto Mike who consoled her in a private language of their own; they had been travelling together for two years, since Ritsu's eighteenth birthday, and had evolved a singular dialect that was part American, part Japanese and part Korean. Mike was thirty-five and podgy and difficult to place. He had been brought up in Alaska but had travelled continuously for fifteen years. And yet the time he claims to have spent in each country didn't add up. If you mentioned Hong Kong he said "Sure, I was in Hong Kong for three years"; "I was in Shanghai eighteen months"; "I spent four years in Istanbul at the Yacht Club"; "I was living in Djibouti nine months" and so on. By rights he should have been at least seventy.

We arrived in Piraeus at one in the morning. The port was almost deserted, the Adriatica office manned by a callow youth sucking pistachio nuts.

"The *Expresso Egitto*," I demanded, rapping the counter. "Has she sailed?"

"Not until eleven, sir," said the callow youth. He looked surprised by my manic questioning. "Eleven tomorrow evening."

I had been misled by a 1983 itinerary. The relief was enormous. Athens suddenly seemed a marvellous place; I loved Piraeus, I loved Patras. We were too revved up by the journey to set about finding hotels, so we searched for dinner instead. In a side street was a restaurant selling whole baby chickens on a rotary spit. Mike liked the look of it; there were similar places in Manila where he'd spent three years.

Mike and Ritsu met as penfriends; they had both had penfriends all their lives. Mike first came to England, aged sixteen, in pursuit of another penfriend: Rosie, the daughter of the ranger of Gainsborough Forest. Mike's father had driven him to Archangel airport on his sixteenth birthday and pointed to a map of the world on the terminal wall. The map was dotted with light bulbs, indicating international airports, and Mike could have a return ticket to whichever one he chose. Mike needed no second invitation, no sir, and by that afternoon he was flying to Heathrow.

He landed in London on Christmas Eve and decided to pay a surprise visit on Rosie. He had her address in Lincolnshire on a scrap of paper, but no telephone number. So he changed into his Alaskan boy scout uniform and hitchhiked up the motorway. The journey took seven hours but by midnight he was standing outside a darkened house in the middle of the forest. He hammered on the door until it was answered by a middle-aged woman wearing a dressing-gown. Mike introduced himself and asked to speak to Rosie. Rosie, said her mother, was asleep, but he was welcome to stay for Christmas if he had made no other plans. Every bed in the house was full so Mike was given a blanket and a sofa to sleep on. He woke up at dawn, excited by the prospect of at last meeting Rosie. He did not have to wait long. Rosie appeared at breakfast with her Chinese penfriend, Chang, who it also emerged was her boyfriend. Chang wore Chinese naval cadet uniform and never left Rosie alone; Mike wore his Alaskan boy scout rig and played gooseberry. That is the trouble with penfriends, said Mike, you never know when you're being two-timed.

Ritsu nodded in agreement, she too had had a nasty experience with a penfriend, a Greek boy. He had written her a letter a month, rather formal and dull, until his seventeenth birthday. Then he had suddenly started mailing foul pornographic descriptions of exactly what he would like to do to Ritsu. Ritsu had found it very distasteful. She and Mike intended to take a taxi to the boy's address and stare up at his block of flats through the window.

After dinner we were strolling in the direction of the taxi rank when we spotted a late-night cinema. It was showing the latest James Bond movie at 3 a.m. and Mike was keen to see it; he had lived in Nassau for two years where parts of it had been filmed. So we bought tickets and sat in the stalls with a score of Greek youths, who found the oddest things to laugh at in their subtitles. At five in the morning we drank coffee and went our separate ways. It wasn't a minute too soon; I was falling rapidly in love with Ritsu and she was too delicate to make a plausible Passepartout.

I didn't begrudge my extra day in Athens. I had a boat ticket in my pocket and time on my side until my next deadline in Port Said. I could afford to idle away a few hours in sightseeing and resting. Besides, I was pleased to be back in Athens. The orange trees in Syntagma Square were covered in blossom and I bought an air mail edition of *The Times* from a kiosk and sat down at a table in the sun. The paper carried an article by the Labour M.P. for Lewisham West, Christopher Price: a spirited defence of the Greeks against the prejudice of the new right. The Greeks, wrote Mr Price, had become the new Jews of Europe, always wrong, never to be taken seriously and pretty disagreeable types into the bargain. Ever since the battle of Navarino there had been an English Establishment preference for the Turks. Now, over the partition of Cyprus, the Greeks in transit at the EEC and over the Elgin Marbles, it was being translated into a political tenet. It is over the Marbles, contended Mr Price, that the full flood of prejudice flowed free. The nub of this argument is that the present Greeks are not proper ones; they are a bunch of orientals who have somehow wheedled their way into Europe. He quoted Godfrey Barker in the *Daily Telegraph* as an example of new right thinking: "The truth, more sadly, is that this illiterate, resigned, enfeebled race, for two millennia a shadow of past Periclean glories, has blindly acquiesced, where it has not destroyed itself." According to this new gospel, the English are the Athenians now, and we alone worthy to keep the Marbles.

I scanned Syntagma Square for traces of illiteracy, resignation and enfeeblement. Two waiters were playing a spirited game of handball with an orange, and every old age pensioner in Athens was perambulating the Square selling national lottery tickets. On the Acropolis itself someone had spray-painted "We've lost our marbles", but it seemed more likely that this was English graffiti than Greek. And yet it is certainly true that Turkey several years ago superseded Greece as a destination for travellers. It seemed ages since anyone mentioned Greek temples; they choose to inspect the classical sites along the Anatolian coast instead.

In the evening I looked up an English friend, Bruce Clark, whom I had known at Cambridge and now works for Reuters newsagency in Athens. He took me to a tea shop where we drank vodka and ate cake. Later we went to his flat, with its unrestricted views of the Agora and he played me rembetika records. He said that the first ten times he had listened to rembetika it had left him unmoved, but the next ten times it had sent a thrill through him and now he listens to little else. There is a vogue for rembetika in Greece at the moment: a lilting oriental wail, played mostly on the bouzouki, which was originally imported from Smyrna in 1922 after the Anatolian disaster. The expelled Greeks had lived in a ghetto in Piraeus, smoking wargilehs and crooning rembetika. A recent film, also called *Rembetika*, had turned a cult into a national craze and now every taxi driver in Athens broadcasts rembetika on his cassette machine.

Another singular development, said Bruce Clark, was the huge number of Athenian transvestites. In Athens homosexuality always for some reason takes the form of transvestism, the two being virtually synonymous. In recent years scores of transvestites have begun to haunt the Athens to Piraeus road, near the Luna Park, and local residents were becoming hostile. Another recent film, *Angelos*, in which the father of a transvestite tears his son's stomach to shreds with rusty scissors in shame, had fanned the hostility.

Bruce Clark was equivocal about the prevailing climate of anti-Hellinism; having lived in Athens most of his life and speaking the language he was naturally disposed to side with the Greeks. But he didn't care either way about the Elgin Marbles; he quoted Byron with relish: "I detest antiquarian twaddle. Let's have a swim." His hobby is collecting Tintin books; he has nineteen foreign language editions of *The Crab With The Golden Claws*, including Urdu.

On the wharf at Piraeus, where the *Expresso Egitto* was receiving passengers, all was in turmoil. Huddles of Egyptians were waiting to embark with the booty from a weekend's shopping in Athens; their hand baggage included three-piece suits, Venetian blinds and kitchen sinks. One man had a rickety monkey on his shoulder which he insisted was less than two years old and should therefore travel free. Gangs of perspiring stevedores frantically winched corded boxes, barrels and bales of coarse cloth into the hold; crews of riggers made fast innumerable oil drums, office equipment and lengths of galvanized pipe. On the gangway, teams of longshoremen drove Land Rovers on board, climbed out through their windows and braced the wheels with wooden chocks.

The *Expresso Egitto* was on the last leg of a cruise from the Zattere in Venice and was well supplied with pasta. The menu in the self-service coffee shop listed six varieties and nothing else. But she was a good ship and well stabilised; it promised to be a comfortable thirty-six hours.

The only available cabins were two-berth and my room-mate had arrived first; his seven large trunks covered the entire floor space and both bunks. His overnight bag was perched precariously in the basin. The whole cabin, furthermore, smelt like a flower shop: a flower shop stocked with dead hyacinths. It did not take long to discover the source.

"You have girlfriend, wife, mother or sister, meester!" Ali was opening one of his trunks. "They like Egyptian perfume for present?" The lid of the trunk displayed rows of tiny bottles and phials of oriental scent: essence of mango blossom, rose petal and le must de water melon. Ali was a travelling scent salesman.

I was not sure that I could survive a thirty-six-hour sales pitch so I threw myself on the mercy of the purser. He was most understanding, especially when a trifling financial token of my appreciation changed hands, and found me a single cabin with a porthole of my own.

The *Expresso Egitto* was a large ship, with two hundred passengers at least. Half of these were Egyptians who did not leave their cabins throughout the entire voyage. From time to time you glimpsed them through an open door, mummified from head to toe in blankets or cooking noxious dishes with flagrant disregard for the fire regulations. The European passengers congregated in the San Basilio Bar or the adjacent card lounge where the British contingent were getting up bridge rubbers and pelmanism tournaments. The only source of irritation was a circular tape of piped music which broadcast only three songs. The most irritating was a disco number with such a repetitive lyric it was bound eventually to drive you mad, like a fiendish Chinese water torture. The lyric was:

"He said Captain, I said what?
He said Captain, I said what?
He said Captain, I said what?
He said Captain, I said whaddaya want?"

The European passengers came in all shapes and sizes. A party of Dutch students, with bicycles in the hold on which they intended pedalling to Khartoum, lay on their backs and performed cycling exercises to tone their calf muscles. At dinner that night in the dining-room a couple of Ipswich businessmen invited me to join their table. They were good ambassadors for Mrs Thatcher's Britain: the proprietor of a road haulage company which delivers microfilm and surgical instruments all over Europe, and an insurance broker with a cold. I enjoyed their company; they were well travelled and open-minded. Their pastime was writing letters to newspapers. Jeffrey, leaner faced than Brad, had already had several letters published in county papers, all on the subject of road haulage. Now he was aiming for bigger things; his ultimate goal was the *Daily Telegraph* but that was the Machu Picchu of correspondence columns. And he wouldn't be satisfied merely with his letters being printed, Jeffrey wanted nothing less than a correspondence, letters of reply, a full blown dialogue in hot metal. The trick, he believed, was to introduce a slightly grey area of dispute into your letter, a bait on which potential correspondents could nibble. They would write a letter back and then, bang, with your superior debating skills you nailed the opposition. Politicians, said Jeffrey, did this all the time.

After dinner we were drinking coffee in the bar when a blast of Mozart caught us unawares. "Ah, the Jupiter Symphony," said Jeffrey. The classical lobby, who had been petitioning the barman all afternoon, had won their skirmish against disco Muzak. We had passed Cape Sideon and the coast of Crete during lunch; now there was nothing but sea in every direction. There was quite a warm breeze blowing from the south-west. A few passengers strolled about on deck in cardigans or stared mournfully over the rails at the wash. By moonlight the Mediterranean appeared purple, the deep Berber purple of North Africa.

We put into Alexandria ninety minutes ahead of schedule, then bobbed at anchor for several hours while the port police completed their formalities. We were moored alongside a Chinese vessel, the *Xinfeng*, and watched the customs officers cross in a small launch clutching briefcases of Egyptian currency. They took up residence in the dining-room where several card tables were commandeered as immigration, visa and currency exchanges; every passenger being required to convert the equivalent of one hundred and fifty dollars into Egyptian pounds. In return they were issued with numerous receipts, each authenticated with expensive stamps payable in foreign currency. Since there was no way of telling, say, how many Austrian schillings were needed to achieve an acceptable threshold of Egyptian pounds, the procedure was interminable. The British contingent was particularly censorious.

"It is only to assist you," said the chief of police enigmatically. "Elseways you'll be pestered by the black market."

It struck me that Phileas Fogg was never subjected to currency regulations throughout his entire journey, travelling only with twenty thousand pounds in cash and letters of credit from Barings Bank in his carpet bag. Over the loudspeaker an Egyptian voice reminded us to register our "cryptic reading matter" before disembarking.

By noon we had been assigned a berth on the quay; we had been waiting for a Russian liner to sail for Odessa. Customs were laborious and took another ninety minutes to clear. But by lunchtime I stood outside the port compound, a free man in Africa with both feet firmly planted on *terra firma*.

4 | *In which a painful visit is paid to an Egyptian dentist, and a new face joins the crew of the Aqaba Crown.*

I was pleased to be in Egypt. The dusty streets around the port were jammed with mule carts and counters of Alexandrian oranges and carpenters hammering on chairs and urchins peddling horoscopes. Goats grazed in dustbins and huge stems of bananas were everywhere suspended from meat hooks. There must have been a paper chase in the town earlier that morning, because the streets were ankle deep with little scraps of waste paper, which swirled about in the traffic like totaliser slips at a race meeting.

I hailed a bright orange taxi with rounded wings like a bumper car, and asked for the station. We drove along the Corniche at gratifying speed, past crescents of white-painted apartment blocks reminiscent of Nice and sidewalk cafes with potted plants staking out claims on the pavement. Alexandria was once the seat of government during the summer months and the Corniche is dotted with former embassies and ministries falling into neglect. The station is large and colonial, a legacy of British occupation, with an elaborate portico and columns sculpted to resemble palm fronds. My taxi driver had followed me into the booking office, and when it emerged that my train to Cairo would not leave for two hours, suggested that I might like to inspect Pompey's pillar and the Catacomb of Kom El Shuqafa.

Pompey's pillar, which as a matter of fact has nothing whatever to do with Pompey and was erected by the Roman prefect Posthumus in honour of the Emperor Diocletian, was part of the once-splendid temple of Serapis. Some historians contend that it originally formed part of a portico of four hundred columns, but frankly this is unlikely since there is no trace of the other three hundred and ninety-nine columns, nor even of one other column. Other authorities claim Pompey's pillar was part of the famous royal library of Alexander the Great, but this too is something of a kite since the pillar in question post-dates it by several hundred years. It stands on the crest of a mound of rubble, surrounded on all four sides by structurally unsound Alexandrian tenement blocks, from which scores of "guides" appear at the first whiff of a tourist and bawl conflicting dates. Once I had absorbed all that is known, and rather more than is known, about the chronology of Pompey's pillar, my taxi driver exclaimed "Half time" and bore me to a Pepsi stall which he had no hesitation in recommending.

The Catacomb of Kom El Shuqafa is no less vexing to antiquarians who are once again in the dark. A guide, on receipt of a few piastres, led us down a winding staircase into a deep chamber and indicated a crater in the ceiling.

"The catacomb," he said, "was not discovered until 1900 Ay-Dee, which is eighty-four years before. It was discovered when a donkey fell through that hole in the ceiling."

On behalf of the British contingent I felt honour-bound to enquire after the fate of the donkey.

"It was killed, of course," said the guide. But then he added, "quite painlessly."

From time to time during this sightseeing expedition, whenever we passed a traffic cop, my driver had wound down the window and slipped a green 25 piastre note into the policeman's hand. This was the ancient Alexandrian custom of greasing the palm that directs you, and did not apparently strike him as an imposition. My taxi driver just grinned and hooted anything that moved. On the return journey he said, "Forgive me mister, I have a favour to beg of you. Write me a citation please." He produced existing citations from the glove compartment: picture postcards of the *Sea Princess* on which cruise passengers had inscribed "To Ahmet. Great driving. Marjorie and Bob."

"*Sea Princess*," chuckled Ahmet. "The love boat." I wrote something appropriate on a postcard of Brindisi and he added it to his collection. Then he dropped me at the station.

The train journey from Alexandria to Cairo crosses the fertile plain of Northern Egypt and takes three and a half hours. I had booked a first-class window seat and ate my way through a packet of Matinee biscuits while the countryside slipped by: flat, lush fields bounded by irrigation canals, from time to time relieved by a solitary minaret or an intricately tiled garage or a dovecote shaped like a tandoori oven. Peasants in home-spun dbjallahs went about their humdrum task of scything sparling, or embarked upon epic treks to some distant market to sell a cucumber. The conductor on the train distributed glasses of tea and boiled sweets.

I didn't really want to go to Cairo, it was an irksome detour, and it would have been much simpler and pleasanter to take the coast road direct to Port Said. But the Sudanese government had declined to issue a visa in London, referring me instead to their consulate in Cairo. Obtaining a visa, their London representative had assured me, was merely a formality; it would actually be more convenient for me to collect my visa in Egypt than to plough across London to Cleveland Row, he said. So I had decided to spend one night in a small hotel I know of near the Khan El-Khalili Bazaar, on a small square formed by three mosques: the Mosque of El Akhmar, the Mosque of Kalaun and the Mosque of Sultan Barkuk. It is not a very comfortable hotel, the El Hussein, but I like the area. At night the square is lit by nephta flares and it is amusing to sit on the hotel balcony, with its wooden balustrades, and listen to the sound of car horns. The bedrooms have gaudy tapestries of Mecca on the wall, and enormous Toshiba fans, purchased under some earlier regime and never unpacked. They stand in the corner of every room, between the basin and the wardrobe, still wrapped in polythene and without plugs.

After dinner, as is my custom in a strange city, I took a taxi to the smartest hotel and wandered about in the lobby. In Cairo the smartest hotel is the Nile Hilton, not to my mind a very stylish place but it accepts credit cards so the drinks are free. I was quietly bolting a Bloody Mary and flicking through a copy of *Time* magazine when an Ethiopian gentleman brought his walking stick down on my table with a resounding thwack. "It's disgusting," he said. "It's obscene."

I assumed he was objecting to my drink on theological grounds so I smiled apologetically and said something to the effect of "I'm so sorry. But I've been travelling all day, I do apologise, we Christians are so lax."

But it was not my Bloody Mary which had enraged him, it was my *Time* magazine.

I had not studied the cover very closely when I bought it, but now

I could see that it was indeed highly emotive. The African continent had been superimposed with a black woman's face and she was turning away in shame. The Island of Mozambique was suspended somewhat unattractively beneath her nose. The cover line said "Africa's woes: coups, conflicts and corruption."

"It is, it is . . ." the Ethiopian was temporarily at a loss for words, "it is a high school essay. No, it is not a high school essay, it is an *elementary* school essay." He pulled another stool up to the bar and impounded my magazine for his own censure. "It is, quite simply, lies," he said. "A pack of lies from beginning to end."

I hadn't read the article at the time, so was in no position to form an opinion. But the Ethiopian didn't know that, so I said I thought it made a number of points worth making, though it doubtless went too far. The Ethiopian looked furious so I added, "Typically American and over the top, of course." The Ethiopian was thirty-four and had mad curly hair; he was in import/export and was not resident at the Nile Hilton. Like me he was simply wandering about in a suit, drinking above his station. As soon as he left I read the offending article. It was certainly damning. Written in the aftermath of the Nigerian coup it portrayed the modern African as a despondent imbecile, craving Western goods he could not afford and was not prepared to work for, loafing in the towns while the countryside ran wild, listening to transistor radios until the batteries ran out since they could not be replaced. Nothing, said *Time*, was possible without baksheesh, or dash, or chai, or bonsella, or any of the other dozen African euphemisms for bribes. Even in the poorest African capitals, government officials could be seen in convoys of Mercedes Benz limousines, scattering cyclists and pedestrians as they swept past. Owning a Mercedes is such a potent African status symbol that a new Swahili word has been coined to describe the elite that drives them: *wabenzi*, literally, men of the Mercedes Benz.

The Ethiopian was outraged, but he had a theory. He believed that the American journalists who sat in their big offices in New York and wrote these articles were not writing about Africa at all. "They are writing about the American black, beating the American black with an African stick. They want to show that the black man can't run anything himself and needs the white American to rule him. That is their intention. They are uptight. They don't write in their magazine the good things about Africa. They don't write that nobody in Africa has psychological problems. Not one single African is in psycho-ther-apy. Name me one African in psycho-therapy," he challenged me.

I conceded that I could name no African in psycho-therapy.

"Anyway, where are you going in Africa?" he asked.

I decided not to mention Ethiopia, in case he felt compelled to furnish me with letters of introduction, so I outlined my proposed route through the Sudan. I said that I would pick up a visa tomorrow morning and arrive by sea next weekend.

"A visa for Sudan in one day?" The Ethiopian laughed cryptically. "One month more likely and you will need baksheesh."

There are two major drawbacks to the Hotel El Hussein: the mullahs allow no strong liquor to be sold within sight of the mosques, so the hotel is dry, and the 3 a.m. Muezzin call is quadraphonic.

"Christ, will somebody turn that racket *off*!" The British and American residents, spending their first night in Cairo, threw back their shutters and slammed their suitcases.

"*Allah. Allah is great.*" The Azan persisted in the face of infidel objections. "*There is no other God but Allah . . .*"

A green neon crescent, perched on a minaret, illuminated the whole square and a lame hound barked at this surrogate moon. All over the city, from the tombs of the Caliphs to the City of the Dead, the howling was taken up by other dogs, straining at the leash. There is little rest for the nasrani at the Hotel El Hussein.

The visa section of the Sudanese Consulate is sited directly behind the Sudanese embassy in Cairo's Garden City. It consists of a kiosk in a muddy lane with a large grille, built like a cage, behind which presides a solitary visa official. Milling about on the broken pavement, trying to attract his attention, were two or three hundred supplicants: of which the large part was Sudanese plus eighty or so Europeans. Several rival queues wound their way to the window, and occasional skirmishes broke out which were rapidly defused by Egyptian militia carrying machine-guns. It was not an encouraging spectacle.

I joined the back of one of the queues and spoke to the Dutchman in front of me. He was on an overland trip to Nairobi and had so far been waiting three weeks for his visa. The average delay, he said, was twenty-one days but people had been known to wait six weeks. My boat, the *Aqaba Crown*, left from Port Said that night at midnight; there was obviously little point in following the Dutchman's example. I considered abandoning the visa altogether and arriving in Port Sudan without one. But if the Sudanese port police refused me entry, which seemed more than likely, I would have no option but to rejoin the *Aqaba Crown* which was sailing on to Hodeida in North Yemen. The Yemenis had already refused me a visa, and in any case there was little prospect of finding a passage from Aden to Bombay. After Hodeida, the *Aqaba Crown* returned via Jeddah to Port Said so I would have written off twelve days for nothing. There were no two ways about it, I had to obtain a Sudanese visa in the next eight hours.

I was glad I was wearing a suit and tie. Most of the Europeans in the queue were overlanders in jeans and cheesecloth shirts and had a world-weary look about them. They were conditioned to long delays; probably accepted them as part of the experience. I hate delays. I become irritable standing in short queues in the bank. I shoved my way to the front, brandishing my British passport and mumbling "So sorry, embassy priority, total cock-up" until my nose was pressed to the grille.

The Sudanese visa official was writing a letter — it looked like a thank-you letter — and chose to ignore my poignant throat-clearing. Eventually I caught his eye. I explained that I had a boat to catch that night in Port Said and could I have a priority visa? He passed me a mimeographed application form, demanded eight pounds, and said, "First you will need letter of recommendation from British Embassy." Then he added, "You must be quick. We finish at twelve o'clock and tomorrow and day after closed." The time was ten minutes to eleven.

The British Embassy in Cairo is an enormous white-fronted folie de grandeur, in the style of Latrobe, situated at the end of Latin America Street which is seven minutes sprint from the Sudanese Consulate. The Union Jack fluttered reassuringly from the rotunda, and the entire staff was standing in the forecourt energetically hosing down cars. A clerk accompanied me to the British Consular office, which was decorated with posters of red London buses, and typed me up a letter. The Embassy, it read, had no hesitation whatever in endorsing my plan to enjoy four days tourism in the Democratic Republic of the Sudan.

I sprinted back to the Sudanese visa section, along the muddy lane, and once again elbowed my way to the grille. The official studied my document. "Tourism?" he read. "Come back three weeks." He shut my passport in a drawer and returned to his letter-writing. I protested. My ship, I said, sailed in seven hours. He had led me to believe a visa was possible.

"That is business visa," he said unsmilingly. "Not tourism visa."

"But I am business. Shipping business."

"This letter from British Embassy say you are tourism, not business." The visa official was obdurate. "Come back three weeks."

"Then I will change the letter," I said and sprinted back to Latin America Street.

Cairo is sticky in mid-morning. Cars were parked on pavements, rendering them impassable, so you had to squeeze between bumper and wall or walk in the road. Taxis hooted unceasingly and without purpose beyond making a noise. Urchins shouted "Hey, mister, you are welcome, buy postcard?" The entire staff of the British Embassy was energetically polishing windscreens.

The Consular clerk was sympathetic. He was concerned that the Sudanese would resent my chopping and changing, but agreed to issue me with a business recommendation. He asked whether I had any letters of introduction from my company. I didn't, but suggested running one up myself. I had a sheet of Standard writing paper in my pocket so I borrowed an Embassy typewriter and wrote "Nicholas Coleridge is import/export shipping publisher of this organisation." Then I counter-signed it with half a dozen invented names and added "Valid until January 1st 1985". On top of a filing cabinet I noticed a British Embassy seal so I applied a few of those for good measure. I was particularly pleased with the expression "Import/Export". It lent a free-booting authenticity certain to impress the Sudanese.

The Sudanese visa official was moderately impressed, though he still had misgivings. He said, "Four passport photo please." I had only three on me; I had imagined they would be enough. There were plenty more in my hotel but that was on the other side of Cairo. It was fourteen minutes to twelve.

I wandered down the muddy lane searching for a paparazzi. The Egyptians are avid photographers. They snap you in restaurants with antique cameras on tripods, and try to sell you the print. At the end of the muddy lane was a desolate four-lane highway with an arcade of shops on the far side. None of them looked remotely like camera shops, and even if there were any I doubted they could supply instant polaroids. There was nothing doing to the left or right, so I weaved across the road, dodging the traffic, and went into a grocers store. And there, standing in the corner, was a Xerox machine: not the latest model, it is true, but it seemed to work. A notice said "Photocopy, 25 piastres". My last hope was to Xerox the three pictures and pray the copies were clear enough to qualify.

The ancient machine was left to warm up for a few minutes, then lumbered majestically forwards. The copies were better than I had expected and I sprinted back to the Consulate.

The Sudanese visa official appraised the new picture. He said, "This is photopicture, not passport picture." But then, on a whim, he accepted it. Then he said, "Twelve pounds please."

I said, "But I have already given you eight pounds."

"That was application for tourism visa. Now you apply for businessman visa. Twelve pounds please, sterling."

I paid. Of course I had no option. The visa official said, "We will issue visa. Collect at 2.30 this afternoon." He gave me a cloakroom ticket as a receipt.

That morning at the Nile Hilton, residents dawdling over prelunch aperitifs were diverted by the abrupt arrival of a rumpled figure in a white tropical suit, and hobbling with the aid of a maplewood stick, who dragged his broken body across the marble lobby. A film of dust covered every part of his clothing, and also his face and hands, and it was only by a pair of New & Lingwood walking shoes that he was distinguishable as a European at all. There was no telling his age, or where he had come from. Many theories circulated: some thought they recognised in the dust the red sandstone of Basra; others believed he might have wandered from afar afield as Gaza or Tubruq. But it was the hotel doorman, who has considerable experience in such matters, who resolved the conundrum. "This gentleman has just procured a visa from the Sudanese Consulate. Help him to the bar."

It was a great feeling of achievement merely to get inside the Sudanese Consulate. Waving my cloakroom ticket, I was escorted up a flight of stone stairs to the holy of holies of the visa section: the despatch office. Half a dozen officials peered out from behind the desk piled with application forms and letters of recommendation from embassies, from time to time applying a round, brown cypher with their saucer of tea. The room was stifling. An overhead fan, capable of three revolutions a minute, paddled the fierce heat from cornice to cornice; most of the time it served as a trysting place for mosquitoes. I was given tea but did not drink it; allowing instead the vapours to soothe me with a facial sauna. I had now two out of the three crucial stamps, but Mr Essam had the third seal in his pocket and Mr Essam was in a meeting. He was expected any time. "Sit down mister, you are welcome." Mr Essam returned at half past four; he had added his seal before he had even taken tea and looked startled by his elan. I thanked the Sudanese visa section for their cooperation, with no trace of cynicism because I was genuinely grateful. They said, "You are welcome Sudan, mister."

About ten miles from the outskirts of Cairo, the Port Said road runs into desert. I stopped the taxi and looked back at the shimmering osmosis of smog and diesel fumes suspended above the capital. Cairo thumbs her nose at ecology; she is a swirling labyrinth snarled with traffic, bumper to bumper, and drivers sitting good-naturedly in their vehicles with both elbows on the hooter.

The desert is one long rambling army camp which extends forty miles from Ismailia to Port Said. On both sides of the road were rows of tanks, as many as five hundred parked in a single line, and recruits in string vests doing physical jerks and sentries smoking behind sandbags. The Ismailia desert is the most sensitive military zone in Egypt. The Israelis penetrated it with uncomfortable ease in 1967 and it is a vital buffer for the Suez Canal. Taxis may not leave the highway which suited me fine; I had no time to strike out into the dunes. The only scenery, apart from rifle ranges, are radar installations and the tumbledown hoardings for Pyramid Bank and MISR Import/Export which line the road.

At Ismailia we gave a lift to two Egyptian soldiers in berets, who sat in the front with the driver, holding hands. Their hair was shaved so close to their skulls that patches of skin were exposed; their boots gaped at the toes and had no laces. They smoked the driver's cigarettes until the packet was finished, then leant over the back seat asking impertinent personal questions, such as was I circumcised and why not. When they got out, after their free thirty-mile hitch, they asked me to tip them for their company.

Port Said has a Mediterranean breeze and apartment blocks reminiscent of Cannes. It was virtually abandoned from 1967 to 1975 when the Canal was closed, and still has a slightly temporary air, as though several thousand Egyptians were squatting in the French Riviera. The buildings along the waterfront are surprisingly unscathed by the troubles and there are rows of arcaded offices, with wide lattice balconies, overlooking the moorings. The combination of the area's sensitivity and Egyptian bureaucracy make Port Said an exceedingly difficult place to find a passage south. Travellers persist in the notion that, because ships pass through the Canal en route to almost every destination in Africa and the Far East, they can quite easily rent a cabin, or sleep on deck or even work their passage as crew. Several Europeans were making the rounds of the shipping offices, enquiring about routes to India and reaching the conclusion that they would have to fly. I had read Gavin Young's book *Slow Boats to China* in which it had taken him five days and an amazing stroke of luck even to reach Suez, and when he arrived at Jeddah without the correct papers he had been compelled to fly across Saudi Arabia to Sharjah. This, for my purposes, was out of the question: I wasn't allowed to take an aeroplane and I needed to sail from the Horn of Africa to Bombay.

I had contacted the Cunard Steamship Company, who I knew had ships in the Red Sea, and they put me in touch with their CAMEL subsidiary: Cunard Arabian Middle East Line, who generously offered me a passage from Port Said to Port Sudan aboard the *Aqaba Crown*, calling on the way at Aqaba and Jeddah to unload containers. Ideally, I suppose, she would also have called at Djibouti, which would have saved me a long and potentially dangerous overland leg through Ethiopia, but to retrace Fogg's route by sea as far as Port Sudan was a major boon and I gladly accepted.

I had been warned that delays on container ships are endemic, but that was a calculated risk. There can be delays to get into port, when the ship rides frustratingly at anchor for days queueing for a berth. There can be delays in the Suez Canal, waiting for a place in the convoy, and delays awaiting missing cargo. The *Aqaba Crown* was making her way to Port Said from Felixstowe via the North European ports and Piraeus, and I was to present myself at Cunard's local agents, Port Said Shipping and Navigation Company, who have offices on the harbour.

My taxi driver located the offices with great difficulty, despite the fact they are large and prominent, and the car filled up with guides anxious to direct us. As each one failed, he did not leave the cab shame-faced, but co-opted another friend off the street like a nightmare conga, until six of us were squashed into the back seat and none the wiser. It is a commonplace that you can never lose your way in an Arab town, because there is always somebody to guide you through the maze. This is no longer true: modern Arabs are strangely ignorant about their surroundings and have no sense of direction.

The offices of the Port Said Shipping and Navigation Company are in a modern complex owned by the Hilton Group. Unfortunately, there is no adjacent Hilton Hotel, or anything within stars-reach of it, as I was to discover shortly. A wraparound wall of burnished glass belies the polar air conditioning of the office, where several smartly dressed clerks were processing telexes. The fittings are chrome and teak, and I was encouraged by the sight of my name written in block capitals in a diary.

The news, on the other hand, was not so encouraging. "The *Aqaba Crown*," I was informed, "is late."

"How late?"

The shipping clerk shrugged. "Maybe tomorrow, maybe day after, maybe longer. We have received no signal."

I bought myself dinner in rather a grand restaurant with pink tablecloths, next to the port, called Maxim's where the veal was well cooked but twice as expensive as London. By eight o'clock there was still no news so I laid contingency plans. If the *Aqaba Crown* was three or four days behind schedule I could not afford to wait: I could see my whole itinerary unravelling as far ahead as Singapore, like a snagged jersey, and it brought me out in a cold sweat. The only solution was to plot an overland route to Port Sudan, but this was fraught with uncertainty. It meant taking a taxi at least a thousand miles, and both roads to the Sudan are a nightmare: the coast road, via Marsa Alam, petered out on my map at an oasis; the longer route, via Aswan, was said to be closed following a fire on the Lake Nasser Ferry. In any case, I had been looking forward to my cabin on the *Aqaba Crown*.

I had taken the precaution of pilfering a napkin full of black olives from the Nile Hilton, and I was moodily chewing these when there came a sharp crunch. My back tooth had split in half on a stone and suddenly I was in intense pain. It was this moment that an Egyptian cameraman, who had been stalking me all over town with his box brownie with a view to selling me a print, chose to spring up from behind a table.

"Got you," he laughed. "Centre frame. You buy picture?"

I said, "Can't you see my flaming tooth's just fallen out?"

He replied: "It doesn't matter. It is a back one, it won't show in the print. Or we can touch you up chemically, small additional charge."

If you need a dentist in a hurry in Port Said you could do a lot worse than Dr M Shawki Abu Saif. But you could also do a lot better. His surgery is in the same street as the American Consulate, above a shop called El-Bedweihy, and when he is not practising dentistry Dr Abu Saif is importing bathroom tiles. His surgery doubles as a show-room for his stock which is cemented, in little blocks of six or eight, sufficient to display the whole motif all over the walls.

Unfortunately Dr Abu Saif was clean out of most of the medications he needed to mend my tooth, so the appointment began with a shop-ping expedition to a pharmacy where I purchased antiseptics, oil of cloves and a bag of cotton buds. Unfortunately Dr Abu Saif was also clean out of piastres, such was his haste to get the job in hand.

He mixed the ingredients in a plastic bowl, beat them into pulp with a pestle, then braised them over a small spirit lamp. At last he said, "Now we are beginning," and clamped the broken tooth with a strange appliance, somewhat like the key for tapping air from a radiator, and filled the vacuum with his paste. He told me to clench my teeth and bite hard. Then he walked out onto the balcony, which is the roof of the shop called El-Bedweihy, and shouted "Faud, Faud." Faud was his apprentice and, in his own good time, joined his master. Faud was as thin as Dr Abu Saif was corpulent and between them they jammed my jaws together, Dr Abu Saif pressing from above, Faud squatting underneath and pressing up. We sustained this undignified tableau for twelve or fifteen minutes.

"No eating for two days, remember," cautioned Dr Abu Saif. "Just drinking whisky."

Heaven knows where he supposed I'd find whisky. The Ritz, Port Said's only non-dry bar, was permanently shuttered. I went to find a hotel. The Holiday Hotel, the town's best, was full. The Abu Simbel, next door, was empty. It is not known whether the Abu Simbel was named after Ramses II's thirteenth century B.C. temple, or vice versa, both are very old. The manager did not think I would enjoy staying in his hotel and insisted I see the room first. When I accepted it, because it was by now ten o'clock and my tooth was throbbing, he held me in contempt.

Ten minutes later there was a knock at the door. Two envelopes had arrived for me. The first was from the shipping agents. The *Aqaba Crown* was less than eighteen hours behind schedule and would arrive tomorrow evening. The second was a large buff envelope. Inside was a complimentary print from the photographer. Even he must have realised there was no market for it. An anguished young man was caught bent double in an attitude of crippling pain, delving into his mouth with an index finger. I tore the picture into tiny pieces and sank them in the Canal.

Mr Sayeed Hezazy Hassan, Managing Director of the Shipping Agency, is a very natty Egyptian with perfect manners. He apologised for being away when I first called, he had been inspecting their offices in Jeddah. He is a broad man with black corrugated hair, greased smartly across a fleshy skull. He wore a grey herringbone jacket and a grey cashmere cardigan; his gold Cartier wristwatch and maroon snakeskin blotter were as discreet as they were expensive. His English is fluent; he spends several weeks a year in London, put up in a Cunard Hotel. "But I won't stay at the Cunard International at Hammersmith any more," he joked. "It is too far from the West End. Now they billet me at the Bristol, much more comfortable you know."

He made a telephone call to the port authority and I was immediately issued with seaman's papers, essential for boarding at Port Said. I was to be registered as Assistant Purser. "It makes things easier, you understand, passengers confound the system." He told me to be waiting in the lobby of the Holiday Hotel at midnight, at which time the *Aqaba Crown* would pass immigration and I could join her by launch.

"Oh, incidentally, where are you leaving the ship?"

"Port Sudan."

"Is that wise?" asked Mr Sayeed Hezazy Hassan. "It is a terrible place. I saw a couple of Sudanese at Jeddah airport this morning, they were pushing car tires on their trolley as hand baggage. The country must be having big economic problems. It reminded me of Egypt under Nasser, when we had to go to Greece or Italy for our spare parts."

The lobby of the Holiday Hotel is Port Said's first choice rendezvous for meeting friends and business colleagues, according to its brochure. That night, however, it was all but deserted. I split a bottle of Stella Export with a curly fair-haired American in his mid-thirties, John Droughton from Florida, who was waiting to join the yacht *Nabila*. He was one of multi-millionaire Adnan Khashoggi's private helicopter pilots, and the fifty-crew *Nabila* was expected to clear the Canal at dawn. Droughton's problem was that he had the wrong papers: he had helicopter seaman's papers and the port police were insisting he joined the yacht from an air base.

"But how the hell am I supposed to do that, flap my arms? The helicopter is on board."

Every quarter of an hour he rang Khashoggi's office in Los Angeles and they dialled the yacht on a direct line. "Streuth," said John Droughton, "why the hell did Khashoggi want to come here anyway? He said we were going to Rio in January for the Carnival. Now he's changed his mind and it's Sri Lanka." He said that if I'd seen the new James Bond film, *Never Say Never Again*, I would have noticed the *Nabila* in Nassau harbour, with his helicopter parked on top. I replied that I had seen the film last week in Piraeus.

"Piraeus," said John Droughton, his eyes shooting up to the ceiling. "That's another hole."

At half past midnight I was collected from the lobby by a shipping clerk on a push bike. He put my carpet bag in the basket and we walked through the empty streets of Port Said wheeling the bicycle. The only people about were teenage militiamen, who loitered behind pillars and played skittles with machine gun bullets. Immigration was a formality, with my seaman's papers I was waved through, so we stood on a launch belonging to Jim Cairo and Sons, the port taxi service, and waited for the *Aqaba Crown*. She had drawn number sixteen in the convoy of twenty, and they passed into the Canal at twelve-minute intervals. It was full moon and the whole harbour was illuminated like a mezzotint as tugs escorted oil tankers larger than Blenheim Palace through the narrow isthmus from the port. There were Russian freighters delivering arms to Ethiopia, Japanese tankers full of butane, Yugoslavian cargo vessels weighed down with pickled fish. At four in the morning the *Aqaba Crown* steamed into view, the smallest and most compact ship in the convoy. Jim Cairo's launch pulled alongside, the gangway was lowered and I was aboard.

5 | *In which the* Aqaba Crown *is further delayed while port-hopping down the Red Sea.*

The *Aqaba Crown* is a German ship with a German crew, on permanent charter to Cunard. She is one of the most modern container vessels afloat, launched last April, with a bridge equipped like Dr Who's Tardis with black perspex control panels and Krupp radar. Captain Wohlgemuth was waiting on the bridge in the dark: he is a stocky grey-haired Berliner, born the year that war was declared, and he was looking slightly harassed. Negotiating the Suez Canal is fraught for a captain; it is an eighty-seven mile assault course beset with inefficient Egyptian pilots who come aboard to assist navigation, scores of pettyfogging formalities and precision timing. There are three convoys a day through the Canal, two southbound, one northbound, and the slightest delay on the captain's part means relegation to the next sailing.

All the lights on the bridge had been switched off to reduce glare, and a powerful searchlight erected on the prow. Both banks of the Canal were marked with green and red torches, like landing lights on an airport runway, and we began to cruise through Port Said at minimum throttle. Seen from the bridge of the *Aqaba Crown*, the wooden houses and shipping offices along the front were even more surreal than by day, with the palm trees and ornate balconies lit up in sharp relief by the searchlights of the ships. To port and starboard we were chaperoned by a flotilla of bath-sized tugs, which wheeled and tacked below the hull like small dogs snapping at the hooves of a carthorse. We were gliding so silently into the jaws of the Canal that you could hear the occasional lorry pulling out onto the Cairo road, three miles away, and revving into the desert.

Meanwhile, back on the bridge, the Egyptian pilot was getting down to the serious business of negotiating his baksheesh. He was dressed up in naval uniform with epaulettes, stained with flecks of rice and onion; his walnut shaped bald pate aped the physiognomy of the late Anwar Sadat. His presence was clearly superfluous to our progress, since Captain Wohlgemuth was steering his ship most competently with the help of radar and charts, and the only role for the pilot involved thumping his walkie-talkie from time to time, with a view to repairing it.

The custom of rewarding the pilot with whisky and cartons of cigarettes is a bone of contention on the Canal. If you don't supply them, the pilots become obstreperous and delays occur, notwithstanding the fact that spirits are off-limits to Moslems. The same pilots who insist on tuning the captain's radio to the Muezzin call at 3 a.m., and praying on the floor of the bridge, still expect baksheesh. This is not for their own consumption, but is sold in bulk on the black market, as many as two hundred bottles a day. The latest ruse by captains is to stock up with the cheapest duty-free whisky in Rotterdam, and transfer it into Johnny Walker bottles. Since the pilots don't drink the whisky themselves, the substitution goes unnoticed.

I was shown to my cabin, a spacious air-conditioned suite comprising a sitting-room with a desk, a bedroom and bathroom. Small portholes gave onto life boats on one side and the deck on the other, which was loaded four-deep with containers; we were sailing at ninety-five percent capacity. In the corner of the cabin a mini-bar fridge was stocked with spirits and beer, which were to cause me some anxiety as the voyage progressed. Beside the bed, which was built like a cot with wooden bars in case of rough weather, lay a plastic fly swat bearing the legend, "Camel Containers, there are no flies on us."

It was already dawn by the time the immigration officers had completed their formalities and left the ship. The launches peeled away as we entered the narrow Canal and cruised under our own steam at a steady five knots towards the Red Sea. It was agreeable to climb into bed in this comfortable cabin, with the engines throbbing gently in the hold, bottles rattling reassuringly in the fridge and the eerie creaking of cargo on deck.

By the time I woke up the *Aqaba Crown* was riding at anchor in the Bitter Lakes, a huge inland lagoon like the flooded crater of a volcano, midway between Suez and Ismailia. Even before the Canal linked them with the sea, the Bitter Lakes were salty and were avoided by the nomadic tribes and spice caravans which frequented Biblical Goshen. It is here that the southbound convoy waits for the northbound convoy to pass them, before completing their passage to the Red Sea. I drank coffee on the bridge while the Chief Officer, Rolf Steinberg, a giant of a man with his hair tied back in a pony-tail, identified the other vessels. All the ships which had preceded us along the Canal the night before were also at anchor. Most of them, said Rolf, were heading for the Far East. I asked our relative speeds and he said that only one ship out of the whole convoy was faster than us, and she was the *Nedlloyd Rotterdam*. We could make sixteen knots, she could touch twenty. I inspected her substantial grey hull through binoculars, with no premonition that she would be indirectly responsible for extending my journey by twenty-six hours.

Captain Wohlgemuth joined us on the bridge wearing sandals; he was always informal at sea, only donning uniform for arriving at ports. He said he had known some of the seamen who were trapped in the Bitter Lakes in 1967 as a consequence of the Six Day War; fifteen ships were marooned there for eight years when the Israelis dug in on the East Bank, mines were laid and one vessel was bombed. For the first eighteen months all the ships maintained full crews, always expecting to negotiate their release, and organised a mini Olympic Games between the multinational hands. When the situation became hopeless, most of the men were airlifted out and the vessels were lashed together and maintained by a single skeleton crew. The irony was, by the time the Canal was re-opened in 1975, most of the ships were obsolete.

We expected to resume our passage after lunch. These meals, in the officers' mess below the poop deck, began at twelve o'clock and made no concessions whatsoever to local cuisine. All the stores had been taken aboard in Hamburg, and were defiantly European: chicken soup with rice, roast chicken with potatoes, and rum and raisin ice-cream. The mess boy was a charming Kiribatian called Beia who derived, as did all the crew apart from the officers, from those remote South Pacific Islands a thousand miles north-east of Australia.

I was allocated a deck chair on the stern and this became my daylight domain for the next four days. From here I could watch the wash parting behind the ship and see both banks of the Canal stretching ten miles into the Ismailia desert before diffusing into haze. Sandbanks

dotted the horizon as well as occasional coils of barbed wire and burnt
out tanks, remnants of the Six Day War and the Egyptian counter-
attack of October 1973. By dusk we had arrived at Bur Tawfiq, the
concrete suburb of Suez which marks the end of the Canal, and in
the distance were the neon signs of Suez itself, illuminating the desert
sky with an effervescent glow like theatre footlights.

Pilots again joined the ship, eager as before to facilitate our passage
and fill their Adidas bags with spirits. The Egyptian government charges
twenty thousand dollars for a ship to negotiate the Canal; but, just like
any fifty-piastre hotel in downtown Cairo, every employee is apparently
paid on tips.

By morning we were passing the Strait of Tiran, the mouth of the
Gulf of Aqaba. To our left lay the barren wilderness of Sinai, domi-
nated by the Holy Mountain, now once again under Egyptian control.
The government have lately announced ambitious plans for developing
Sinai as a holiday resort but the problems are prodigious. There is no
water or food apart from plagues of locusts and desert dew; even reaching the sea takes forty days and forty nights by four-wheel drive jeep,
and the paleolithic villagers who inhabit the coast are to the manna
born.

On the opposite side of the Strait is Saudi Arabia, the arid empty
quarter which extends three hundred miles south to Al Wajh, per-
ambulated only by the dwindling bands of hard-core Bedu who haven't
emigrated to the Beverly Wilshire or Earls Court.

Twenty miles further up the Gulf two more frontiers hoved into
view: Israel and Jordan. The chi-chi Israeli holiday village of Elat and
the Jordanian port of Aqaba face each other across the Strait, barely
five minutes apart. With field glasses you can watch the Israelis wind-
surfing on their stretch of white sand, or toasting under straw umbrellas;
the Aqaba coast is King Hussein's favourite water-skiing spot, where
he is shielded from terrorists by a flotilla of military speedboats on
either side of his wake.

Aqaba was our first stop to off-load containers, a straightforward
exercise which should have taken about twelve hours. Just as we were
steaming towards harbour, however, an ominous grey hull appeared
in the Strait and overtook us. This was the *Nedlloyd Rotterdam*, tying
us in knots with her superior tonnage and making full speed ahead to
the only container berth. We were well and truly bounced: Aqaba
operates a first-come, first-served policy and the *Nedlloyd Rotterdam*

was weighed down with cargo. The minimum delay, estimated Captain Wohlgemuth, would be twenty hours.

But it wasn't twenty hours, it was twenty-six hours of riding frustratingly at anchor in the sweltering gulf.

"You should be here in the summer," said the Chief Officer. "Then it's like an oven."

Even in January your shirt stuck to your back as you leant over the rails, while the stevedores fished for sprats from the harbour wall during their lunch break, and steel cranes winched the containers onto trailers.

Aqaba is a courteous town which has tripled in size in the last five years but the development has been sensitive. Like most Arab ports it has a stage-set quality, as though the apartment blocks and minarets and palm trees aren't attached to any foundation but are merely propped up on the sand. A rugged mountain range rises steeply behind the port, and it takes only the mildest leap of imagination to strip the whole town off the shore and revert to virgin desert. Shipping traffic has increased dramatically since the closure of the Shat Al Arab, when Aqaba became Iraq's only port of entry. More than half Aqaba's cargo is in transit to Baghdad, and the Jordanians are reaping a fortune in toll charges. Most of the traffic is armaments destined for the war against Iran, but is coyly registered as soft drinks on the customs carnet. "They must have some pretty weird canned drinks," joked a Camel executive. "I saw some containers labelled Seven-Up and they had tank-barrels sticking out." Camel themselves won't deliver weapons, leaving it to the cowboy container lines. "Apart from anything else the Saudis won't allow armaments to dock at Jeddah and arrest ships which have previously transported them."

At last it was our turn to dock. Although I was anxious about the wasted hours these were, in Fogg-speak, "anticipated and allowed for"; I had built a thirty-six hour delay into the Red Sea schedule. By the time we started unloading we had already slipped forty hours including the hiatus in Port Said, but the stevedores were working double shifts and there seemed every prospect of clawing back some lost time.

Cunard's Aqaba operation's manager, a charming Jordanian called George Dahal, took the ship's officers plus me in my role as honorary purser to dinner at a Lebanese restaurant in the port. We ate mezze and discussed stowaways.

Stowing-away is a growth industry along the Red Sea. Port Sudan has become so notorious for it that every vessel is searched from bridge to hold before sailing, and never fails to turf out two or three. The world's top stowers-away are Mozambique nationals trying to get home; lately they have become so desperate that they'll board any ship at all heading anywhere.

"We were caught out for the first time on the *Aqaba Crown* last voyage," said the Chief Officer. "We combed the ship, found two men hidden in the lifeboat, but forgot the crane. A stowaway had climbed up during the night and locked himself into the cabin, with enough provisions to last a week."

The curse about stowaways is that, once they're discovered, it is the shipping line's responsibility to repatriate them. Without a visa to disembark anywhere else, they have to be procured transit papers and flown home. If he is re-visiting the stowaway's port within thirty days of discovery, however, Captain Wohlgemuth has a sharp procedure for dealing with them. "I insist they sign on as crew members, which simplifies formalities, and keep them locked up below deck. We feed them, of course, but no cigarettes and no beers, nothing like that. By the time we drop them home they're thankful to go, and it's cheaper than providing air tickets."

Runners-up in the stowaway stakes are the Chileans. In the days when Captain Wohlgemuth ploughed the South American coast, they were always slipping aboard.

"But you know Chilean men have one secret flaw," he told an incredulous table. "They all wear women's knickers, black ones, underneath their ponchos. So when I inspected the hold and noticed a pair of black knickers dropped behind a crate I knew we had stowaways on board. So we brought a tannoy down below and ordered them to give themselves up, but there wasn't a squeak. They were trying to sit it out and since most of the cargo consisted of huge sacks of cotton, it was impossible to tell where they'd burrowed in. So then we made another announcement: we said we were going to gas them out, and started pumping compressed oxygen into the hold. Within seconds they had surrendered, believing it was poison gas, and we dropped them off at the next port."

George Dahal had an even more astounding stowaway story, which had happened in Aqaba only the week before.

"The stevedores were unloading cargo as usual," he said, "when a lot of splashing and yelling was heard, and an African was threshing about in the dock. Naturally they lowered a rope for him and when the man had climbed ashore he claimed he had been thrown overboard from a ship anchored half a mile into the Gulf. He said he had stowed away in Ghana, and when he had been discovered the captain and first mate had beaten him up and dropped him over the rails.

"This kind of thing is considered very serious in Jordan, and the captain and mate were arrested for manslaughter. They protested that they had never seen the man in their lives before, but the weight of evidence was against them. For one thing, this African was a most articulate young man, aged only twenty, but already he spoke fluent English, French and Greek as well as his own tongue and he made a very good impression in court.

"I had gone along to watch the case because I was curious about it, and when the judge was making his decision I just happened to be standing in the corridor near the Ghanaian. Now he didn't know that I speak Greek and he was talking to a friend of his, confident that nobody could understand him. He was telling his friend that he hoped to be awarded seven thousand dollars damages this time, because on the previous occasions he'd pulled this stunt he'd never got more than six thousand dollars. I rushed back into the court and fetched the judge who followed me into the corridor and heard it too. This African later admitted he had done this trick five times before, stowing away and jumping overboard near the port with his criminal story. And on every other occasion the deception had paid off."

It is five hundred and sixty-seven miles from Aqaba to Jeddah and the journey took thirty hours. Deft dock work in Jordan had repaired the schedule a little and the *Aqaba Crown* was tracing the Saudi Arabian coast at maximum throttle. We were cruising about twenty miles from shore to avoid treacherous reefs, and the whole country corruscated steam like the bonnet of a car with a dry radiator. I sat stoically on my deck chair, massaging my sangfroid while eating walnuts and skimming the *Jordan Times*. A new bridge column had been launched that week, in which four fictional Arabs demonstrated a rubber in the Amman Sheraton, with heroic dialogue. "No one could accuse Sonny of being shy in the bidding, he bid the slam with the confidence of a man who expected to make it."

The cast-iron companionways of the ship were heating up like a griddle as we forged south, and anyone rash enough to step outside in bare feet would dance like the victim of a pirate raid.

We knew we were nearing Jeddah when a flock of seagulls suddenly appeared from nowhere to swoop for fish in the ship's wash. The port loomed ten minutes later out of the haze, first just a blur of vertical shapes, then a sprawling urban souk of minarets, industrial chimneys, cranes and office blocks. The skyline resembles Dallas or Houston: burnished glass towers, designed by the world's most expensive architectural partnerships for corporations requiring instant visible prestige. And yet, as we sailed closer, these buildings were not all American in inspiration. There were also perfect examples of neo-Islamic post modernism; classical Hyatt Hotel shells with an elaborate minaret or deep trellised window tacked onto the roof. At street level, I have no doubt, waste paper and mounds of garbage lay unattended in potholed parking lots, but I was not to confirm this at first hand: the Saudis will issue no shore passes to seamen. Or at least, while in theory they might, such passes always take ten hours longer to process than the ship is staying in port.

A Saudi pilot in a white phobe and three days' growth beard joined us for the hazardous passage into port. Jeddah is sheltered behind a barrier of shallow reefs, with only a narrow entrance blasted through for shipping, and countless vessels have come to grief negotiating the creek. Saudi pilots, of course, are not tipped in whisky. The Shariah alcohol laws are truculently enforced; even containers of beer destined for other ports may not enter Saudi waters. The penalties for being caught with spirits are clearly displayed: forty strokes each for gin and whisky, one additional stroke for every additional bottle of beer. The *Aqaba Crown* bonds her alcohol in good time before landing, but, just as we approached the port, I remembered my mini-bar fridge had been overlooked. With mounting panic I totted up the penalty: ninety-two strokes plus a flat half bottle of Becks. I ran hell for leather to my cabin and stowed them underneath the mattress.

Jeddah harbour is a peculiar combination of relentless modernity and hide-bound bureaucracy. The orange Ferranti gantrys and straddle carriers are the most sophisticated in the world, operated by immigrant Filipino guest workers. While Aqaba can unload ten containers an hour, and Port Sudan barely manage three, Jeddah achieves an effortless thirty-six. The docks are spotless, swept night and day by shrinking Yemenis with horsehair brooms. There are none of the piles of rope and rusting anchors which usually characterise ports, and each compound is separated with security netting from the next to prevent fraternisation between crews. Beyond the port's compound an eight-lane freeway struck out through the desert towards Riyadh, on which an endless traffic jam of juggernauts manoeuvred from lane to lane in a cloud of exhaust fumes. The radio officer, Seegers Friedrich, cautioned me to keep my door locked at all times while in port. Sometimes the Islamic religious police, the Matawa, board the ship posing as stevedores and summarily search the cabins. Although, on Cunard ships, there is nothing incriminating to find, these spot checks are unnerving.

We cruised out of Jeddah at midday to begin the final one hundred and fifty-seven mile leg to Port Sudan. "I think you will notice the difference from Jeddah," laughed the captain as I dawdled on the bridge.

"Ya, ya," agreed the crew, "you certainly will."

I certainly did. We berthed at midnight and the whole port was apparently illuminated by a pair of hand-held car torches. As my eyes became accustomed to the dark, however, I saw a band of the most desperate brigands imaginable lurking behind packing cases: feline Arabs in jalabayyas with curved daggers at their hips or Dinka tribesmen from Juba. It soon became clear why the harbour was in virtual darkness; even the dimmest light is an instant country club for every winged insect in the Sudan, so the stevedores choose to keep their watch by moonlight.

An hour after docking, the quarantine doctor came on board, applied his grubby thumbprint to the vaccination certificates and demanded cigarettes. Once it would have been whisky he wanted, but six months ago, under pressure from Riyadh, the Sudan went dry. Overnight, government troops impounded every bottle of spirits in the country in a lightning raid, from every shop, bar and hotel, and drove them to the banks of the White Nile in Khartoum. There, with great ceremony and Islamic self-righteousness, thousands of litres of whisky, gin and vodka were poured into the river. Six weeks later a new decree went out. The mullahs had realized that the Nile irrigates all the fields in the fertile plain, and since the crops were now contaminated with alcohol these too must be gathered and destroyed.

At 3 a.m. I returned to my well-appointed cabin for the last time, to pack. It seemed I had lived there all my life and I felt like a man being evicted from his ancestral hammock. As I left the *Aqaba Crown* at first light, there was a throttling cramp in the pit of my stomach and it was definitely nothing I had eaten.

6 | *In which nothing very significant happens in the Sudan. But all of it to the point.*

At every port down the Red Sea I had been regaled with anecdotes about Captain Roberts. He is Cunard's representative in Port Sudan: a swashbuckling mariner of the old school, always posted to the trouble spots, I was told. I expected a red-haired bearded giant terrorising the stevedores in backstreet Sudanese. Instead Captain Roberts is a short, gritty Scot; the sort of man who is made news editor on top regional newspapers. He escorted me from the *Aqaba Crown* to clear customs in a dingy shed. Before the Sudan he had spent several years in Jeddah; as soon as he was posted here the Shariah alcohol laws followed him across the Red Sea. Was someone, he joked, trying to tell him something? He is a man who misses his whisky. Even the small British club, on the end of the port, had been raided the previous month and fifty thousand pounds of spirits seized.

Captain Roberts drove me through the tumbledown outskirts of Port Sudan to the main square. Clouds of dust were billowing up from the mud roads, making it difficult to see.

"Oh God, it's the blasted hubbub," said Captain Roberts. The Sudanese hubbub, sometimes known as the Khamsin, can whip up at a moment's notice, bringing everything to a halt. People were everywhere squatting beside the road and winding their headclothes around their faces, to sit the sandstorm out. It looked like turning into a bad one, remarked Captain Roberts.

I was dropped off near the market, spread out my maps on a cafe table and plotted a route. I wasn't sorry to be on my own again, with more flexibility, but the alphabet was disorientating. The Sudanese have the third most raffish calligraphy in the world, after the Burmese and the Ethiopian Amharic alphabet; to write a single symbol takes hours if executed thoroughly, with all the attendant swirls and cedillas. Copying out a short story is a month's work; a novel requires a lifetime. This no doubt explains the almost complete absence of Sudanese literature. Instead, the literati slate their creative urges devising exhaustive carnets, identity documents, currency regulations and permits for travel, each taking several days to process. If I wanted to top and tail the Sudan in a hurry, I couldn't afford to get fouled by red tape.

I had originally planned to take a taxi to Kassala, the regional capital of the south, then bear left by taxi and enter Ethiopia near Adaruba which looked sufficiently insignificant not to have immigration control. Since Ethiopia will only issue one-day visas, and then only for Addis Ababa which is the sole legal point of entry, I was obliged to travel the length of the Ethiopian coast to Djibouti without one, so it was crucial to penetrate the border with discretion. The more I studied the route, however, the less I liked it. The train to Kassala would be slow and it might be hard to find a taxi prepared to take me so close to Ethiopia. That part of the country is completely in the thrall of three rival guerrilla armies, all waging dual campaigns against government troops and against each other. One is a small but maniacal scission of Islamic fundamentalists, said to be funded from Iran by the Ayatollah Khomeini, who believe President Numayri's Moslem revival has not gone far enough. The second is a dwindling detachment of Coptic Christians pledged to halt the march of Islam. The third and largest group is Colonel John Garang's five thousand phalangists, whose objective is nothing more prosaic than pillage and rape. Two weeks earlier they had successfully ambushed a government outpost and massacred the occupants to a man, dragging off the laundry women into the hills to an indelicate but prolonged fate. Government troops had retaliated on their own initiative: raiding the villages near Abyei believed to be sympathetic to the rebels, razing them to the ground and rustling their goats. Morale was so low throughout this foray, however, that several troops had slipped away and defected to Garang's guerrillas.

On reflection, the coast road seemed infinitely preferable. Although only a track, which would add several hours to the schedule, it had three advantages. I could take a taxi all the way to the border; Garang's phalangists are the only guerrillas active in the area; and I could disclose my ultimate destination in stages. It was sweltering in the square. The palm trees on the perimeter drooped dusty and bedraggled. The table was already covered with spent bottles of Alkola: a local brew that is sweet and syrupy, and tepid from being stored in the sun. Flies buzzed unceasingly, settling on the maps and crawling inside the kola bottles and laying eggs in my ear. The cafe reeked of incense. It is the custom in the Sudan not to smoke a hookah but to inhale the vapours of Coptic incense from a copper brazier. Rooks cawed on the tin roof of a vegetable stall, swooped to the ground to gather some bit of offal, and then with rattling wings flew back to the roof. Youths were potting them with an air rifle from the pavement, but were rotten shots and pellets zinged among the tables. It must have been my tropical suit which made me a magnet for hawkers. I refused, oh a dozen times at least, the solicitations of urchins who wished to shine my spotless shoes, clacking their brushes against Padawax tins. Old men in jala-bayyas and turbans petitioned me again and again, frankly disbelieving that I did not require horse-hair riding crops, leather wallets, pottery gourds, Nubian heads, shoe trees made out of ibex horns, ivory brace-lets or miscellaneous splinters of genuine coral. Antique, Sudanese women extended skinny hands and with a whimper recited dismal screeds learnt by rote. Blind men, the maimed, the halt, all were led up to my table in a pitiful maundy procession to receive token alms which can only have prolonged their misery.

On the edge of the square was a small rank of taxi drivers, and they too had not hidden their services under a bushel. Small boys, com-mission agents for the drivers, hissed "Tagzi mister, tagzi. OK, where to?" Until I could stand it no longer.

"All right. I have taxi."

"OK, where to mister? Airport?"

"No. Suakin."

Suakin is the old Red Sea port of the Sudan, abandoned by the British in the mid 1930s and lined with coral beach huts. There is nowhere much to stay, apart from the government rest house, and it is little visited except as a jumping off point for the Suakin Archipelago: a pattern of reefs in the Gulf famous for shark fishing. My plan was to take a taxi straight to Suakin and then, by the deft application of American dollars, persuade the driver to continue first to Tukar, then on to the border town of Karora. My driver, Buri, was young and rather uppity and certain to rue the Islamic revival; he had a Moody

Blues cassette in his cab of such poor quality it had obviously been taped and re-taped many times en route to Port Sudan. In London, Buri would have worked behind the bar in a nightclub or casino; here his sole ambition was to have sex with Europeans. He had achieved this only once, I am glad to say, with a Dutch girl on the beach, but it had set a prerogative for pestering any female backpackers with fair skin. His English was good, though not as fluent as he thought. His range of subjects said more about European overlanders than about Buri; he talked about Bob Dylan and Joni Mitchell and free festivals as though they were still topics of great moment in the West.

The drive to Suakin was prolonged. Buri's taxi, when it exceeded speeds of fifty miles an hour, began to shake. The road, though good, was dusty, the hubbub blew grit into the radiators and stalled the engine. On our left was a narrow strip of desert and beyond that the sea. Fishermen had built short jetties straight out from the beach and were dozing on the prows of their dhows or drying barracuda on the sands. The Suakin beaches used to be a great favourite with the European community for barbecues; now they are closed at dusk so that the army, it is rumoured, can smuggle drink through a break in the reef.

I asked Buri whether he ever fished and he was insulted. He would only join a fishing expedition to chaperone a European girl. Shark fishing, he said, was dangerous. If you fell overboard, snap, that was the end of you; the dhow couldn't turn quickly enough to haul you back in and, once they have tasted blood, the sharks would buff the vessel until it capsized. No native fishermen would risk rescuing a colleague, even a son, from the sharks of the Suakin Archipelago.

We reached Suakin just after twelve o'clock and I told Buri I wanted to strike on another forty miles to Tukar. He was not at all taken with the idea and I had to delve slightly deeper than I'd intended into the wad of five hundred American dollars rolled up inside a pair of Hilditch & Key boxer shorts. The road to Tukar was certainly dismal and I could understand why he feared for his cab. It is nothing more than a track through the desert, no longer in sight of the sea, and vicious pellets of gravel ricochetted against the chassis. The track was marked by a small tor of rocks every few hundred yards, but as the hubbub blew up it was hard to see from one tor to the next and he crawled along at ten miles an hour. Once or twice we passed jeeps from a doomed agricultural project, but they didn't loom out of the dust until they were alongside. It was like being trapped inside a Christmas snowstorm — one of those glass tableaux you pick up and shake — but with swirling sand instead of festive sleet. Occasionally the hubbub let up for a few minutes, long enough to see a low range of mountains across the desert. Once I spotted a skeleton of a camel, but when we stopped to poke it, it turned into a dead bonfire.

Tukar is more prepossessing than I had expected. The main drag has an arcade of small shops selling oranges, custard cream biscuits, and Alkola. Buri drained his in one, so I bought him another. It seemed sensible to break the bad news on a bloated stomach: that he was driving me to the Ethiopian border.

At this Buri put his foot down, but not on the accelerator. He pointblank refused to go any further. He was already eighty-five miles from Port Sudan and wouldn't arrive back until tomorrow morning. He had never driven along the road from Tukar to Karora, but had heard it was terrible and anyway it crossed the mountains close to the guerrilla camps. Hours passed, platitudes were exchanged, we reached a compromise. We would stay in Tukar overnight and continue the next morning. As well as dollars I had promised a bottle of Pick-Me-Up, a strange restorative from the Queen Mother's chemist in St James's, which I said was extremely alcoholic and could only be imbibed by the spoonful. On the label it said: "This celebrated preparation is a splendid reviver in the morning, and taken shortly before lunch and dinner also serves as an excellent aperitif." I had been given it as a going away gift in England, and Buri was impressed. I told him it was five times stronger than arrack, and he couldn't drink it at the wheel.

If you are looking for a remote hotel in which to die amidst the maximum discomfort and squalor, you need look no further than the Sahara Hotel, Tukar. I have stayed in many bad hotels in the seamiest backstreets of Shiraz and Erzurum, and claim a certain discernment in the matter, but nothing I had experienced began to compare with the Sahara Hotel. For dirt, for stench, for every privation of hygiene and plumbing it is in a class of its own. In the corners of the bedrooms were mounds of crumpled tissue paper and dead insects; the basins are not connected to the pipes and have for years been used as spitoons; the floors are of trampled earth and the bed formed of three uneven planks. The management are as surly as they are untrustworthy; the cook, a crumbling witch with half her face fallen away. None of this would be in the least bit remarkable for Southern Sudan if the rooms didn't cost seventy-five Sudanese pounds a night: thirty-eight pounds sterling. The tariff was clearly displayed at reception. The price would have been steep at six Sudanese pounds, and yet, in this obscure doss-house in the desert in a bankrupt country, they were charging twice as much as a family hotel in the Lake District with hot water, clean linen, a lounge full of Reader's Digests, and a choice of Special K or prunes for breakfast. Perhaps guests stayed at the hotel so rarely they needed to extract maximum revenue. Certainly I was the only paying resident; the other rooms were occupied by staff. It was their vile retchings and spittings that I could so clearly hear through the walls.

Shiva Naipaul, in *North Of South: An African Journey*, was the first writer to perceive Africa's sense of unreality about money. He cited a shoe-shine boy in Nairobi who demanded six dollars for "special deluxe service". Now, it seems, the whole of north-east Africa is peopled by shoe-shine boys; taxi drivers who doze half the day in the front of their cabs, without fares, and then ask ten pounds for a five-minute ride; bell-boys who corner you in lifts and jostle aggressively for tips; hotels in the desert charging seventy-five Sudanese pounds for a Salvation Army spike.

I went downstairs to the hotel restaurant for my third Alkola of the evening. Time threatened to pass slowly. The hubbub continued to swirl. Buri was sleeping on the back seat of his cab. The locals were in convalescence from some deadly strain of bush fever and looked hostile. I was reaching the end of my book and would then have to fall back on a copy of *Great Expectations* made simple, using only "the basic one thousand vocabulary for school certificate", purchased in Port Sudan.

Suddenly into the middle of this desperate scene walked an English girl. She wore her hair in a native scarf but couldn't have been from anywhere else. She looked twenty-two, and she sat down at a table across the room and studied an Arabic grammar. I don't habitually accost strangers merely because they are English, but the remoteness of the hotel and the swirling hubbub outside made me curious. After twenty or so minutes, I walked up to her table and introduced myself.

"Did you have to approach me like this?" she said bitterly. "Now they'll think I'm a prostitute. They suspect that already." She refused a drink on the same grounds.

Jane Watson was doing Arabic at Girton, but was on a year's sabbatical from Cambridge to practise speaking the language. She was teaching English in a local school while researching her thesis: "The place of the modern Sudanese poet and novelist in society." The thesis was a problem. She had already reached the conclusion that there is no place for the modern Sudanese poet or novelist in society. The topics that the few Sudanese authors choose to write about are questions of Western philosophy, and in the end the temptation to move to the West, or to take up a lucrative university post in the Arabian Gulf, was irresistible. So they quit the Sudan where their books are in any case unavailable. Of the neatly typed reading list Jane had been given at Cambridge, only a couple of books were in print.

She seemed quite unmoved by an English voice, though she certainly hadn't heard one for several months. She did not ask me where I was from, or where I was going or who I might possibly be. After a while she said she must leave. I stood up too to say goodbye. She snapped, "For God's sake, you cretin, stay at the table for a bit, or they'll think you've scored." Then she walked outside into the raging hubbub.

The next morning we set off towards the mountains playing one of my English tapes, which I made clear was staying with me. It was Elton John. "I want to kiss the bride," sang along Buri chastely. "I want to kiss the bride."

The hubbub had lifted and so had his spirits. We drove through another doomed agricultural project where millions of UNESCO pounds were being frittered away on a field of shrivelled maize, and on through the fleapit village they call Akik. Then the mountains became quite steep and Buri stopped tooting his horn on blind corners in case it alerted Colonel John Garang's five thousand philandering phalangists. Fortunately they were nowhere in evidence and were presumably too busy queueing for their turn with the laundry maids to bother pillaging a lone taxi. Once I fancied I heard jungle drums gossiping across the ravine but, true to pantomime tradition, it was only Buri's heart beating. Two hours after leaving Tukar we arrived on the outskirts of Karora. I asked Buri to pull up half a mile short of the village, turn straight round and go home. I didn't want a taxi with Port Sudan number plates drawing attention to my arrival. Buri needed no second bidding and burned off back towards the mountains. Five minutes later I remembered he'd still got my tape. Later that evening, by way of compensation, I discovered I'd walked off with the Sahara Hotel room key.

7 | *In which the length of Ethiopia's Red Sea coast is traversed by taxi. And mention is made of crocodiles and Cubans.*

Karora isn't much of a place but there was a certain cavalier thrill from kicking my heels on the doorstep of Ethiopia. Most of the village is Sudanese but, shortly before it peters out, there is a dusty no-man's land and beyond that, Eritrea. Karora is the vortex of Eritrea, the jumping-off point for the flood of refugees fleeing the civil war. The Sudanese attempt to register them as they cross the border, but the Ethiopians prefer to wash their hands of their northern frontier; the war against the Eritrean rebels, who are fighting for independence for this former autonomous Italian province, has been going badly for the government. The rebels now control the whole countryside north of the Port of Massawa, and they would have taken that too but for a massive Soviet airlift. Ever since the last Emperor of Abyssinia, Haile Selassie, was deposed in 1974, Ethiopia has been run by a sinister clique of Marxist generals known as the Dergue, shorne up by Russian and Cuban military attachés. Their various attempts at solving the Eritrean question have, however, flopped. The fighting has dragged on and on to become another forgotten war, no longer reported in serious newspapers, which suited my purposes fine: Eritrea is the Achilles heel of Ethiopia.

I sauntered furtively across no-man's land and down the main street, an operation which did not take very long and was anyway ill-conceived. There was a strip of about thirty mud houses and shops on either side of a mud track, where a spontaneous market had formed. Women squatted on their haunches amidst cauls of dirt selling nuts from shallow sacks, or little piles of okra and pots of Nivea cream.

Despite my nonchalant air, I was not taken for a native but was beckoned in a friendly manner. The people are much lighter in colour than the Sudanese; the women were dressed in elaborate qemis and shemmas: lengths of rough cotton worn like Inca ponchos, brightly dyed with embroidery at the neck. The men are tall and poised, with finely chiselled noses and are as different from the bloated, bulbous Sudanese as two adjacent nations could possibly be. Some of the men were selling rock salt from baskets which is used as a surrogate currency in country areas. Stupidly I had forgotten to pack a tin of Saxa in my carpet bag, so I set about trying to change money.

This was a problem. In almost any other part of the world you would have been besieged by money-changers by now, desperate for dollars. Here, with very little freedom of movement or exposure to the outside world, the dollar, unlike salt, has lost its savour. I tried to buy some monkey nuts and fruit but there were no takers either for the Jordanian rhial or the Italian lira; some Ethiopian birr were crucial.

At the far end of the village was a modern breeze-block building with two Chevrolet wagons parked outside, the first transport I had seen. It was possible that this was an Ethiopian immigration post, in which case I should wide-berth it, but on the other hand the wagons seemed the only way out of Karora. I asked one of the growing retinue of youths trailing me up the street if the building was Ethiopian. He shook his head, then made a hideous charade of a throat being cut. This mime was taken up by the rest of the party, until they were all shooting, garotting, spearing and back-stabbing the length of Karora High Street.

The breeze-block building turned out to house a small electrical plant, not yet operational. It had been built with Russian money seven years earlier but never completed, though three men were paid every month to maintain it. They thought it a good joke to be subsidised by the enemy government to do nothing. It was the Ethiopians who had given them the Chevrolet wagons, one of which was now "kaput". Their only duty, it seems, was to drive down to the administrative capital in Asmara every few weeks to collect their retainer, and I asked when they were next going.

"Not for a few weeks at least," said Jiji; their leader. Jiji was a well built man with crinkly black hair and was wearing a none-too-fresh aertex shirt. His face was unusual in that all the features were crowded into the middle, framed by a slack tire of black skin. When he heard that I wanted to change dollars he became solicitous, and offered four birrs for each dollar: twice the official rate. I accepted and he was pleased; in Asmara a dollar changes hands at five times the published rate on the black market. But I did not convert nearly as many dollars as he suggested, because I needed to maintain financial leverage.

We drank tea and ate bananas at Jiji's desk, clearing away trays of elastic bands and a 1979 forward planner. The crowd of youths, who had naturally followed us into the office to witness the currency deal, hung back at a discreet distance. The only man who joined us for tea was Jiji's assistant, Adwar, who seemed personable enough and grinned through gapped teeth. Later I learnt he had had the two lower middle teeth removed aged eight, in accordance with the local custom, by a mysterious tooth doctor who travelled from village to village performing this dentistry in return for a spear. As well as grinning, Adwar could peel oranges with a knife in a single coil: a useful fellow to have around in a war zone and I dubbed him Honorary Passepartout.

Over breakfast I told Jiji that I wanted to be driven to the Djibouti border. He was understandably rather taken aback since it is a distance of five hundred and sixty miles, nearly all of it on rough tracks across grassland, but on the other hand he could hardly use pressure of work as an excuse and his addiction to green dollars was well developed. He suggested leaving in a day or two and maybe only going as far as Asmara. I suggested leaving immediately and driving non-stop. I expected the idea of driving all day and all night to dismay him, but in fact he approved it. We could complete the journey, he thought, in forty-eight hours if Adwar came too as reserve driver, and they steered in shifts. He took it for granted I had no visa, and if we were avoiding hotels and towns it made it less likely we would be stopped. We negotiated a price of forty dollars for Jiji, seven dollars for Adwar and thirteen dollars for petrol, which seemed quite reasonable considering just across the Red Sea in North Yemen, sixty dollars doesn't even buy three gin and tonics at the Holiday Inn.

Jiji made me wait in his office, on a burst chair with the foam stuffing falling out, while he went to buy petrol; he wouldn't let me come too in case I saw how cheap it was. Adwar meanwhile went off to the market to collect nuts, bread, some squashy tomatoes and several bottles of Pepsi-Cola. The large crowd of youths was still hanging about, and when they were left alone with me became friendly. It was noticeable that there were girls in this group too, impossible in a

Moslem country. At least sixty percent of Eritreans are Christians of the Ethiopian Orthodox Church, a church of singular tolerance. In fact it was their Monophysite heresy in accommodating Islam, Egyptian and Jewish creeds that had led to the schism from Rome in 451 AD.

Jiji and Adwar returned after half an hour and stewed more tea, but I was anxious to be off so gulped my glass quickly and went and sat in the wagon. There were two passenger seats in front and the trailer which had been partially loaded with cans of petrol. I folded my map so it could conveniently be referred to in sections, and stowed the carpet bag of money behind my seat. I wasn't particularly worried that Jiji would rob me, but it seemed prudent, in the circumstances, to reduce the scope for thieving whilst I was asleep. In a few minutes we set off down the main drag, hooting wildly, Jiji shouting goodbye to every third man in the village, and I saw how unnecessary my hugger-mugger arrival from the Sudan had really been.

For ten miles from Karora we drove through threadbare grasslands where herdsmen presided over cadaverous cattle, then followed the track into the mountains. Here was scenery of astonishing beauty: steep, jagged escarpments rising almost vertically on both sides of the road, like a continuous battlement, behind which lay even higher ridges. It was obvious why the Ethiopians could never subdue the rebels.

After a couple of hours motoring through mountains, I started reading *The Times*, a copy of which I had bought in Port Sudan. It was ten days old and very creased and had in all probability been retrieved from a waste paper bin in a hotel bedroom and re-cycled for sale. In a section called Spectrum I read a flattering profile of Frank Bough explaining why he made such a plausible breakfast television presenter. On the next page there was a letter from the Chaplain of Keble College, Oxford, headed "A Tide Of Misery From Ethiopia". He was appealing for aid for the war refugees crossing from Eritrea into the Sudan. The university Chaplain had visited some of these refugee camps himself in the long summer vacation and found "mother and baby clinics with only a month's supply of drugs; doctors, when they existed at all, forced to perform major operations in squalid conditions; attempts to provide schooling in makeshift buildings with scarcely a textbook to use". He ended his letter with a plea for urgent resources "if the desperate consequences of drought and war are to be mitigated in any way."

I asked Jiji about the refugees but he pretended not to know what I was talking about. He said there had always been migration from the Sudan to Eritrea, and vice versa, the people were instinctively nomadic. The worst droughts, he said, were in the south, not in Eritrea. (This is true. It was the disastrous droughts in the south in 1972 to 1974, when an estimated three hundred thousand peasant farmers died, that hastened the downfall of Haile Selassie. But it is a strange thing about the south. In virtually every country in the world, apart from Britain, it is the poor arid fractious south that causes all the problems: Iran, Iraq, Egypt, Italy, India, the Sudan and now Ethiopia. I wanted to make an epigram out of one man's south being another man's north, but didn't think Jiji's English or my wit was quite up to it at that moment.)

We were making good time — were, in fact, ninety minutes ahead of my slapdash Ethiopian schedule — when we passed Mount Matite and descended into a huge forest. The change of vegetation was total: from moonscape to subtropical bush shot through with eucalyptus and jacaranda trees and trails of bougainvillea. There were waterfalls cascading hundreds of feet into the jungle below and packs of gelada — bleeding heart baboons — ran across the road at the approach of the car. Adwar, who was by now taking a turn at the wheel, swerved to run one over, which seemed unsporting; he justified himself by a bullish baboon skin market in Asmara.

Running parallel with the road for a few miles, was a tributary of the grey-green greasy Anseba river, a repulsive stagnant swamp shimmering with bilharzia, and I asked what the score was on crocodiles.

Jiji rummaged in the glove compartment and produced a crocodile foot sawn off just above the knuckle and mounted on a plinth of copper. He claimed to have shot the reptile himself but sounded half-hearted; later he forgot all about his boast and said such paws were freely available in the lobby boutique of Asmara's three-star Keren Hotel. Eritrea isn't really crocodile territory but the south-west of Ethiopia, around the Ghilo river, is the densest crocodile country in Africa. There you find the vicious twenty-foot species, the Ruwasa, with hides like handbags, which can be shot twice clean through the mouth and still not keel over.

Jiji began telling me a story about an American anthropologist and his contest against a Ghilo river crocodile, then trailed off as he struggled to find the right word. Over the next thirty hours I returned to the story over and over again, pestering him for extra details until I felt I had learnt as much as was possible given the complexity of the tribal spirit world. This, but not in his own words, and elaborated just a little by me, was the story:

"An American anthropologist in his early twenties had been sent to a remote part of the country, near Axum, to join an expedition seeking to prove that the Abyssinians were the seventh 'missing' tribe from the Book of Exodus. The field study was funded by an American millionaire or some similar philanthropist and not by a university or institution, all of whom were rather disdainful of the project. The millionaire backer, however, who was directing operations long distance from his home in Iowa, had been inspired by the legend that the Ark of the Covenant is preserved somewhere in the dry desert around Axum, so in the face of academic censure, most of which in any case passed him by, he set about recruiting the best team that money and his impatience could buy.

"He did not attract the high-fliers of the profession, the young Evans-Pritchards or Tom Wolfes with ambitions for a professorial chair. Instead his advertisements posted on university noticeboards were answered by anthropological carpet baggers, entrepreneurs and remittance men, who were tempted by the favourable salary scale. The expedition had five members, of which the American anthropologist in question was the fourth in seniority. They flew into Addis Ababa with a great variety of equipment, and after a few weeks spent making enquiries in the capital, managed to engage a dozen porters at several times the going rate. Then they set off, in a huge cavalcade, up to Axum where they pitched camp in the Axum Hotel. It was obvious to everyone right from the start that the expedition was ridiculous. There was no Ark of the Covenant and no possibility of finding one. The important thing was to wire back encouraging developments every so often, to keep the backer happy and the money flowing. So the anthropologists conducted field studies in the bar of the Axum Hotel and in the many brothels of the town, and made idle excursions by taxi to see the Ancient Baths of the Queen of Sheba which are also in the area.

"After about ten weeks of this, however, the millionaire backer showed signs of restlessness. His telegrams became terse and his demands for information insistent. To keep him quiet, the expedition leader, who was an inveterate fornicator and drunkard, who had never risen from his bed until midday, telegrammed that they had discovered inscriptions on the walls of the baths suggesting that the Ark was several hundred miles to the West, in the middle of the jungle, and that they were persevering with their scriptural structuralism.

" 'Studies be blowed' wired back the millionaire: they should proceed immediately to the village of Adi Selam. He said he had been monitoring events on his 1:1,000,000 wall map and had a hunch that the Ark was there.

"This put the expedition on the spot. They couldn't remain at the Axum Hotel because their bill was paid directly by their backer and the management was reluctant to sanction deceit. There was nothing for it but to leave for Adi Selam, which is a godforsaken spot with no hotels and just native huts to sleep in. They arrived a week later, after a most uncomfortable journey, and leased some straw huts and played gin rummy.

"Now Adi Selam is only a few miles from the Zalema river, which is notorious for its crocodiles. The natives will not travel in canoes except in convoy and the women who beat their clothes clean on the rocks are frequently dragged off by these wily reptiles and consumed. With the flick of their tails they can break a man's back, and in many of the remoter villages along the river the crocodile is worshipped as a god.

"Shortly after the anthropologists arrived, the crocodiles suddenly started becoming doubly ferocious. They capsized canoes and dragged goats off the bank and, it was said, began to invade the villages at night, slithering several hundred yards into the corral and attacking children in their beds. It didn't take the villagers long to work out who was responsible. The anthropologists had upset the river gods and there must be an oblation.

"Not all the elders of the village agreed. Some were making useful pocket money by renting their wives and daughters to the randy anthropologists, at a fixed rate, and were enjoying their menthol cigarettes and brandy. But when the atrocities persisted, the headman of the tribe agreed that something must be done and he sent for the anthropologists to report to his hut. There he told them that a sacrifice was required, at the earliest time convenient to both parties, which in the headman's case was dawn the following morning. One of the anthropologists must jump from the river bank and wrestle to the death with a crocodile. Then the five men were escorted to a hut on the edge of the village where they were guarded by several heavily-garred natives.

"All night the anthropologists argued about who should be sacrificed.

The leader of the expedition said that, as the most distinguished of them academically, he could not forfeit his life; the youngest argued that, as the fellow with the shortest innings, it would be unreasonable to take him off so early. In the end they drew cards for it and the fourth American anthropologist, who is the hero of the story, drew the three of diamonds and sealed his fate. Then the rest of the expedition told him how much they had always thought of him, and what a great guy he was, and they were quite sure death would be instantaneous.

"In the morning, with much ceremony, the whole village lined the river to spectate. Children climbed trees for a better view and old men imparted oral traditions of previous sacrifices. The victim was led to the bank and, just as the sun came up, he was thrown into the water. About thirty crocodiles immediately glided towards him and his terrible end seemed inevitable. But suddenly, and for no apparent reason, the crocodiles turned tail and swam away up river, as though something had stung them. The villagers were dumbfounded. It was clear that this man was himself a river god — a maluth — and he was helped exhausted out of the filthy water and draped with a leopard skin cloak and carried to the headman's hut where he was drip-fed goat's milk from an ivory gourd.

"That afternoon the headman's own three daughters, who were preposterously nubile and certified virgin and scarcely older than fourteen, were ushered into the hut for his delectation, and later the same evening the headman pleaded with him to marry them.

"The anthropologist's colleagues scoffed at the idea. Their only thought was heading back to the Axum Hotel before anything else happened and they couldn't believe he might choose to stay. But the fourth anthropologist thought it over, and in the end he couldn't find any good reason to go home. He wasn't married. He had very little money by American standards. His professional standing fluctuated between abject and nil. So he accepted the headman's offer and several days later married all his daughters at a monumental feast, and settled back to an agreeable life doing nothing, while his wives herded his cattle, and washed his blanket and thatched the roof of his hut with dried reeds.

"Every two years or so the anthropologist quits the village for three weeks and travels on his own to Addis Ababa. The journey takes ten days each way. There he books a room for the night in the Hilton

Hotel, takes a bath, dials room service for a dry martini and watches television in bed. In the morning he collects his new American Express card from his box number at the central post office, settles the bill with plastic and makes a cash withdrawal on the card for a hundred pounds. Then he writes out a cheque for the total amount and mails it straight to American Express so no debt is outstanding. The interest he accrues from his modest investments in the States easily covers his bi-annual binge in Addis Ababa. The hundred pounds cash he spends on several bottles of whisky for his father-in-law, and some prize steers to bolster his herd. He is always pleased to get home to the village. At night he deviates slightly from local custom by sleeping with all three of his wives at the same time, but this eccentricity is overlooked by his fellow tribesmen. Above the lintel of his hut is the escutcheon of the crocodile god: a severed reptile's head with glass beads in the place of eyes."

We had emerged from the forest and were heading across grasslands back towards the coast and the Port of Massawa. I would have preferred to skirt Massawa altogether, because it is a government base, but there is no alternative road and in any case Jiji needed to buy motor oil and provisions. It was getting dark and I wanted to put several miles between ourselves and the port before I dared doze, so we made a plan. Adwar and I would hole up in a cafe several miles short of Massawa while Jiji took the Chevrolet into town to shop. Then he would pick us up, hide me under a rug on the floor of the wagon, and drive through Massawa as rapidly as possible.

The plan worked well. Adwar and I drank tea in a cafe close to the beach and I taught him clock patience. Jiji returned within the hour bearing bags of nuts and sesame seeds, several slices of flat spongy bread called injera, and a bowl of foul-tasting cold porridge topped with green cooking oil. I did not eat this, but Jiji and Adwar spread dollops of it on their bread. Later I heard this dish is prepared in a pottery gourd disinfected with human urine. After supper we got back into the wagon and I took up my rather informal position near the gear stick.

Jiji drove with great speed but carefully; it would be fatal to be flagged down by the police at this stage. I saw nothing of Massawa: I believe it has a striking imperial palace in the Egyptian-Swiss style;

and only got the impression it smells of diesel. Three miles into the suburbs, I was just about to sit up when Adwar forced my head down again with his thumbs. We were crossing the railway line and there was a delay at the level crossing. There was a rumbling of armaments and trucks overtaking us and a great deal of shrill whistling. After ten minutes the commotion stopped. Adwar wouldn't let me up for another five miles. "Russians," said Jiji. "Russians and Cuba. From Ogaden." The Ogaden, in the extreme south of Ethiopia on the Somali border, is another disputed territory, invaded by the Somalis in 1977 and only recaptured with Soviet help. Now they were heading for Eritrea.

It was well after midnight and we had been driving for eight hours. I asked Jiji to pull over onto the soft shoulder and we rearranged the sleeping accommodation, which meant ejecting Adwar to the wagon with the petrol cans and gaining extra leg room for me. It seemed ridiculous, as I dwelt on it, that this was the only feasible way of following Phileas Fogg's route south, but there was no other. None of the ships fast enough to be viable put in at Djibouti; Saudi Arabia and the Yemen were closed; and I had to round the Horn of Africa. So I wound a towel around my carpet bag to make a pillow and slept fitfully against the passenger window. The frequent potholes on the road made real rest impossible and the serrated edge of the ashtray in the door kept cutting into my elbow. I abandoned all hope of sleep at first light, around 4.30 a.m. We were driving only a hundred yards from the sea past a formation of misty islands; it was surprisingly cold so I put on a jersey and meddled with my battery razor. Within half an hour it turned hot so I removed the jersey again and lowered the sun visor. It would have been fun to have swum, the sea looked warm and calm, but it didn't seem a wise move.

We were making excellent time. The road had improved and there were now high hopes of leaving Ethiopia by late that evening. The only cause for unease was the Djibouti border which would certainly be manned by Ethiopian immigration officers who would notice my lack of visa. There was no way of predicting their reaction. At worst, they could take me to Addis Ababa for interrogation, fine me and deport me on the next flight to London. It would be a dismal and slightly humiliating way of concluding the adventure.

"Police. Lower down mister."

Jiji tried to push me to the floor but it was too late. We had been spotted by an on-coming jeep and were being flashed with headlamps.

To our left was a lighthouse and a cluster of small huts but otherwise there was nothing but grasslands, rough grazing and thornbushes, as far as the eye could see. The policemen wore black leather, but underneath they wore T-shirts and their dark glasses were not sinister like the El Salvador Treasury Police, but had a touch of high fashion; or rather low fashion, these Polaroids were knock-on merchandise. There were three of them. The Chief of Police carried a riding crop.

They stuck their head inside the van, then told us to get out. We stood on the side of the road while they threw my luggage and the bag of nuts onto the track. It was inevitable they would ask to see my non-existent visa. Then I noticed, on the backseat of the jeep, a huge Toshiba music centre: the kind of portable cassette player the Arabs and Indians so much admire. Alongside was a pile of cassettes: local dance music for the most part but also a Beatles tape, Sergeant Pepper.

"Ah, Beatles," I said. "English pop music."

The Chief of Police looked pleased. He swaggered over to the jeep and inserted the tape.

"Let me take you down, where I'm go-ing to," blared the speakers. "Strawberry Fields for ever." It sounded more nasal than I remembered.

"John Lennon."

"John Lennon." The Chief of Police repeated the name. Then he said, "Bang, bang." News of the assassination had reached Abyssinia.

I retrieved my carpet bag from the road where it had been thrown and fished for a tape. The first one I put my hand on was David Bowie. I presented it to the Chief of Police who tried it out.

"DRI-I-I-VE in Saturday-ay."

He was delighted. I spread out the map on the bonnet and asked him for directions to Saroyta. It was another twelve miles straight along the track, though you could hardly have taken a wrong turning because there weren't any. The Chief of Police decided to escort us. We followed the jeep all the way to the village, waved and kept on going. But the policemen weren't watching; they had pulled up in the market place and were showing off the tape.

There were four small sentry boxes at the border, two of them Ethiopian, two of them Djiboutean. They were separated by about forty feet of tarmac, with a toll gate at either end. I knew this because I had asked Jiji and Adwar to drop me five hundred yards from the border, so I could approach on foot allowing time for reconnaissance.

It was about an hour after dusk. We had covered the last two hundred mile stretch from Saroyta in under seven hours, including an inland detour around a dormant volcano and twenty miles of fossilised lava. I had divided my reservoir of dollars into two piles: the main supply at the bottom of the case, a small float on top. This was going to be the ultimate test of money opening doors. Three Ethiopian soldiers, all of them rather diminutive, sat on upturned packing cases smoking cigarettes and scratching their heads.

It cost fifteen dollars. I played the scatty Englishman, affable but bemused, who had arrived at Addis Ababa and quite simply never been issued with a visa. For some reason or other I had slipped through the net, don't ask me how. Perhaps it was because I had arrived transit then extended my stay, who knows. The police in Saroyta had okayed my passage but if a small fine was called for then I'd gladly pay up without further ado. I was frightfully sorry if I'd inadvertently fouled the system in any way.

The captain of the three guards told me to follow him into the sentry post. It was a square concrete building with a stone bench along the length of one wall like a country bus station. Various official notices were pinned to the back of the door, and there was a tin tray with glasses laid out for tea. And there was no telephone. I could see a short wave radio set but nothing with which he could easily make contact with Addis Ababa.

I repeated my daft story and stressed how anxious I was to be getting along; there was still a long drive to Djibouti. The captain passed me an exit form to complete and then, almost apologetically, revived the subject of the fine. I took out a bundle of bank notes, taking care he didn't see how many there were. It was obvious that there was no set scale for this offence and the captain was making it all up as he went along: he was just going to pluck a figure from the air. To start the bidding I put ten dollars on the desk, then added a third five dollar note. The captain seemed satisfied, folded them in half and attached a paper clip.

The customs pole was raised, I lifted up my carpet bag and the ridiculous swordstick which had long ago become a liability and difficult to carry, and hot-footed it into Djibouti, the toe-rag of Africa.

8 | *In which a visit is paid to a house of small virtue.*
And a dhow is sought across the Arabian Sea.

The drawback of entering the Republic of Djibouti from Ethiopia is the absence of any welcoming committee. Since the border is closed, there is no taxi rank. Nor is there very much else, apart from desert and salt mines, all the way to Tadjoura.

Djibouti is generally described as a poor man's Aden and is mentioned in the *Book of Lists* as one of thirteen top destinations to avoid on your travels. It did not surprise me that Phileas Fogg, with his unerring nose for a hell-hole, should have chosen to call there. Rather like a nightclub, Djibouti keeps changing its name with a view to attracting more customers. Within recent memory it has variously been trading as The Kingdom of the Afars and Isaacs and as French Somaliland. I hadn't much been looking forward to my time in Djibouti. In the event, it turned out to be rather an amusing hole, judged by its own lights.

One of the frontier guards kindly offered a lift to Faga, a village opposite the Bab Al Mandab Strait, and there I found a taxi prepared to take me to Djibouti itself. (Confusingly, the country is now named after the capital.) The taxi was a black Zodiac and soon we were rattling along a rough road past plains of evaporated salt. This section of the coast used to be sea-bed, and Afar people harvest the saline deposits in baskets and sell them to each other. Because Djibouti is insignificant and included in no pocket diary, I made the mistake of underestimating its size. I had hoped to reach the port in less than an hour, but after two hours we'd only got as far as Tadjoura and the driver decided to drop me there instead. He said I could easily take a ferry across the

Gulf to the capital, and that this would furthermore save me hundreds of Djibouti francs. This mention of a saving, coupled with his shifty expression, should have been enough to alert me that something was wrong. No sooner had the taxi left in a cloud of grit than I learned the ferry was out of action.

Tadjoura seemed rather an interesting town, with a large truck park and a large camel park side by side. There are also seven mosques but these were invisible from my downtown vantage point. I was contributing to a five party summit conference about taxi fares around the Gulf, when an English voice said, "If you're heading for Djibouti could I cadge a lift?"

Charles Van Krieff had wavy ginger hair and carried a briefcase. His brogues were expensive but very worn; later he explained this was due to constant rubbing by shoe-shine boys. He was not a tourist but was in Djibouti on business, though he was vague about this. He had no permanent base in town but said his commitment to Djibouti was one hundred percent, and he lived in a hotel called the Pensione Dorra. Djibouti's crucial geographical position at the tail of the Red Sea was certain to pay off, sooner rather than later, especially as the Russians tightened their grip on Somalia.

"NATO will have to take this place over," said Charles Van Krieff. "It's only the French who are stalling them. And if the Yemen goes red, then that will be it. Moscow could close the Red Sea tomorrow."

He said he was thirty-five and had been hanging around Africa for six years collecting contacts: some of these, he implied were in the highest echelons of government and would be worth their weight when the economy perked up. At some earlier time he said he had been in a guard's regiment, and after that a hippy. He did not respond well to the army surnames I bounced off him, but was sound on cheap Iranian hotels. After this grilling he never mentioned his army career again, but spoke expansively of North India which I have not visited.

For someone with such a commitment to the place, Charles Van Krieff was not enamoured of Djibouteans. He said they are homicidal, second in this respect only to the Somalis.

We reached the outskirts of the capital and I asked for the name of a hotel. Charles Van Krieff was adamant I should stay at the Djibouti Sheraton, dismissing my scruples about finding better "copy" elsewhere than an American chain.

"Come off it, you won't travel faster in a mud hut. In fact it could slow you down. If you're searching for a ship you must flash your Sheraton room key." Then he invited himself to dinner courtesy of my Barclay card Visa.

The Djibouti Sheraton is typical of a modern African hotel. It is built to a grid pattern from reinforced concrete, with an outsized lobby influenced architecturally by the domestic terminal at Heathrow airport. At the last minute, however, just as the plans were leaving his studio, the architect must have remembered that the hotel was destined for a primitive place, and made appropriate additions. So there is a swimming pool changing hut with a grass roof and a wooden sculpture outside the dining-room made from spears.

Charles Van Krieff and I had dinner in a restaurant called Le Punt, where we ate grilled prawns and drank lager. Afterwards we looked in at the hotel nightclub, Le Guepard, which the receptionist recommended as the best anywhere on the Red Sea. However it turned out to be on this occasion empty and, after a lot of commotion, we were allowed to tear up our cover charges and leave. Charles Van Krieff wrote down his telephone number at the Pensione Dorra, but when I subsequently rang him it was unobtainable.

I went to bed but was awakened half an hour later by knocking at the door. I shouted, "Come in," but there was no response except more knocking. Eventually I got up and opened the door. A waiter was standing in the passage with a guest list.

"May I ask you your room number, sir?"

I told him.

He asked could I repeat it.

I said, "For crying out loud, you must know which room this is. It has the number on the door."

"We have to check," said the waiter. "Sorry to disturb you." And then he continued his errand the length of the corridor.

This constant cross-referencing was, I soon discovered, a hallmark of the Djibouti Sheraton. You couldn't move without declaring your room number several times.

"May I buy some stamps at reception?"

"Room number, sir?"

"Have you got the time?"

"Room number?"

Even at the Olympic size pool, where I swam a couple of lengths before breakfast, a flunky trotted from end to end until he had recorded my number. The effect of all this questioning was disconcerting. Luxury hotels are only truly luxurious if they make the visitor feel carefree. At the Djibouti Sheraton you felt "there by the grace of God go I", and that the moment you checked out you would be booted into the street.

Another disconcerting thing about the Djibouti Sheraton was that none of the waiters were at all familiar with the menu. If you asked for a club sandwich they looked disbelieving, as though you had just invented this item to fox them. Even when you pointed it out, they pretended it was a "special" and not normally available.

After breakfast, while it was still cool, I began my search for a boat to Bombay. There is still quite a lot of traffic on this route, and I had been told I should have no difficulty. As so often, the optimistic prediction at a London dinner party soon shrivelled beneath caustic exposure to reality. Several dozen large dhows were tied up against the port, but none of them were going to Bombay. One captain with horribly blackened teeth thought he might sail in twenty days' time, but the rest were indefinitely awaiting a full hold of cargo. None was encouraging about an early sailing; on the credit side, however, they at least agreed that such a voyage was viable.

I had read somewhere (I think in an article by John Hatt) that animal skins are regularly smuggled from Djibouti to India and vice versa. Since the governments of both countries clamped down on export licences for cheetah skins, a large trade has grown up in smuggling them to and fro. So now it is easy to buy Indian cheetah skins at the market in Djibouti, and African cheetah skins in Bombay.

It occurred to me that if I could locate a pelt merchant, he might put me in touch with a ship.

The stallholders with skins for sale were not cooperative. They said they didn't know where the skins appeared from, their job was selling them and would I like an ibex rug? I informed them that the bottom fell out of the trophy market more than ten years ago, and I could get one for half the price at Sotheby's Belgravia. They were very interested to hear this and noted down the address.

Feeling rather dispirited I had a cup of tea. The cafes in Djibouti have a Parisian feel and one was offering croissants, though when these arrived they tasted like bagels. There are still several thousand French Foreign Legionnaries garrisoned in the town and all the cafes double as brothels for their benefit. The reason the drinks are so expensive is that the brothels don't allow reservations, so they make a hefty profit in the bar while punters queue for upstairs.

There was a Djiboutean in the bar wearing an embroidered cap and a pair of leopard skin shoes, and on the off-chance I pointed to the shoes and growled. This should have indicated that I sought a skin smuggler. He was quick on the uptake and led me out into the street. We walked at speed through dusty alleyways for about twenty minutes until we had virtually left the town; houses petered out and there were palm trees. Eventually we arrived at a corrugated metal hut with a window like a ticket office and, sure enough, a head popped out and asked for twenty Djibouti francs. I bought two tickets and my guide led me inside. It was Djibouti Zoo.

A passer-by suggested I consult the British Consulate. I had no idea we had a consulate in town and was certain they couldn't help, but the notion was intriguing. To be posted to Djibouti must surely be the shortest straw in the service, unless of course it was a shortcut to promotion. I imagined eager Consular Secretaries, still in their early twenties and sticking out the discomfort with the promise of Rome to follow. Or perhaps Djibouti was a diplomatic punishment block, staffed by cashiered alcoholics from Jeddah or ex-First Secretaries caught in bed with an ambassador's wife. Definitely it merited a detour.

Everybody in Djibouti knew exactly where the British Consulate was, but none of their directions were compatible. I had visited the Belgian, Norwegian and Italian Consulates before I realised this was another wild goose chase. Britain sensibly maintains no diplomatic presence in the Republic of Djibouti.

I suddenly remembered that I had been given an introduction to a Madame Bustier, a French resident said to be on good terms with all the local captains. My informant, who now lives in the Virgin Islands, could remember almost nothing about her except that she had been the mainstay of Djiboutean society in the fifties. However, she was not listed in what passes for a telephone book; the hotel operator suggested she might be ex-directory.

The barman at a cafe called Khamsin had heard of Madame Bustier, however. His face lit up with recognition at mention of her name and he instructed me to return to his cafe at seven o'clock that evening. When I arrived bearing charts of the Arabian Sea, I was immediately escorted by the barman's son to another cafe closer to the port. This establishment did not have a name above the door and was located in a basement. There was a strong smell of incense and many of the clientele were chewing qat, the narcotic leaf which is so popular in Djibouti and the Yemen. There were very few chairs and all of these were taken, so I stood inconspicuously against a wall debating which of these zombies might be Madame Bustier or a master mariner.

The barman's son, my chaperone, was involved in an argument with the doorman; every so often he pointed at me and there was renewed bitterness. Eventually the barman's son was handed some money and promptly left.

I took matters in hand and requested an immediate audience with Madame Bustier.

The doorman who had so recently paid off the barman's son laughed. Madame Bustier, he said, had left Djibouti long ago; for all he knew she was dead. Nevertheless, I believe I detected a slight deference for her memory. Madame Bustier had owned these premises in their heyday, when customers dressed for dinner and all the girls knew how to repair a black tie in the early hours.

The club, I was told, was under new management and catered for an inferior class of punter. Several French Foreign Legionnaires stumbled down the stairs to endorse this observation and were joined by Somali girls. In the corner were wooden cabins.

The doorman, who was also the barman, offered me a drink. I now realised that my escort to the club had been tipped for introducing me, so I felt obliged to spend some francs in compensation. Some rum-based punch was mixed in a bowl but I chose Coca-Cola. In due course a Somali girl joined me and I bought her one too. I thought that even in Djibouti there could be no favours in return for Coca-Cola and this proves to be so. The Somali girl kept whining "Rum, rum, bum, rum," but when this was not forthcoming she wandered away.

After about an hour the management offered complimentary plates of cocktail snacks to all customers who had bought drinks. These were very plain and unpretending, consisting of hard-boiled eggs and chillis. I was eating the egg and leaving the chillis when a stranger joined my table.

He said: "Are you the Englishman who is looking for a boat to Bombay? Because I am sailing in three days' time."

Ahmet Singh was half Indian and wore a grey suit jacket over his jalabayya. My first impression was a good one and I never had reason to change it. I offered him a drink and he ordered a Coke. He said he had been hunting for me all over town. He had heard an Englishman needed a passage, and was surprised I'd chosen to drink in this particular nightclub. I explained the confusion over Madame Bustier and he seemed relieved: my Captain was evidently a prude.

His ship was called the *Socotra* and she was a one hundred and ten foot motorised dhow. If I sailed with her I could have a cabin to myself and the trip would take between five and seven days. I asked what we would be carrying as cargo and Mr Singh said cotton, dates and bags of salt. This seemed most unlikely and, in due course, my suspicions were fully justified.

The *Socotra* would not be sailing to Bombay itself but to Alibag, a smaller port about thirty miles to the south. Mr Singh explained that the harbour charges were much lower there and there was less chance of delay. Then we discussed money and I offered a two-tier system. If we left in three days' time I would pay one price (three hundred and fifty dollars); if we left tomorrow I would pay another (four hundred and fifty dollars). This would be handed over in two instalments: the first as I stepped on board, the second as I stepped off in Alibag. Mr Singh came to the conclusion that the cargo he was awaiting wasn't worth a hundred dollars to him, so we agreed to sail the following night.

My last day in Djibouti I spent buying provisions for the journey and attending a lunchtime barbecue at the Djibouti Sheraton. On a notice board in the lobby was a collage of photographs of "distinguished guests" who had graced the hotel in recent months. One was a junior minister for French trade, frenetically shaking hands. At the barbecue, however, the most frenetic guests were a swarm of tsetse flies who circulated sociably from arm to arm.

9 | *In which the Arabian Sea is crossed by motorised dhow. And time passes more sluggishly than elsewhere.*

Captain Ahmet Singh's crew on the *Socotra* were also half Indian and half Moslem. One of them, Rajiv, was Ahmet's brother; the three ratings were also in some way related to the Singhs; a fourth, Sami, was a spectral youth who cowered miserably throughout the voyage except when he was listening to my Hitachi Walkman. Sami was employed as cabin boy, mess boy and steward combined; his main duty consisted of stirring an episodic stew to which new ingredients and spices were added daily.

I had decided not to overburden the galley by sharing this tagines, and as soon as I was shown to my cabin, unpacked several bags of provisions. Shopping in Djibouti is cathartic before a long voyage since the choice is surprisingly good. Djibouti is the packet biscuit capital of East Africa, though these are mostly broken; only the wrapping saves them from crumbling away altogether. Nevertheless, I had managed to buy bread, processed cheddar, dates, oranges, cheese biscuits, nuts and Coca-Cola, and had furthermore procured Marmite in Aqaba and saved some apricot jam from the Djibouti Sheraton, and it looked like enough for six days.

The *Socotra* was a wooden dhow with a sail which could be unfurled when helpful and a muscle-bound engine. At full throttle she could achieve almost nine knots and, apart from occasional rests to let the motor cool down, she chugged onwards night and day. There were three cabins on deck, or rather sunk into the deck: one shared between watches by Ahmet and Rajiv Singh; one for the ratings and one occupied by me; there was a cubbyhole in the stern for Sami. My cabin had a foam mattress raised on a ledge with drawers underneath, several hooks, two small windows at deck level and a tool box. The only other facility on the *Socotra* was a small washroom which Sami spent several hours a day sweeping out with a palm broom.

We set off with the minimum of fuss, heading first towards the south coast of the Gulf of Aden, which is disputed territory between Djibouti and Somalia, to avoid some shallow sandbanks. I hadn't registered quite how long the Horn of Africa is: we would have to sail two hundred miles before we even reached the Arabian Sea, and this through difficult waters. Captain Ahmet Singh explained that the Somali current can attain speeds of seven knots, becoming part of a clockwise circulation system that continues all the way to India. Therefore it was crucial to use the current to our own advantage rather than sail against it.

By the time I woke up we were passing the island of Socotra, after which the dhow was named. Socotra is now occupied by South Yemen, despite sovereignty claims by Somalia; it is used by the Yemens as a military base and shipping is forbidden to pass closer than twelve miles.

While I was talking to Rajiv Singh I noticed a stack of raw meat on deck and asked whether it would be better stored somewhere cool. Rajiv laughed heartily at this suggestion and repeated it to Sami who sniggered. The meat, he said, was for throwing overboard in case of shark attack, as a diversion. All Arab dhows carry raw meat as basic equipment; they buy it for next to nothing from butchers when it is too high for human consumption.

The *Socotra* was not a comfortable ship for a passenger, since there was no sundeck. The flat tops of the cabins were lashed with cargo and the companionways were too narrow for sitting out. The choice, therefore, was lounging in bed inside the cabin or talking to Ahmet or Rajiv Singh in the open wheelhouse. Both these options lost their novelty after about an hour, by which time one craved either silence or company. A solution which worked well for the first two days was sitting with the Singhs in the sun, while avoiding conversation by listening to the Hitachi Walkman. Sami, who was a closet raver, suddenly got very into Dexy's Midnight Runners and listened to them non-stop until he ran the battery flat.

From then on, diversions aboard the *Socotra* were at a premium.

I'd finished all the novels I had bought in Port Sudan, and the only reading matter available in Djibouti was a copy of *Newsweek*. I tried to ration my perusal of this journal to one article per hour, but it was tempting to plough on. By lunch time on the second day I had read every column inch in the issue, and now hungrily picked the corpse clean like a scavenging hyena. I read articles that I wouldn't normally have tackled in a million years; new developments in computer software, bacterial breakthroughs in cattle disease, an incredibly turgid book review of a bibliography of Dostoevsky, which had to be digested in sections. Even then some shreds of offal remained on the carcass.

I wondered whether I was the only person, apart from the staff, ever to have read the names of every one of the two hundred and eighty-seven editors and writers listed on the *Newsweek* masthead. After that I memorised the retail price of *Newsweek International* around the world. In future, whenever I am in Iceland, Finland or Yugoslavia I will automatically be able to produce 40.00 Kr, 10.00 Mk or 130 Yd respectively without needing to refer to the cover.

I made a list of all the things one could do aboard the *Socotra*. These were as follows:

1. Eat nuts. You can easily kill several minutes prising the shell off a pistachio nut.

2. Talk to the Captain and ask him how we were doing.

3. Stare out to sea.

4. Doze.

5. Read *Newsweek*. I was hoarding a paragraph about zip codes, printed in microscopic type, for a rainy day.

It was also of course possible to combine some of the above activities, for instance reading *Newsweek* while eating nuts, or talking to Captain Ahmet Singh while staring out to sea. But on the whole I did not squander my pleasures and enjoyed them singly.

After we'd left the coast of Africa behind, there was nothing to focus on in any direction except Arabian Sea. There are no islands, no rocks, no coral reefs or oil rigs. The sea is extremely deep, mostly exceeding nine thousand feet, which makes for calm water; there is little swell and almost no tide. Also, because we were close to the water, we hardly listed at all and the only subsidence was due to the vibration of the motor.

The Arabian Sea is nevertheless a mysterious ocean, less well charted than the Atlantic or the Pacific, mainly because the surrounding countries are inhospitable to expeditions. One strange phenomenon is the periodic mass death of fish. Twenty-five years ago, said Captain

Ahmet Singh, twenty million tons of fish suddenly floated to the surface, including sharks, wahoo, billfish and tuna. Nobody knows exactly why this happened: scientists believe it is due to poor oxygen; seamen blame volcanic eruptions on the sea bed; cranks suspect Soviet activity at a secret underground submarine base. What is remarkable is that the same thing has taken place every half century since the middle ages, and there are numerous historical references in Arabian archives.

Rajiv Singh was the only member of the crew who was married; his wife and three children lived in Djibouti with her parents while he was at sea. There was also a third Singh brother, currently languishing in bed with a broken ankle, a salutory object lesson to the inhabitants of Tadjoura not to back into the main road when a lorryload of Seven-Up bottles are passing.

Close inspection of the cargo confirmed that it was not, in fact, composed solely of cotton, dates and salt; there was also qat, for Arab expatriates in India, and several animal pelts. These mostly originated from Kenya and Somalia, were smuggled up through the Ogaden and processed in Djibouti. Judging by their smell, most of the skins had been inadequately cured and would quickly begin to moult, so from the customer's point of view they can scarcely be worth buying.

Although we had compasses and charts on board, Captain Ahmet Singh made little use of them. He had been sailing this route for so many years, originally as an apprentice to his uncle, that he knew it instinctively from the current. The stars, which are incredibly bright in the black Arabian Sea, are also an important navigational aid. Later I was told that the Djibouti to India route was charted as early as the ninth century by Arabian sailors, in manuals called Rahmangs, which contain virtually all the same information used today.

On the fifth day I rose again to find a slight breeze and the sail in action. This meant that we were within two hundred miles of land and the wind was blowing up from the Indian Ocean. It also meant that the sea became slightly choppy and spray broke over the prow of the dhow. To celebrate, I had a long interesting read of *Newsweek*'s zip code announcement; by the time I finished it we were several hundred yards nearer Bombay.

On the sixth morning, just after dawn, we were within sight of land. Captain Singh could tell from the coastline that we were about twenty miles too far south, so we tacked to the left with a following wind and headed for Alibag. Three hours later we put into port where some slightly rum cronies of Captain Ahmet Singh immediately carted away the cargo.

I bought an omelette for Sami in a cafe, made my farewells and sought a taxi rank.

•

10 | *In which the whole width of India is traversed by railway. And disparities emerge over the duration of the journey.*

A taxi was easily engaged in Alibag and we arrived in Bombay via the town of Pen in just over an hour. As we approached the city, however, I was surprised by how little traffic was about on the streets; in fact my black Alibag Austin was the only vehicle in sight. Nor were there any Indians: the pavements were empty, the shops shuttered, the food kiosks deserted, the whole populace vamoosed. Since Bombay has eight million citizens crammed onto an island the size of Parsons Green, it was most mysterious, as though an acid monsoon had strafed the metropolis and everyone fallen out.

I had asked to be taken to Victoria Station, Bombay's central terminus, and here at least was activity: if four thousand Tamils crashed out on benches can be so described. The Tamils and Indian railways were the only sectors not observing the bandt, a massive one-day strike called by the Hindus in protest at state land compensation. The government were compulsorily purchasing some fields on the Bombay perimeter, to extend the docks, and the whole city was protesting about reparation. This explained the Empty Quarter.

Victoria Station is a cavernous gothic edifice of grey stone, with soaring buttresses and medieval revival gargoyles. It is usually compared to Ely or Chartres Cathedrals, but it reminded me of a provincial art gallery or theological college; it has a gloomy, dripping air and you expect rhododendron bushes. Instead there are scores of red-coated porters carrying sacks of maize on their shoulders, picking their way through the slumbering mass wrapped in blankets or brewing up tea on the station platform.

I joined a ticket line at a window marked Madras, but was directed instead to an office on the edge of the station. This is the tourist bureau, a uniquely Indian notion whereby Europeans are given priority booking seats. For every train out of Victoria Station, two berths are reserved until three hours before departure, in case any free-wheeling Aryan should wish to travel. This suited me fine, and I consulted Mr Daitari (his name was displayed on his lapel) about timetables.

"Please be seated, Mister, sit you down." Mr Daitari indicated a three-legged chair stabilised with old timetables. He was a wiry, nervous Indian with highly polished brass buttons of the Central Railway Company; his hair was Brylcreemed into a solid apostrophe on the crown of his head. On the wall behind his desk hung three sandalwood framed pictures: an 1897 railway map of India, the river front at Benares and a bleached-out photograph of the Chattar Manzil in Lucknow.

"Now, Mister, you are in perfect repose and able to tell me your required destination."

I said my required destination was Madras.

"That will present no problem," said Mr Daitari, "but not tonight. Two other Londoners, Mr & Mrs J Adams, have just reserved those actual seats, perhaps you are knowing them?"

I said I didn't believe I had yet had the pleasure and Mr Daitari conceded that this was quite possible, London being such a great city. "But it is a small world," he reminded me.

I bought a ticket for the 22.10 Madras Mail for the next evening and Mr Daitari detailed a runner to join the queue. He said the train would take twenty-seven hours to cover the one thousand three hundred and fifty-six miles, and would depart from platform twelve. I worked the hours forward in my diary: it was going to be a tight connection for my steamer to Singapore — five hours — but Mr Daitari reassured me that the Madras Mail was famously reliable, it never ran more than twenty minutes late. We drank a cup of milky tea until the boy returned with the ticket: first-class air-conditioned sleeper-berth number seventeen: and then I made to leave. Mr Daitari held my elbow with a surprisingly meaty hand.

"A word of warning before you go, Mister. Indian trains are very safe, especially first-class, but there are bad fellows the world over. And some of these persons are in India at this very moment. You have probably heard already of the Tamil Tigers?"

I confessed ignorance; they sounded like a baseball team.

"Very bad fellows," said Mr Daitari, "from Sri Lanka. Also the Cobra Group from Sri Lanka. That country has got too hot for them, so they bought their dacoity to India, stopping trains and stealing jewellery."

I asked Mr Daitari what steps he advised for my safety.

"Now I am telling you," said Mr Daitari, "the Cobra Group have a secret sign, a snake tattoo on their upper arm, it is a sure giveaway. If you observe the Cobra Tattoo, don't dally, sir, open the compartment door and jump for your life."

I wasn't sorry to be trapped in Bombay for twenty hours. I was hot and sticky and worn out and an instant departure to Madras would have been tiresome. I longed for a bath and wanted, if possible, to have some laundry rapidly turned round. Finding a taxi out of the station was difficult since they were all observing the bandt, but eventually a yellow blackleg cab cruised by and I asked for the Taj Mahal Hotel.

The Taj is one of the great hotels of Asia. It stands directly opposite the Gateway of India, the great triumphal arch erected to celebrate the royal tour of George V and Queen Mary, and like every successful hotel east of Athens has an old and a new wing. The original Taj is like a Hindu-fied station hotel, with elaborate wooden balconies and mahogany telephone kiosks; the new Taj is a bright white skyscraper, wherein the Club Sandwich Coffee Shop for American visitors. Burly bell captains in turbans, cummerbunds and frock coats bawl out taxi drivers, and footmen tiptoe silently to and fro with blackboards, paging guests, with cowbells tinkling from their caps. There is a large marble lobby, and well sprung sofas, and discreet staff who know instinctively whether you have a right to be there. In other words the Taj is a proper hotel, with employees who find nothing demeaning about hotel work and don't merely consider it a convenient cover for freelance blackmail.

I took a room in the old wing and kicked off my shoes and lay on the bedcover: a fitted, quilted cover with a flap for the pillows of the type you only find in such hotels. The brass bedside lamps had a solid look about them and did not threaten to flicker or fuse when you rolled over. I had a long, hot bath and shaved, then pottered around the room in a towel until I felt ready for the next bath. There is no more elevating sight in the world than a pile of thick large fresh white hotel towels, folded on a shelf, and it seemed a pity not to use them all. In no time at all my entire wardrobe had returned from the laundry.

In the evening, dressed in clean clothes, I drank some Bloody Mary in the bar and mused on how congenial a proper barman's job must be. Moslem bars seemed ridiculous by comparison: waiters, waiters everywhere but not a drop to drink; just coconut shies of Pepsi bottles and Miranda orange and comical nonalcoholic cocktails made out of rosehip and lemonade; the sort of drinks Americans devise for their children, with names like a Mickey Mouse or a Goofy Sling. For dinner I ate a well spiced mutton curry and watched elegant Maharanis in saris having dinner à deux with their husbands, and sharing private jokes. After the boys-own tyranny of Islam, it was heart-warming. A graceful Bengali girl, with bells on her fingers and rings on her toes, danced sensuously to insistent Hindu music, and was photographed by Californians with disc cameras. The Kashmiri white wine arrived chilled to a perfect temperature.

(It must by now be obvious that I was demented by my escape from Africa and sentimental with exhaustion, and the first proper shot of alcohol into the bloodstream for a fortnight: gaga in fact.)

At midnight I strolled lightheadedly along Ramchandani Harbour Road. It was a balmy night, the sky was pink and the sidewalks crowded. There were quite as many hawkers as in Port Sudan but they played different cards: men charmed cobras at your approach and, if you so much as glanced, required payment; children sold spirographs and postcards and tiny fistfuls of nuts which they delved out of grubby pockets; youths sedulously commended bathroom weighing scales. "Test your weight, Mister, test your weight." Slightly further along, but still hardly more than fifty yards from the hotel lobby, I suddenly came upon rows and rows of sacks, ranged along the pavement. It took several seconds, in my euphoric mood, to click that these contained people: hundreds upon hundreds of bodies shrivelled in foetal positions or huddled in doorways. These were a few of Bombay's half million homeless, mostly widows and orphans, who wander the streets by day begging for annas, and flop on the curb by night.

As I passed by, one or two children shook themselves awake and called for money, which naturally I provided. Maharashtra children have very large sad eyes and it was uncomfortable the way they smiled so prettily for so little. After a few minutes, other, older, people roused themselves and joined the queue, elbowing the children and becoming unpleasantly adhesive. I sent these interlopers empty away and returned to the Taj more melancholy than when I had set out.

By the time I woke up it had turned muggy, which was a strong argument for spending the day outside Bombay. I took a launch across the harbour to Elephanta Island to inspect the rock temples of Shiva. The island is tropical and bristling with palm trees and a steep pathway of two thousand stone steps leads from the jetty to the temples; several American tourists were undertaking the ascent by sedan chair, in bone-shaking discomfort. The pathway is lined, every fifty yards or so, by cold drink stalls which become proportionately more expensive as you approach the summit, so there is no advantage to be gained by holding back. The most interesting panels in the temple, it is said, depict Trimitru the three-headed Shiva, taking the form of Brahma the creator and Vishnu the preserver. Brahma and Vishnu were evident enough, but who was this standing in the centre of the panel with a pot balanced on her head, surely not the Trimitru Shiva? No, it was an Elephanta village woman earning an honest rupee. Every villager on the island hangs around the temple, angling to be pho-tographed, for which the fee is ten rupees or one rupee, depending on whether you asked first.

These people have become brilliantly adept at adopting photogenic poses, to suit every shutter speed, and hurl themselves with great resolve between camera and temple at the sight of a lens. There are also wild baboons on the island, but these too have been adopted by the villagers and require a photographic modelling fee at the same rate.

I took a taxi to Victoria Station in such good time that my driver decided I would like to see Falkland Road en route and made a detour on his own initiative. I was pleased he did. This famous brothel strip in downtown Bombay exceeded my most lurid expectations; both sides of the road for several hundred yards are lined with cages, inside which a thousand or so prostitutes are displayed for window shoppers. Small groups of men leered through the bars, paying their money and taking their choice upstairs to dingy cubicles. A fetid light seeped out from these upper rooms and every so often a beady moustachioed face and the flash of a sari could be glimpsed through a chink in the shutters. My driver was in no doubt that only youthful bashfulness restrained me from stepping inside, and even went so far as to make overtures on my behalf through the cab window. I pretended panic about the train, and told him to step on it.

At first sight, the Madras Mail was a hothouse version of Falkland Road. The first-class air-conditioned coach is not divided into separate compartments but is a single unit of ninety-six couchettes, separated by green Fortuny-style curtains. Berth number seventeen was located in the corridor and only a midget could stretch out on it. All about, swinging their legs from upper bunks or lifting heavy plastic suitcases from the platform, were my fellow passengers: government civil servants, Bombay asset strippers in white cotton shirts, importunate old women who draped their belongings from the hook above my couchette. The air-conditioning unit would not become operational until we had gathered speed and the compartment was sudorific: I thought enviously of Shadrach, Meshach and Abednego in the burning fiery furnace. My shirt was already wringing wet and there seemed no prospect of hanging anything up or changing into loose clothes.

Deliverance arrived in the shape of the guard.

"Upon my word," he said, "this gentleman is too lofty for berth seventeen. You will be more comfortable in number fifteen."

He was right. Berth number fifteen was a corner bunk, a good eighteen inches longer and better still had storage racks. These were only partially monopolised by my three bunk-mates: a perfect pair of twin sisters from Solapur and a distinguished white-haired engineer, Mr Saipur.

"You are coming I think from London," said Mr Saipur, "and missing the rain. You would welcome, I perceive, a real pea-souper."

Over the next two days Mr Saipur became a key ally on the Madras Mail; his ossified salad days English grew on me. He was reading *The Hound of the Baskervilles* which doubtless put him in mind of pea-soupers. His favourite author was P G Wodehouse: "A great stylist, no one to touch him on style," said Mr Saipur.

On the dot of 22.10, with a tremendous jolt, the Madras Mail began its wheezing retreat from Victoria Station. The train gathered speed then squealed to a halt. We were at Dadar Junction where a second wave of Bombay passengers embarked, slamming doors and opening and shutting windows. The guard blew his whistle, the train tooted. Again we jolted and wheezed, the carriage listing from side to side, bristling over points like a car on a cattle grid, braking and accelerating by turns. Half an hour out of Dadar the overhead lights were turned off and passengers settled down to sleep.

Only then did it occur to me that I had no bedding. Naively I had expected sheets and blankets in first-class and had brought nothing. The perfect pair of twin sisters from Solapur, wise virgins both, had tasselled cushions and duvets; Mr Saipur unbuckled a rug; for me, two nights exposed on a plastic pallet looked inevitable.

"Would my spare counterpane be of any use to you?" asked Mr Saipur. "It can become a little chilly in the wee small hours."

The Madras Mail jerked eastwards. I groped my way along the corridor to the oriental style lavatory and changed modestly into pyjamas. Just as I was completing this precision operation, the engine braked and my Gucci biro shot out of a pocket and down the hole onto the track.

I made a pillow out of shirts and a towel and tried to sleep. From every corner of the coach came the sound of belching; long complacent rumblings from the very pit of the stomach. There is no social stigma attached to belching in India, and the compartment soon reeked with the stale stench of born-again biryani. Two hours passed. The Madras Mail stopped and started every twenty minutes and the belching persisted like bullfrogs on a summer's evening.

I turned onto my side to face the wall. The slope of the couchette made this indescribably painful since the ribbing of the mattress dug into my hip. With every minute that passed the agony became more intense; a shooting pain which sent shivers through the whole stomach, occasionally abating a little, only to return with even greater sharpness.

After half an hour of this, there could only be one explanation: I had acute appendicitis.

The symptoms were all too clear. I had never had my appendix removed and it was self-evidently inflamed. I ran a cold sweat. If I sat up, the pain transferred from the stomach to the small of the back. The train stopped at a station. I twitched the curtain and saw it was called Bhigwan. The platform was deserted, the booking office lit by a strip of low voltage neon. I eased myself out of bed, put on walking shoes, fumbled for travellers cheques and clumped towards the door. I would leave my luggage on the train, stagger onto the platform in pyjamas and take a taxi to the nearest hospital, wherever that might be. Bhigwan was not a name I associated with para-medicine, but emergency surgery was imperative.

Suddenly, however, there was another tremulous lurch and the train was pulling away from the platform. There was nothing for it but to struggle back to bed until the next halt. The process of crawling onto the couchette was the most lacerating five minutes of all.

In the morning I woke to find the conductor handing me a vacuum flask of sugary tea and a chapatti. I felt as fit as a fiddle; the appendicitis was phantom, a simple case of Bombay duck. I sipped the tea and looked out of the window. We were passing through flat featureless pastureland, stretching miles into the distance, relieved once every seven or ten minutes by a trundling bullock cart. We were about fifty miles south of Gulbarga. The perfect pair of twin sisters had already left the train, "while you were in the land of nod," said Mr Saipur.

The whole carriage now smelt of Colgate toothpaste. The Indians are great teethbrushers and I queued for the sink behind passengers who scrubbed and rinsed for several minutes at a stretch. With the coach only half full, the upper bunks were stowed away, making welcome headroom.

I ate an orange wafer biscuit and remarked, by way of conversation, to Mr Saipur "twenty-seven hours is a long time in a train, isn't it?"

"Thirty-one hours you mean," said Mr Saipur.

"Thirty-one? I'm certain I was told twenty-seven."

Mr Saipur consulted his timetable. "No, no, definitely thirty-one. Only the afternoon mail takes twenty-seven hours."

I fell back against the seat like a character in an Edwardian melo-drama whose mortgage the villain has just foreclosed.

This meant there was barely an hour between the arrival of the Madras Mail and the sailing of the MV *Chidambaram.*

I had bought my ticket for the *Chidambaram* in London as a vital connection. In fact the date of the sailing had to a large extent deter-mined my date of departure from the Reform Club. This Shipping Corporation of India vessel makes a round trip from Madras to Sin-gapore only once every twenty-one days and is the solitary passenger ship between those two ports; to miss it would be a disaster. I had furthermore enjoyed lugubrious correspondence with the Corpora-tion's city agent, Mr Oza of St Mary Axe, EC3, who had offered a bewildering choice of accommodation: "First-class, second-class A, second-class B, third-class or deluxe." (There are also two bunk classes in steerage, but these are considered too lowly for Europeans.) I had chosen deluxe and furthermore paid four thousand nonrefundable rupees inclusive of breakfast, lunch and dinner. Several times, during the rougher moments of the journey, I had eagerly anticipated my lazy days aboard the *Chidambaram.*

Now, once again, I had to lay contingency plans and the prospects were not encouraging. Unlike Djibouti to Bombay, there is little casual shipping across the Bay of Bengal. Singapore imports nothing from India and India can afford nothing from Singapore. Which left three tortuous fallback routes south-east from Madras.

1. By rail. If I caught the night sleeper to Calcutta, I could perhaps travel by train down through Burma. (If this was possible: I rather thought Rangoon airport was the only legal point of entry.) Then take another train on through Thailand and Malaysia to Singapore. At very least this would take seven days.

2. By ship. Either from Calcutta to Singapore or hanging on in Madras for a miracle (or chartering a boat? or buying one?) or taking the train to Sri Lanka and trying from there. All very spurious.

3. By ship and rail combined. Marginally more likely. If I could find a passage to Penang, then I could take the ferry to Butterworth, then catch a train through Malaysia via Kuala Lumpur to Singapore.

In other words, it was crucial that I catch the *Chidambaram*.

One secondary problem was that I did not actually have a ticket for the ship, merely a voucher and a photocopy of the booking telex. I had been instructed to exchange these for a proper ticket at the Corporation's Madras office in Linghi Chetty Street, but there would be no time for that. I would have to present myself at the gangway and brandish the voucher.

By one o'clock we reached Raichur and the platform was thronged with wild dark-skinned women with hennaed hair and foreheads. The conductor distributed lunch trays with saffron rice and cauliflower curry but I ate peckishly. I had become mesmerised by the clatter of the wheels which seemed to say "Every day, and in every way, I am travelling faster and faster and faster; every day, and in every way, I am travelling faster and faster and faster." But it wasn't true; the train was taunting me; I was going slower and slower and slower; I was crawling, at a snail's pace, towards a cul-de-sac.

Another tune was churning around in my head at the same time; it had been playing on a juke box in Brindisi and I couldn't get rid of it. The meter perfectly fitted the clatter of the points. It said:

Everybody — chuff — chuff — chuff
Is very busy — chuff — chuff — chuff
Getting nowhere. Nowhere
Chuff — Chuff — Chatter —

Mr Saipur was joined after lunch by several of his friends who had boarded the Madras Mail at Solapur. They spoke English to each other and were generous about including me in their conversation. None of the talk was light; they broached one philosophical question after another, with impressive brinkmanship. One minute it was comparative religion, the next it was monetarism, five minutes later we were onto free collective bargaining. Mr Saipur was in his element. I hadn't heard such preposterous fossilised syntax since school debating societies. After each person had finished speaking, someone would sum up the drift of their argument (not always easy) and then a third voice would paraphrase that.

"On a point of information . . ." said Mr Saipur.

"That is not a point of information," rebuked his friend Mr Rampur, "that is a point of order."

They asked for an Englishman's view of the Empire. Did I feel a great sense of loss that we no longer had one?

In fact, I've never given the matter more than a moment's thought, and don't much mind either way, but this was no place for a Don't Know. I waffled on about Britain the dignified, senior power who had ceded her possessions like parents to their grown up children. It was a pretty good load of rubbish, but Mr Saipur and friends seconded the motion enthusiastically, all the way to Guntakal.

"It is most refreshing to hear the views of the fourth estate," said Mr Saipur. (But really, of course, this was the fifth column.)

The fields beyond the track had become very dry; they were cracked like crazy paving with deep fissures and there were mud huts that looked as though they'd crumble if you so much as touched them. Once or twice pools of smoke rose from the outskirts of mud villages. This part of India is very wild and poor and I read somewhere that suttee was making a comeback because widows preferred to burn with their husbands than burden their children. I questioned Mr Saipur about this and he poo-poohed the idea, which was a relief because my itinerary couldn't stand a Phileas Fogg rescue mission.

In the late afternoon I again became anxious about catching the ship, and sat on a bench by an open door with the conductor. The continual stopping and starting was unnerving. Although, to be sure, we were covering reasonable distances through the window, progress was somehow never reflected on the map. We would jolt through several hours' worth of local stations, but still remain in the same square of Tamilnad's *Cartography of South India*.

I retired early to bed with an extremely exciting thriller about Iran, called *On Wings of Eagles*, which passed the time but heightened my phobia. I became convinced that Mr Saipur was a member of the Cobra Group, and while he was putting on his pyjama jacket looked out for the snake tattoo. There was a distinct mark on his upper arm. It was probably a vaccination, but could have been a skin graft. The brakes squealed and we arrived in Cuddapah.

The Madras Mail made better progress during the second night and by dawn was less than thirty miles from the city. My carpet bag was packed and rupees carefully pared into convenient bundles. A further piece of good news was that the harbour and the station are reasonably close to one another: ten or fifteen minutes by taxi.

But then, in the middle of nowhere, we stopped dead. There was no station, no signal box, no sacred cow on the line, it was inexplicable. Twenty minutes passed, then thirty. Mr Saipur suggested we might be changing gauge, but the explanation had a hollow ring.

Beyond the track was a shallow ha-ha, prickly with thorn bushes, and beyond that an empty asphalt road.

Thirty minutes turned into forty, then three-quarters of an hour.

In the distance, about two miles up the road, it was hard to judge because the country was so flat, was an approaching vehicle. At first it looked like a bullock cart, but as it got closer it turned into a grey Austin.

Just supposing I jumped out of the train with my cases, scrambled down the ha-ha, across the field to the road and held up my arm like Visvamitra at the court of Dasaratha. Maybe I could get a lift to the port. But there again, if the car refused to stop and the Madras Mail simultaneously shuddered back into motion, I would be stuck in the middle of nowhere, or more precisely in the middle of Tamil Nadu province.

As the Austin got nearer, the solution backed off. I felt none of the decisive thrust one is supposed to experience at such moments; there was more adrenalin in a glucose Redoxon.

"On a point of information," trilled the positive canton of my brain "every car in South India is an unofficial taxi and will stop automatically."

"On a point of order," retorted the negative, "any driver rich enough to own a car will not put himself out for a fistful of rupees."

I stood up, sat down, then rose again. The whistle screamed, the carriage lurched, the grey Austin sped past on the road and the train was moving.

Madras Central Station is more parochial than Bombay Victoria, and the forecourt is lined with yellow motorised rickshaws. These two-stroke three-wheelers are known as auto-rickshaws, and have small hooded side-cars for passengers. I commissioned one of the two hundred available auto-rickshaw riders to despatch me to the harbour.

"Singapore ship please. The *Chidambaram*, OK?"

"OK."

We chugged towards Marina Beach with great purpose. It was pleasant to be cycling through an almost empty city; the rush hour wouldn't start for another hour. Next to the beach was an aquarium, and there was some impressive Moghul architecture, mostly government offices and ministries.

The auto-rickshaw rider leant round over his saddle. His teeth were stained black with betel juice.

"Chola Hotel, Mister?" He was double-checking the destination.

"For God's sake no, the Singapore ship, harbour, port, sailing, quay, wharf, ten minutes."

"Not Chola Hotel?"

"No, no, no, please, no, I implore you . . ." For the second time on this trip, words failed me. "Singapore ship, Singapore ship." My voice trailed away into a whimper.

We turned round and chugged back towards the harbour, visible now by a forest of cranes. Every fifty yards we stalled and the motor had to be re-started manually. Many years ago I owned an unreliable orange moped. It never started when you turned it on and shuddered orgasmically after you'd cut the petrol. I hated it very much and it is now, I believe, jacked up in the underground car park of the National Magazine Company in Carnaby Street, W1, minus its tires. This yellow Madras auto-rickshaw brought back the full horror.

The harbour gates loomed, but were on the far side of a railway line and the level crossing was shut. A freight train lumbered past. After a hiatus of almost a minute, the level crossing was laboriously opened by the signalman's daughter.

We reached the harbour gate. The auto-rickshaw driver could take me no further and had no change. I told him to keep it.

The *Chidambaram* was tied up against the dock, but there were no passengers jostling on the quay; everyone was aboard. Stevedores were unthreading rope ballasts from the gangway.

"Wait for me, wait for me." My tongue hung out like the desert survivor in the Perrier commercial. Could this ship be a mirage?

"You've cut it pretty fine I must say, sir," said the Purser at the head of the gangway. "Is that all your luggage?"

I waved my telex and mumbled something about failing to exchange it for a ticket.

"Ah yes," said the Purser. "You're on the passenger list. The steward will show you to your cabin."

11 | *In which the Bay of Bengal is crossed by steamship. And a visit is paid to a snake temple in Penang.*

My fellow passengers in deluxe class were not gay, which is to say they did not get up fancy dress evenings or deck quoits competitions; that was left to the first- and second-class travellers. In fact the deluxe passengers could fairly be described as a stodgy lot: we rose late, and snobbishly paced our own enclosure on deck, and dined alone. Most people aboard the *Chidambaram* were travelling alone, often with heavy baggage in the hold. Some were Indians, resident in Singapore, who had returned home to wind up their dead parents' estate and were shipping ornate pieces of heirloom furniture back to the Republic.

There were some Dutchmen on board who kept themselves to themselves, and an Australian couple, Roger and Margaret, both in their fifties, who had been touring Asia for a year and months ago realised that they hated the sight of each other. Both latched onto me as a potential ally. They would set off round the deck after breakfast, in different directions, and arrive at my deck chair at the same moment from opposite companionways; then they would scowl, and pretend to walk on, and sneak back with some fresh complaint about the other, and collide again. Roger and Margaret were the only deluxe passengers who shared a table in the dining-room; they sat with their elbows on the white tablecloth not bothering to pretend they weren't thoroughly fed up; they watched the other diners like hawks; hoping to catch someone's eye, so they could suddenly remember something important they had to tell them (such as to remember to wind forward your watch one hour at midnight) and pull up a chair at your table.

Roger was a construction site manager, Margaret was a schoolteacher; they lived in Perth (I could draw you a ground plan of their bungalow but wouldn't dream of inflicting such tedium) and had planned this sabbatical for five years; it had taken that long to engineer simultaneous leave. Margaret was looking forward to Sarawak and the Philippines. She had been misinformed that they are restful. It would have been much simpler and cheaper if they had flown straight home and sought psychiatric help in separate clinics. As it was they cast a desperate pall over the English-speaking passengers (which was virtually everyone; after three days Margaret latched onto the Anglo-Indians) and made the bar a dangerous place to congregate.

The deluxe cabins on the *Chidambaram* were twin-berthed with beds rather than bunks, and arranged so that three cabins open onto a communal sitting-room. The ship was not full, being the low season, so I had a cabin to myself; the communal sitting-room was never used at all since nobody dared risk the possibility of having to make conversation.

(The exception to this was Roger and Margaret's sitting-room on the starboard side of the ship; they waited to pounce on the two adjacent passengers as they walked through to their cabins; after two days of this, both demanded to be transferred, one to an inferior class which meant the safety of a different deck.)

The passage from Madras to Singapore heads straight across the Bay of Bengal for about nine hundred miles, sails between the Andaman and the Nicobar islands, then heads south-east to Penang. We would put into Georgetown for a day, with an opportunity to disembark, then sail on down through the Straits of Malacca to Singapore. The journey was scheduled to take five and a half days.

After the excitement of the Madras Mail it was a welcome relief to amble about on deck and join the interminable grumbles about the food. Some passengers spoke of getting up a petition to present to the captain. I didn't actually think the food was all that bad, but it helped to pass the time and nothing ever came of it.

During dinner on the second evening I noticed a tall, sandy-haired man in his late forties, sitting at a table at the far end of the dining-room. I hadn't seen him before, and he subsequently told me he'd been ill: "A touch of flu," he said, "soon sweated it out." He was wearing beige cavalry twill trousers and a blue striped shirt and a blue tie. His chin was shaved very close in the military manner, so there was no trace of six o'clock shadow though it was well after eight o'clock.

I wondered whether he had just shaved especially for dinner. (I don't normally have a beard fixation, but so many of the other passengers had strong growths that a smooth skin stood out.) His face was slightly too intellectual for the army, unless he was a young general or some kind of tactician; his expression was distinctly hang-dog, or rather melancholy, which also weighed against a military provenance. His forehead, which was a high one, was sunburnt. I wondered whether he was a diplomat, or one of the new wave of neo-fascist art history dons at Cambridge University, or some other species of academic. But I was not to discover for another twenty-four hours.

During that time we sized each other up. There was an inevitability that we would speak; the deluxe section of the *Chidambaram* is quite small, and society limited. I was fairly sure that this man, whose name I later learnt was George Prendergast, intended introducing himself in due course, because he went out of his way to be subtly conspicuous: ordering his gin at the bar in a civilised London accent, loud enough for me to hear, and making a slight detour past my table on his way out of the dining-room. I, in turn, tended not to slouch when he passed my deck chair, and decided against reading an airport thriller. I hadn't spoken properly to anyone since leaving Djibouti, and I was curious who this might be. So we conducted a dotty but mannered ritual, like a mating dance, invisible to the other passengers, until an appropriate moment for conversation presented itself.

The public rooms of the *Chidambaram* are large and not much used. The ship had once been a French channel ferry, serving Dunkirk and Le Havre, and plastic sofas from this period had been supplemented with high-backed boarding house armchairs, some of them with antimacassars. After dinner, however, the saloon becomes a casino where you can play blackjack and roulette for very small stakes. In addition to the official tables, some passengers organised lotteries of their own. An Indian "invented" a card game in which a suit of playing cards is shuffled and placed face down on the table. Players make one rupee bets on which card they think the queen might be. Only one bet is allowed on each card and the draw isn't made until all the cards are taken; the winner collects five rupees. A more futile game couldn't be conceived: it was like Find-the-Lady except that even the croupier didn't know where the queen was. After playing this game for some three-quarters of an hour, and never choosing the queen, I went to have my palm read.

A Malay woman was offering this service on a lower deck. She was very wrinkled and had bitten fingernails and her reading was given in the utmost secrecy; though if news of it had already reached the deluxe passengers the secret couldn't have been very well kept.

She studied my palm for a long time, sighed deeply, and at last disclosed her penetrating observation. "You like to travel, I think, and are a long way from home."

I was surprised to find George Prendergast on such a low deck. Water pipes criss-crossed the companionways, so he frequently had to stoop, and he was stepping gingerly between puddles of water and diesel.

I muttered "Good evening" as we passed.

"Good evening," said George Prendergast. "Not up to no good I trust." His manner was slightly condescending but at the same time diffident.

I asked him what he meant.

"Oh, anything can happen this close to the water. Chinese girls, you name it."

I looked doubtful about this. I had noticed no low life aboard the *Chidambaram*.

"Well, maybe not," he said. "But there used to be. Not on this ship, but her predecessors certainly." Then he said, "But I mustn't keep you," and walked briskly on.

There was a small reading-room on the *Chidambaram* with an exceedingly strange selection of books. Some were mathematical text books, others were theological: anthologies of sermons from the pulpit of Mount Mary Church, Bombay, and histories of missions. Most of the fiction seemed to have been bought in bulk from a tea-planter's bungalow sale, and comprised shelves of detective stories. Flattened inside the dust-jackets were several crumbling scorpions and mosquitoes and smears of russet-coloured blood.

The reading-room also boasted one or two games, such as a box of Scrabble without any H's or L's and an incomplete set of playing cards. About forty-seven of the fifty-two cards were extant, so there was little prospect of discovering the gap until after the frustrating climax of a game of patience. Nevertheless, the reading-room of the *Chidambaram* was the humming epicentre of intellectual society for the duration of the voyage, and it was here that George Prendergast asked whether I would care to join him for a drink in the bar.

George Prendergast always travelled with a bottle of Angostura Bitters, he said, which he deposited with the barman for pinking his gin. He kept a reserve bottle in his cabin with his duty-free Gilbeys.

"Have you ever been to the Andamans?" he asked suddenly. "We passed them last night about 3 a.m."

I said I hadn't. Had he?

"Eight years ago I spent a week in Port Blair. Not much to see, I wouldn't go again; but worth stopping over if you happen to be in the area."

George Prendergast had travelled everywhere. There was no country, however well developed or remote, that he hadn't visited at one time or another with his bottle of Angostura Bitters. "I'm a barrister," he explained. "Middle Temple. Not easy to get away, but if you dig in your heels and are firm about turning down briefs, you can manage it. I take six weeks holiday a year, always go abroad somewhere. You can do that if you're unmarried, it's one of the perks." He took a gulp of his pink gin. "Dash it, he's overdone the pink again. Well," he added, ruefully, "I suppose now I'll be able to travel even more."

In all the hours I spent drinking with George Prendergast, he spoke only of himself. In every other respect he was an extremely courteous man, and I think he simply couldn't see beyond his own obsession. He wanted someone to talk at, and I just happened to be conveniently on board. I understood enough about his circumstances to be a tolerable dummy, and learnt not to interrupt, and he was happy to sit with someone on a wooden bench on deck, drinking gin and eyeballing the horizon.

This is the story of George Prendergast (which is not, incidentally, his real name, but is not dissimilar to it) as told in four consecutive episodes, explaining the circumstances by which he came to be a fellow passenger aboard the *Chidambaram*.

George Prendergast was brought up in Devonshire (he insisted on the -shire) twenty miles outside Plymouth. His father was a partner in a leading firm of stockbrokers and spent the weekdays in London, so school holidays were spent mostly with his mother and elder brother. The Prendergasts' house was Jacobean and had been occupied by Prendergasts for a couple of hundred years, and before that by a local magistrate when that part of Devon was overrun by smugglers. Steep wooden steps wound down a cliff to a sandy cove, which could only be approached via the gardens of three houses on the peninsula, so to all intents and purposes it was a private beach. When the tide was out the sand stretched nearly half a mile to the sea, and when it was in, waves broke over the rocks and submerged the bottom few steps of the cliff path; it was a magnificent place to be brought up, said George Prendergast.

Both the other families with houses on the peninsula had children, so there was always someone to play with. George Prendergast said he had been rather shy until he was fifteen, but had always got on well with Lucy Hughes. Lucy Hughes was a year younger than he was, and her parents had moved to Devon just after she was born. The Hugheses and the Prendergasts had become close friends and wandered in and out of each other's houses as the mood took them.

"I was eighteen when I realised I was in love with Lucy," said George Prendergast, "though I didn't actually call it that at the time. I had just left school (he was a Wykehamist) and we were almost always asked to the same parties. Since Lucy lived next door I naturally gave her a lift in my car, and dropped her home afterwards. We talked a lot about the books we were reading; the Hugheses didn't really go in for reading, so I lent her books and then we discussed them. It was amazing really how shrewd she was, her taste was excellent, considering she hadn't been to a proper school.

"Mostly the parties we went to were beach affairs; lamb chops and dancing afterwards to a gramophone. They weren't smart, you understand, you went along in your rubber-soled shoes and a pullover, it can turn quite chilly after the sun's gone down. Lucy and I invariably danced together, not in an awfully sexy way but just as friends. And we sat together at dinner. I suppose people could have said we were a bit standoffish, and ought to have mixed more, and perhaps we should have. It probably looked rude. But we didn't see it like that; we simply preferred each other's company to anyone else's.

"Then I went up to Oxford and we didn't see quite so much of each other. Lucy's mother wasn't well, she had meningitis and Lucy stayed in Devon to help look after her; I always thought it said a lot for her character, not many girls would have done that. Another thing that impressed me about Lucy was that she taught herself French. I had lent her some Flaubert and she solemnly sat down every evening, after supper, and ploughed her way through it with a dictionary. By the time she was half way through the first novel she was going quite fast and in less than eight months she read the language almost fluently. That's what I mean when I say she had potential.

"The Oxford Colleges didn't used to hold Commem balls every year in my day, rationing still hadn't ended after the war, but we did have one my final year and I invited Lucy. She was very excited and travelled up from Plymouth on the train, and had gone to great trouble having a new dress made up in London, and posted back and forth to Devon for fittings, and she looked splendid. I had never seen Lucy looking so lovely. She wore very little make-up, though it was the fashion to overdo it, and her face was slightly sunburnt from the beach. And she was completely unaffected. I only realised quite how natural she was when I saw her next to the other girls. She didn't pretend to be sophisticated (though she couldn't possibly have been called a country bumpkin), she just hadn't spent any time in London, it was as simple as that.

"We had dinner before the ball in someone's rooms. You know the way these things are organised, far too many people, everyone roping in everyone else, terrible scrummage. Lucy ended up sitting between me and a fellow named Wallace. Simon Wallace. I didn't know him well, but enough to know he was a crashing bore. He wasn't particularly well off, but had taken up flying. He belonged to some club at Oxford aerodrome and used to fly over the college and make a big deal of it. I hoped Lucy wasn't going to find him a strain.

"I needn't have worried; they got on like a house on fire. I don't mean she ignored everyone else, but she was well and truly taken in. Simon Wallace was a creepy fellow, gave me the willies to tell you the truth, and he wouldn't leave her alone for a second. Took her away to dance and tried not to bring her back to the table; if anyone else danced with her, he was always waiting to scoop her up. I warned Lucy he wasn't thought much of round the college, but she just smiled sweetly and didn't seem to hear. Anyway, the ball went off pretty well overall, I thought, and next morning I put Lucy on the train to Devon, and she wrote a very charming thank-you letter and I wrote her back. Her letters, I should have said, are one of the best things about Lucy. She writes as she talks and talks as she thinks, which is a very rare combination indeed.

"Then I heard Lucy had been in Oxford. Someone had seen her at the aerodrome with Simon Wallace. She had been up for a spin in Wallace's plane; they were pretty certain it was the same girl I'd taken to the ball. I was stunned, and jolly angry too, because it was deceitful of Lucy to come all the way to Oxford without telling me. I admit I was hurt. And I was insanely jealous.

"I couldn't decide what to do. The jealousy grew inside me every day; it made everything else intolerable. The final exams were over and the whole university was celebrating, but I wouldn't join in. I stopped shaving; I stopped eating in hall in case I saw Simon Wallace. I was amazed Lucy had left her mother. She had made a big thing of organising a nurse when she came up for the ball; now she apparently thought nothing of skiving off. Didn't she realise I was in love with her? It was true I had never told her so, but it was a standing joke all over Devon. The funny thing was I had never even kissed her; probably because I knew her so well. That was the trouble with a brother and sister relationship like ours; it was difficult to make the transition."

George Prendergast ordered another gin. It was no effort listening to his story because it was so well constructed. He never rambled. His barrister's training made him adept at marshalling facts, and I got the impression he had brooded on the events for so many years that he was virtually word-perfect.

"The term was ending in a few days and I decided to go straight home to Devon. Normally I spent a few days in London on the way, but I was anxious to check up on Lucy. I thought that if I spent a whole month with her on our own territory, I could soon outman-oeuvre Simon Wallace. I also resolved, when the time was right, to step up the passion side a bit; that was one lesson I had learned from the Wallace incident.

"But when I got home Lucy wasn't there. Her mother said she was staying in London for a few days with an aunt. Mrs Hughes said how delighted she was that Lucy had at last agreed to take a break; she had been begging her to all year, but Lucy was much too selfless. Lucy came home at the weekend. She was exactly the same as ever, just as easy to get along with. She always wore white aertex shirts on the beach and scrunched sand under her toes. I didn't say anything about her being spotted up in Oxford; it seemed wiser not to make a thing of it. And then, after dinner, she suddenly said, 'Oh, you know that chap who sat on my right at the ball, the one you don't much like?'

" 'Simon Wallace,' I replied, though the name stuck in my throat.

" 'Well it's the silliest thing,' she said, 'but he's asked me to marry him, right out of the blue, and I said yes.'

"Of course I was stunned. It was so amazing, so unexpected, so final that I could think of nothing to say. I suppose I congratulated her and so on, though I don't remember doing so. In fact, I don't remember anything much about the preparations for the wedding, or Simon Wallace's visit to Devon, or Simon Wallace swimming off our beach, or the gruesome ceremony itself. The brain has a compassionate way of erasing whole sequences of events, when it's necessary to your mental health, and the next thing I remember is the little house the Hugheses bought for Lucy and their son-in-law in Notting Hill at the north end of Peel Street.

"At first I contrived to see Lucy when Wallace wasn't around, which meant lunch; but it is a beastly journey from chambers into the West End and anyway Lucy didn't like it. It mattered very much to her that Wallace and I should be friends and the implied snub of the lunches upset her. Then they had their first baby and lunchtimes were out for good.

"I think they must have been quite poor. They never ate in restaurants except when I took them, and they never went on holiday. Wallace had some kind of job in the City, I heard that he wasn't very good at it, and he had no money of his own. This didn't stop him from being perfectly objectionable, and I liked him no better in London than I had in Oxford. His remarks were stupid and boorish. Everything he said betrayed his lack of understanding. He thought it smart to hold reactionary views. His opinions on the law were frankly absurd; they would have been comic if they hadn't been pathetic. He reacted to newspaper stories before finishing the first paragraph. He name-dropped swells in the City he hardly knew. He picked Lucy up on views that were ten, no a hundred times, more informed than his own. And the most extraordinary thing of all was that Lucy didn't seem to mind.

"I realised that if I wanted to go on seeing her, I would have to pretend to like Wallace. Lucy made that perfectly clear one evening when I was short with him. So I made a real effort, and gave him lunch in the City, and played golf with him once or twice at weekends. And all the time I was waiting for Lucy to see through him, and to come running to me.

"She was more lovely now than ever. She radiated health. She had no help, either with the baby or with the housework, but never looked tired. Serene, I think, is the right word. And she was never dull. She loved dancing, especially to jazz. There was a jazz club in Charlotte Street and it became a tradition that I would arrange for a babysitter, take her and Wallace out to dinner and then go on dancing. It was murder watching her dance with Wallace. I kept thinking that, had I not invited her to the Commem ball, it would be me who was married to Lucy and not Wallace. My only consolation was that it was only a matter of time.

"Then Lucy had her second daughter, followed two years later by a son. They called him George, after me, and I am his godfather. Which reminds me," said George Prendergast, "I must send the boy a postcard. I always send him a postcard, he saves the stamps. He will be twelve in May."

"About the same time that George was born," he went on, "I bought a flat in Leinster Place."

The *Chidambaram* had been cruising around the coast of Penang Island and was approaching Georgetown harbour. George Prendergast's story would have to wait. He didn't seem to mind; he knew I was captive until Singapore, there was no hurry. Georgetown harbour is picturesque; the town planners were probably in cahoots with a leading firm of postcard manufacturers. There are villas with thatched roofs leading down to the water, which is fringed with casuarinas, and fleets of bumboats moored from bamboo jetties and the colonial facade of the Eastern and Oriental Hotel.

George Prendergast said he had stayed at the hotel the previous year. "Lucy and I had one of the end rooms on the ground floor," he said.

We were due to stay in port for the best part of a day and George Prendergast suggested we made an expedition to the Snake Temple.

"The snakes are drugged to the eyeballs, but if you haven't seen them they're worth the taxi ride."

The Snake Temple is six miles south of Georgetown. Though notionally still very holy, the Temple is in fact sacred only to tourism. Thirty or forty pit vipers are draped over brass tables and there is a pervasive smell of joss sticks. Most of the snakes were in an advanced state of rigor mortis and had clearly been dead for weeks. A priest told us, on receipt of a few Malay cents, that the vipers were deadly and frequently ran amok. He was not able to explain, however, whether the snakes are worshipped as a deity in their own right, or as a manifestation of some neighbourhood god.

After we had taken photographs of the Snake temple, we returned to Georgetown by taxi and glared at the new seventy-six storey telecommunications tower which is being built on the edge of the town. It has already spoilt the skyline and will be a great problem for future generations of postcard designers. Then we went for a drink at the Eastern and Oriental Hotel.

The Eastern and Oriental (formerly the Western and Occidental) is a very interesting hotel and I should like to have stayed there. The public rooms are dignified and in good repair, and the lawn had just been mown into satisfying straight lines from the terrace. A Chinese waiter, who could easily have been a hundred years old from eating only a diet of dried seaweed, staggered to and fro across the vast lawn bearing bowls of nuts and fresh ice. Exotic Malaysian butterflies fluttered about.

"As I was saying, I bought a flat in Leinster Place . . ."

George Prendergast's flat had a large double drawing-room on the first floor, with a dining-room and kitchen leading off at the back. On the floor above were two bedrooms, two bathrooms and a small study. He lived in the flat alone.

"I did think of employing a housekeeper or a manservant of some sort," he said, "but that seemed such an admission of defeat. I didn't want to be a pernickety old bachelor with a valet, I wanted to live with Lucy. For the same reason I've never really decorated the flat properly. I've bought some good pictures, and have made several collections of antiques in my time, but the flat isn't decorated if you know what I mean. That would be Lucy's job. She's terribly clever at matching materials and made Peel Street look wonderful without spending anything, and I wanted her eventually to have free rein.

"Anyway, ten years went by and gradually I became quite well off. If you don't have a family, and live modestly, capital soon mounts up. I was successful at the Bar, having plenty of spare time to prepare my briefs, and always had several thousand pounds more than I expected at the end of each tax year. That was when I began to travel in earnest. At first I just used to take a fortnight, then it became three weeks, and then a month, and then six weeks' holiday a year; a month in September and two weeks in the spring. I went everywhere. I became quite a joke in Chambers; they call me Marco Polo. I never decided where I'd go until the last possible minute, then picked somewhere off the map and bought a ticket. Friends said I ought to write travel books, I'd been to some quite remote spots, but I couldn't be bothered. You see, the truth is, I don't really enjoy travelling very much; in fact I'd much sooner spend my holidays at home.

"But what would I do with myself? The evenings are all right, I've got plenty of friends; but during the day. You can't spend six weeks in the British Museum. I don't enjoy the cinema. Lucy isn't available for lunch.

"At least when you're abroad you move on. I seldom spent more than a day in one place, I lived out of a suitcase. I made collections of local arts: quite good collections actually, it amused me to read up the subjects and buy only the first-rate stuff. I collected jade and batik, then Islamic miniatures and prayer mats. Some of my prayer mats have become quite valuable, nobody bothered with them when I started; now there's a shop selling nothing else in South Audley Street. North African ceramics are interesting, especially early Moroccan if you can find it in good condition. I've got piles of plates stored in tissue paper at Leinster Place; it's so difficult to display.

"I found travelling on my own lonely, especially the evenings: abroad is the reverse of home in that respect. The first week is always all right, but after that it grips you in the stomach. As soon as the sun went down the loneliness took hold. You sit around from six to eight o'clock waiting for dinner, and it's all over in half an hour. The Islamic countries are the worst. However long you spin out a kebab, it won't last more than fifteen minutes. Then there's another three hours to kill before you can go to bed.

"When I look back on all the holidays I've taken, all I remember is pacing empty streets alone after dinner. Drink only makes matters worse; that's the one thing to be said for the Arab countries, no alcohol. Show me a bottle of red wine and I can mark the precise level where the loneliness bites; half an inch below the bottom of the label. That's when your mind starts to swim and you wonder what the hell you're doing there.

"My only escape was sending postcards to Lucy. I tried to ration myself to two, but it usually ended up as three or four. They took several days to compose; I made several rough drafts. You see the messages were very cryptic and you have to get the balance absolutely right: clear enough for Lucy to decode, sufficiently bland not to alert Wallace. Generally I slipped in a reference to Flaubert; that was private territory between Lucy and I. Then I sent them recorded delivery to make sure they arrived. Mrs Simon Wallace. I hated writing that. Usually I just put "Lucy" and the address.

"As soon as I returned to London I always checked that the post had got through. Lucy was very cool about it and displayed the cards quite openly on the mantelpiece. Once I asked her whether it was wise, but she just smiled and said not to worry.

"Then, last February, Simon Wallace died. Lucy rang me at Chambers. She was very distressed; Wallace had been knocked down crossing Kensington High Street on his way home from the tube station. Of course I went straight round to comfort her, and took matters in hand. The children were all away at their boarding schools, so I drove Lucy to see them in turn to break the news. Meanwhile I sorted out Wallace's affairs, which not surprisingly were in chaos, and made arrangements for the funeral. I was overjoyed by my good luck.

"I couldn't leave Lucy on her own in Peel Street, so I camped in one of the children's bedrooms, which was anyway more convenient for sifting the bumph. Wallace had left his family almost penniless, he hadn't bothered with life insurance or anything and they would certainly have to sell the house to raise capital. Except that they wouldn't have to because I would support them; it was the obvious solution. Lucy said she wouldn't accept charity and I said it wouldn't be charity, because we would be married. I implored her to marry me, after a decent interval of a few months, for my sake, for the children's sake, for everybody's sake. At the end of May she finally agreed, and we were married last June.

"The children came to the wedding of course. They were very happy about it; I'm sure that secretly they prefer me to their father. We didn't invite many other people. It was a register office ceremony and afterwards we had a family lunch in an Italian restaurant, and then Lucy and I caught an evening flight from Heathrow to Delhi.

"Lucy had always wanted to go to India. I had sent her postcards of Moghul paintings, and before the honeymoon she made a start at learning Sanskrit. I wanted to show her all the most interesting temples and we decided to travel everywhere by train.

"I suppose my big mistake was trying to pack too much in. I know Rajasthan like the back of my hand, and have discovered hundreds of out-of-the-way palaces, and I wanted Lucy to see them all. So we slept every night on the train and visited several temples a day. And then we travelled back by train through Uttar Pradesh, and finally took the sleeper from Allahabad to Madras where we caught the *Chidambaram* to Penang."

The garden of the Eastern and Oriental Hotel had clouded over. George Prendergast ordered his third gin while I drank bottled lager. The hundred-year-old waiter looked more exhausted with each epic trek across the lawn, first to take the order, then back again with a tray, and threatened to keel over at any moment. Other, younger, waiters had begun spreading cloths on the tables for dinner, and lighting candles in jam jars to discourage the mosquitoes. George Prendergast carried on talking, no longer noticing or caring whether I was listening: he was completely absorbed in his own story.

"I had booked a deluxe suite on the *Chidambaram*, the same cabin as I've got now actually, which was jolly fortunate because Lucy fell ill the minute we came aboard. We didn't know what it was she had picked up, it could have been a number of things. She didn't have a temperature so it wasn't fever, but it was a nasty virus and she didn't get up until we reached Penang. We checked straight into this hotel and were given the end room, with the verandah, and said we'd stay here a week. Lucy felt much better after she'd unpacked, and in the afternoon we visited the Snake Temple just like today.

"It was a relief to be settled into a hotel with a proper bed. For the previous twelve nights we had slept on trains, which isn't ideal for a honeymoon, so we had rather postponed that side of things until the boat. Then Lucy was ill so we still hadn't, so to speak, slept together since the wedding, and before that, of course, she was either married to Wallace or in mourning.

"We had dinner that night on the verandah, and then took a short walk through the town. I wanted to show Lucy where I used to post my cards to her. You see, I can remember every letterbox; I had already pointed out other letterboxes in Agra and Jaipur.

"And then we came back here and had a nightcap. And then, without any sort of warning, Lucy burst out crying. She sobbed and sobbed and wouldn't let me comfort her, she wouldn't let me touch her.

"I was at a complete loss, I didn't know what the devil I'd done to upset her. And then she said the whole thing had been a terrible mistake, we never should have got married. She wanted to fly straight home to her children and call everything off.

"Of course I told her not to be so silly and that she was probably suffering from prickly heat, but there was no persuading her. She insisted on going home. I was at my wits' end.

"Well it isn't easy to find a flight from Penang, and in the end she had to go via Kuala Lumpur. All the time I begged her not to leave, but she was adamant. She kept saying it was nothing I'd done and that everything was her own fault, and that I wouldn't understand.

"She was right about that at least. I'm still as much in the dark as ever. By the time I got home Lucy had returned all my kit to Leinster

Place and left a letter on the dressing-table repeating it wasn't my fault. And now we are officially separated.

"I still look after the money side of things, I don't mind doing that. In fact I quite enjoy it because it gives me an excuse to see Lucy. She really is the most wonderful girl and I'm sure in time we'll get back together again. It would be crazy not to. Until then I'm keeping in close touch, making sure I'm there when I'm needed. Lucy always knows where she can reach me in an emergency, even when I'm out of the country. Which reminds me, I must buy a postcard in the lobby before we leave, just to let her know where I am."

On the fifth and final day's sailing we negotiated the Straits of Malacca, a funnel of navigable water between Sumatra and Malaysia. Like the Suez Canal it is a bottleneck, linking the Persian Gulf and the South China Sea, made perilous by submerged sandbanks. There have been several collisions in the Strait, none of them serious, though everyone agrees it is only a question of time before two supertankers collide. An even greater hazard is pirates. Sumatran pirates are famously blood-thirsty, paddling out at night from the narrow creeks around Lubu-hanruku, and setting upon the smaller cargo vessels. Because the Strait is a frontier waterway, the Singapore government is unable to pursue the pirates into Indonesia, and the Indonesians seem to be in no haste to act at their end.

"You know Sumatrans never take prisoners," said George Prender-gast. "They throttle you with headbands, snap your windpipe in a trice. If you were asleep you wouldn't even know." Fortunately pirates rarely board vessels over five thousand tons. Nevertheless I took the precau-tion of oiling my swordstick in case an opportunity for heroism pre-sented itself.

Shortly before we docked, a number of new passengers, invisible during the voyage, appeared on deck. Some were British. They looked distinctly shifty and could produce no satisfactory reason for travelling by ship, rather than flying. Some of their explanations frankly exceeded all reasonable limits of credulity: for instance, that they were research-ing books about giant squid or importing transistor radios to Malaysia.

When I revealed that I was going round the world in eighty days, they immediately recognised a fellow con-man and bought me a drink.

Thus we arrived in Singapore.

12 | *In which heels are kicked in the Republic of Singapore while awaiting a cargo ship to Hong Kong.*

The travel writers I admire dislike Singapore, particularly when they arrive from India or the Middle East. It is a strange phenomenon; they despair for pages about the filth and discomfort of those countries, then react furiously against clean and well-regulated Singapore. There is something about the place that gets under their skin. I resolved, by way of variety, to persevere with Singapore and do my utmost to like it.

I took a rickshaw from the Empire Dock to Raffles Hotel.

The rickshaw man asked me, "Where are you coming from?"

I said, "Madras."

"Oh Madras, ha ha. Ha! Madras! Very dirty place Madras." He sniggered superciliously. "You are pleased to be in Singapore." (This was not a question, it was a statement.)

"Yes, very pleased." But I felt disloyal to Mr Saipur of the Madras Mail for acquiescing.

There has been so much high rise development in the old part of Singapore that we had arrived at Raffles Hotel before I noticed it: a two-storey, white stucco quadrangle dwarfed by a dozen half-built Centre Points. Nevertheless it still has a certain post-Colonial charm. If you are looking for the perfect hotel for a honeymoon, with comfortable beds, constant hot water, discreet but attentive service, gourmet food and all the amenities of a capital city, then stay at Claridge's in London or the Plaza in New York. If, on the other hand, you are looking for a ramshackle oriental pension, with wide balconies, dusty palm trees, constant drilling, the smell of diesel, expatriate British rubber planters down from Malaysia, cold Tiger beer and a billiards table, then Raffles is the place. It is not a hotel for a traveller on a tight schedule; the waiters have developed to a fine art the ability to ignore your requests for a gin sling for hours on end; the famous Chinese delicacy, the hundred-year-old egg, was in all probability an invention of Raffles' room service.

Ten years ago Raffles was almost redeveloped into another luxury apartment block; then someone realized there would soon be nothing left for tourists to sightsee so, for the time being, it is a hotel in aspic; a tiny oasis of palm trees and peeling paint in the middle of a twenty-four-hour construction site.

The bedrooms are enormous; they must be the despair of Singapore's Ministry of Housing which puts up taller and taller blocks of flats comprising smaller and smaller family units on reclaimed land. Three calorie-controlled Singapore families could spread out in each room at Raffles. The distance from the corner of the bathroom to the door of the bedroom was twenty-seven giant strides; outside, a wide verandah with yellow and blue bamboo blinds overlooked tropical gardens. Above the door an Aga-sized air-conditioning unit rattled and whined like a ghost train; if you turned it off the room quickly became unbearable and condensation formed on the whites of your eyes.

I was destined to spend a minimum of six days in the Republic of Singapore. The vicissitudes of modern travel mean that no passenger service now exists across the South China Sea between Singapore and Hong Kong. The single-minded Chinese businessmen who commute to and fro with home computers disguised as wrist-watches and hand-kerchiefs as calculators, wouldn't dream in twenty dynasties of trav-elling by ship. Apart from the fact that they can't swim, they wouldn't see the point. In fact the oriental mind has some difficulty in grasping the logic of travelling round the world in eighty days, when Singapore Airways boasts in-flight service that even other airlines talk about, and provides in-flight slippers. A Chinaman staying at Raffles Hotel flew to Paris the day after I arrived, did two days' business, and was sitting by the swimming pool again before I'd moved an inch. Although everyone in Singapore studied Jules Verne's book at school, they sus-pected me of being wilfully reactionary.

The only other way of leaving Singapore, heading east to Hong Kong, is overland up through Kampuchea, Laos, Vietnam and Cochin China. Quite apart from the escalating guerrilla war in the region and the impossibility of obtaining transit visas, the railway system is neo-lithic; it could easily take eighty days to travel from Ho Chi Minh to Hanoi by slow train.

Fortunately, the Ben Line Steamers Company, an Edinburgh-based line of considerable tradition, had agreed to give me a passage across the South China Sea on their container vessel, the *Benavon*. It was this ship that I was now awaiting for the next leg of my journey.

If Egypt is epitomised by the pyramids and India by the Taj Mahal, then Singapore is an air-conditioned coffee shop in a shopping complex; a vast, freezing hall surrounded by camera shops, with rows of plastic banquettes and waitresses serving pastries in napkins. On every table is a cardboard advertisement for other coffee shops, informing you that the Oberoi Imperial Coffee Shop has gone French this week and the Marco Polo Hotel is staging a "Taste of Australia" fiesta ("Ever dreamed of a succulent sixteen-ounce steak cooked over an open charcoal barbecue? Now is your chance to sample the taste experience of a lifetime . . ."). The verb "to sample" is everything in Singapore. As well as sampling Swiss food in the Tanglin Shopping Centre you are urged to sample a rickshaw ride, Malaysian snacks ("No stay in Singapore is complete without sampling satay"), strolling ("Sample a stroll along Orchard Road") and shopping ("You're in shutterbug heaven when you sample Lucky Plaza Arcade"). Sampling intrinsically involves bringing your camera; without a visual record you might as well not have sampled at all. ("Remember, Rasa Singapora is a round-the-clock treat for wide-angle lenses.")

Singapore is the cleanest city in the world: you can walk half a mile downtown before you spot a dropped bus ticket or McDonalds carton. If cleanliness is next to godliness, Singapore is the veil of the temple; but cleanliness has its price. Fines for littering, even the cellophane from a packet of cigarettes, start at S$500 (about £175); smoking in the cinema is S$500; jay-walking is S$400; a dripping tap S$350. Singapore, as its citizens never tire of telling you, has no natural resources; it is a "service island", about half the size of Fulham Broadway, and the very model of a modern major monetarist freeport. Every facility is prudently husbanded. A symptomatic pop-up notice on the hotel dressing-table read:

"Dear Guest. A very warm welcome to Singapore. You'll find our water fresh and sparkling clear. It's also safe to drink from the tap. Our small island has limited water resources. Over S$365 million was spent on new water projects in the last decade. Another 500 million will be spent in the next five years. During your stay kindly assist us to save water economically. Here are some tips:

Brushing teeth — use a tumbler or glass, not a running tap.

Shaving — use one quarter litre only.

Tub bath — may we suggest a shower instead? Rinse, turn off tap, soap up, rinse down — twenty litres."

When I went out for dinner one evening without switching off the bedside light, a scolding notice was placed on the pillow cautioning me for wasting electricity.

Unless you are on business, time in Singapore hangs rather heavy on your hands. The tourist sites can comfortably be inspected in a morning: the Sultan Mosque, the Japanese Gardens, the Temple of a Thousand Lights; you quickly find yourself revisiting mosques and temples that wouldn't merit a second glance elsewhere. The business centre around Shenton Way is much more diverting: the soaring banks and trade headquarters with their burnished glass lobbies and executive Chinese restaurants on the roof; all of them built in the last eight years on reclaimed land. At half past twelve Shenton Way is thronged with immaculately turned-out Singapore secretaries in silk dresses and pleated skirts: the cult of the efficient personal assistant is remorselessly promoted in *The Straits Times*; at half past one the whole district empties again within a few minutes. Almost everyone working in the merchant banks and trading companies is very young: you can reach positions at twenty-six that you wouldn't hold at forty-five in Europe. But there is no levity. The young Singapore businessman looks like a British clerk in an Elstree Studios movie of the early sixties, dressed in white drip-dry cotton shirts, and self-effacing ties. At noon on Saturdays, I am told, they slip into the company cloakrooms and emerge in vividly patterned batik sports shirts. Who knows what role-playing fantasies prey on their minds at the weekend? *Saturday Night Fever* ran in Singapore for a world record season, and science fiction festivals are packed.

Singapore citizens are very friendly; their whole island is a hotel, a shopping centre, they want you to come back. It is safer on the streets at night than any other city in the world. There are no muggings, no rapes, no second chances; prison sentences are statutory and stiff. Chewing-gum was banned in all state-owned flats while I was in Singapore; the Minister of the Environment regretted the prevalence of gum glued to lift doors. Singapore is like a school at which the rules are clearly displayed but if you once overstep the mark, authority comes down on you like a ton of bricks. Strangely enough "coming down like a ton of bricks" is a catchphrase in Singapore: the same Minister of the Environment was coming down like a ton of bricks on squatters living in bamboo huts along the river. All traces of the old Singapore are being expunged one by one; five years ago the food hawkers who sold satay sticks and spring rolls by the roadside were rounded up and relocated in hygienic food reservations; last year the sampans and bumboats were cleared from the river; now it is the turn of the bamboo houses. Each time, however, a few token examples of the old life are pickled by the Tourist Board, for sightseers to sample. The Indian goldsmiths who used to populate Serangoon Road may be a case in point; unless it was an extraordinary coincidence, there is only one goldsmith left in Singapore: I read three separate profiles of him in the space of a week.

The Singaporeans' overriding characteristic is their desire to set a good example; they see themselves as head monitors of South-East Asia. Public service broadcasts exhort them nightly to even higher thresholds of consideration and public spiritedness; half-page advertisements in *The Singapore Monitor* urge them to report anything suspicious; "Noticed a lot of coming and going lately in an apartment near you? It may be a brothel. Ring this number . . ." A Minister for Home Affairs gave a five-minute homily after the evening news on petty pilfering. His tone reminded me of the headmaster who expects to hang his gold fob watch from a goal post and find it still there next year. Another commercial reminded you about litter; there had been an unwelcome spate of this selfish habit in certain areas; we weren't told which ones; no doubt the citizens concerned knew who they were and had burning ears. At my school it was against the rules to suck lollies or eat crisps on the pavement: for some reason this offence was known as "socking in the street" and if spotted you could be fined a few shillings. For the first time in eight years I noticed myself eating only in the sanctioned food reservations, lest a paper napkin should accidentally flutter to the ground.

My days spent waiting for the *Benavon* were well regulated. I wrote until three, drank some fish head soup, bought an evening paper and idled by the swimming pool; on the dot of five o'clock — so precisely that you could set your Rolex by it — the heavens opened and the monsoon began. Everyone scuttled indoors cursing. Then I took a bath and ate cashew nuts while reading the paper. For several evenings strange mutterings and whisperings were audible just outside the bathroom window and one night, determined to discover the source, I stood on the edge of the bath and threw back the frosted glass pane. I found myself staring straight into a maids' dormitory where several wrinkled and partially clothed women were playing Fan Tan under an eiderdown.

The monsoon ceased at a quarter past five and by half past it was sunny and everyone trouped back to the pool. The other residents at Raffles were insouciant; Australians and Americans for the most part plus a few British. Several parties of expatriates from the old country were on holiday from the rubber plantations near Pekan. They were a species of Briton I thought had long ago disappeared, atrophied in the earlier stories of Somerset Maugham: short, bristling military types with moustaches and seersucker shirts. They did not look well off and must have found Singapore expensive; they brought their own bottles of spirits down to the pool and shamelessly hailed the boy for tonic water and slices of lemon. Their wives were pleasant, slightly cowed women who nevertheless managed to enjoy their break from outstations upcountry, spending the day shopping for lengths of cotton for sundresses. At night the men got tipsy and, after dinner, swam noisily. Then, in full view of the patrons of the Palm Court Restaurant, they made clumsy attempts at slipping off their wet bathing bags under towels and in the process freely displayed their private parts.

The Raffles Hotel was agreeable when you found your bearings. The dowdy decor is appealing, though difficult to explain to Singaporeans. They assume British travellers like such hotels for their colonial connotations. Personally I like them for their design: the rooms leading off open verandahs and little plots of bougainvillea. You had to walk the hotel like a tight-rope; one slip or one wrong turn down a corridor and you are in commercial Raffles. Around an innocuous corner is, without warning, a cringe-making display of local dancing (Singapore folk dancing is the second worst in the world, after Corfu); hang a right from the lobby and a stall is offering you "I had a Singapore Sling at Raffles" T-shirts in a variety of standard sizes. Even in a restaurant called The Tiffin Room, which at first sight seems innocent enough, a screen suddenly unravels from the ceiling and a slide show proceeds. "The well known writer Rudyard Kipling," booms a portentous voice, "said, 'When in Singapore, eat at Raffles'." I noticed there was no parallel citation from the well known humorist S J Perelman: "The cuisine at Raffles is the most odious in Asia."

After dinner, however, when the folk dancers have unbuckled their native masks and the kettle drums been stowed away, when the mushroom lights around the swimming pool are turned on and the British expatriates have tucked their genitals safely inside their underpants for the night, and the violins in the palm court are playing for dancing, there is still romance to be found at the Raffles Hotel if you have the patience to seek it out.

But it wasn't exactly Chinatown. The longer I paced the sanitised pavements of Singapore the more I searched for lowlife; somewhere in this city people must have broken ranks; down some dark alley at the wrong end of Jelan Besar, there had to be sing-song girls and machehs (celibate Chinese au pairs), sikoos with shaven heads and soothsayers. But however dark the alley and however wrong-ended the street, there was always the metallic glow of American Express and Bank Americard stickers to disappoint you.

At last, by assiduously cultivating the Chinese housekeeper and consenting to smuggle her into Britain in my carpet bag, she disclosed the names of two or three off-limits night clubs. These were in the Arab quarter, off Crawford Road, and were said to be in full swing as early as ten o'clock.

The Kwai-Phor Club, which sounded the most promising on the list, is located above a shop selling canned tuna and crab; you enter by way of a side passage, dark and uneven, with an open drain running along one wall. At the door, which was ajar, was an old man sitting behind a table: wrinkled, battered and bowed, with cunning rheumy eyes and a green tin full of small change. He waved me to go away, but when I produced my scrap of paper with the address written in Mandarin Chinese, he relented, and asked for seventy-five cents entrance fee. The walls of the wooden staircase were hung with rice paper scrolls of black and gold calligraphy fringed with red ribbon; in a niche on the landing was a small shrine with a household god, joss sticks and down-at-wick candles in copper saucers. At the top of the stairs a curtain was tied back to reveal a long narrow room, extending the width of three houses which was filled with Chinese. Tables for Mahjong and Fan Tan were arranged along both walls above which were suspended dim electric lights. Around each table sat Chinese men stripped to their vests, each with a glass of beer or tea at his elbow and hands of Mahjong tiles, like dominoes, set out in front of them. They played in total silence, the only noise being the clatter of ivory tiles onto the reject pile. In the middle of the room, however, were two lines of hard chairs, arranged back-to-back, and Chinese women quietly gossiping and sipping beer. At the far end was a wooden stage with music stands arranged for some impending cabaret. The room was steamy, cooled only by a couple of sluggish fans, and waiters wheeled to and fro with litre bottles of Anchor lager and bowls of chicken porridge.

I sat down on a chair. Pretty soon a friendly Singaporean in a Javanese batik shirt joined me and asked if I played Mahjong. I said I didn't and he said it would take too long to teach me, and that anyway I would only be cheated. We ordered beer and a bowl of crumbly dried fish which tasted like Bombay duck. It is a tradition, he went on, to cheat novice players, especially gwai-lo's (white devils). He pointed round the room and said that at almost every table players were using secret codes to their advantage. Mostly these are word codes designed to tell your partner which tiles you hold; the words are numbered from one to nine, each representing one of the three main groups in Mahjong: mun — characters; sok — bamboos; and thong — circles. Mutter an innocent code word which had nothing to do with Mahjong, and combine it with a second word to cover the miscellaneous groups called the "big cards": tong, nam, sai and pak — "the four winds"; or hong-chong, fatt-choy and pak-pun. This can be communicated even more precisely through Mahjong semaphore. If you want the pak-pun (white heart), a blank smooth-surfaced tile, touch your forehead which resembles the card; for the fatt-choy, hold your hair, because hair in Chinese is also pronounced fat; for the Ng-thoong (number five circles) point to your navel — the Chinese, it would seem, have five navels.

At other tables, however, the same signs could mean something altogether different, based on a separate system of word association.

Later, in a book by Mr Sit Ying Fong, I read that Mahjong had had a profound influence on colloquial Chinese. "One example, recorded in the Chinese classics, tells of a subordinate officer who once did a bit of creeping to his divisional commander against whom he was playing Mahjong. Knowing the General needed a sam-sok (number three bamboo) to win the game, the young officer quickly discarded this tile. Hence the Mahjong expression 'ta sam-sok' (delivering the sam-sok) meaning 'currying favour'."

At about a quarter to eleven a loud drumming and thrashing of cymbals off-stage heralded the arrival of four Chinese sing-song girls. In the years leading up to independence, when the British ran the administration and millionaire Chinese tokays were left to rule the native quarter undisturbed, sing-song girls were highly esteemed and earned, anyway for their short working life, three or four times as much as doctors and solicitors. They were employed by consortiums of ten or fifteen rich merchants, who met several times a week in secret clubs to hear them sing and then reciprocally entertain them in upstairs "rest rooms". Often Mahjong was played for the favours of sing-song girls, who were themselves fickle in their loyalty to clubs. Rival consortiums tried to head-hunt them and transfer fees reached dizzy heights.

The modern sing-song girl's lot is barely an echo of her former glory; she is obliged to perform in cabaret clubs like the Kwai-Phor, or to devise twittering routines for the tourist hotels. They still cling to their dignity, however; sing-song girls are always well turned out with elaborately arranged hair and raw silk dresses. Their singing is high-pitched and, to my ears, ugly; many of the top notes are inaudible, like a dog whistle. But the Chinese love it; they listen with rapt attention and, at the end, clap loudly. Then the sing-song girls walk in pairs along the hall collecting tips, and I noticed most people dropped at least three or four dollars into the box.

The next morning I paid a call on the Ben Line shipping office. They occupy a suite on the eleventh floor of the World Trade Centre, with magnificent views across the straits towards Sentosa Island. Cable cars whizz past the window and there is constant activity as cargo ships and cruisers manoeuvre in the bay below. The news, on the other hand, was not so lively: the Benavon had been delayed two days in the Suez Canal and was running behind schedule. I received the information phlegmatically and without surprise; really it was incredible how the Egyptians, having delayed my own passage through the Canal four weeks earlier, should again interrupt my schedule at long distance, seven thousand miles further on.

I was given lunch at the World Trade Centre Club by John Tan, Ben Line's Singaporean assistant manager. We sat on suede sofas and ate bacon sandwiches; outside the plate glass window was an astroturf crazy golf course and, beyond that, sauna baths and more panoramic harbour views. These clubs are expensive to join by British standards (though not by American) and extremely comfortable. John Tan is a man of about fifty, affable and good company; he has been with Ben Line most of his working life. He said he had just taken his family on a coach tour of Thailand and they had risen every morning at 6 a.m. to fit in the maximum sight-seeing. His children were all studying for their next round of exams. The "O" and "A" level papers are, as it happens, all shipped to Singapore from Cambridge in containers where they are met at the port by armed security guards. Then the candidates' papers are freighted back to Cambridge and marked. Competition for places at Singapore University is cut-throat and a degree is considerably more decisive in the Republic than in Europe.

I spent my last few days in Singapore reading the papers and dawdling at the port awaiting the *Benavon*. Sometimes, when the wind was blowing up from the south, I fancied I could already hear the unbelievable anguish of the bagpipes floating across the Strait of Malacca. The Singapore papers, on the other hand, were not inspiring. They find the most curious items to run as headlines:

"Medical undergrad loses exam revision notes six weeks before finals," screamed one.

Others were almost surreal in their reporting of high finance. "S'Pore developer pulls off HK property coup." "S'Pore developer Ng Teng Fong has pulled off a coup in Hong Kong. Taking advantage of depressed property markets there, he and his company picked up a prime site for only $38¼ million," read a front page lead in *The Singapore Monitor*.

For a prosaic editorial, however, you can't better *The Straits Times*. They endorsed the Singapore Government's latest education plan with alacrity: to allow mothers who have been to University first choice of schools for their children. The spurious logic behind this scheme is that Singapore women graduates are too involved with their careers to help the country's drive for high intelligence babies. Singapore male graduates, in turn, are not making enough efforts to marry girls with degrees which would, in due course, according to the Government, produce motivated issue. First choice schooling will supposedly encourage graduate women to have babies for the privilege of their children attending top schools, and men to marry clever girls for the chance to jump the queue. "The Government is right to combat natural tendency of graduate males to marry non-graduate females," sam-soked *The Straits Times*. "Singapore needs top quality school children."

One interesting item I did find concerned Andy Lee, the son of Singapore's Prime Minister Lee Kuan Yew, who I suddenly remembered had been a contemporary of mine at Cambridge, with rooms on the same staircase. I never knew him well, but remembered him as a gangling grinning youth with a squash racket. He was one of those distressingly efficient people who make ingenious notices for their door, informing you where they could be found at every minute of the day, with an arrow that variously points "in the library" or "having a bath" or "in the college bar". The only other thing I remembered about Andy Lee were the sacks of rice and sweet and sour pork he had delivered from a restaurant in Soho, which he stir-fried in a saucepan in the kitchen. Now, on his own territory, I learned that Andy Lee is not only number two in the military general staff, but the hero of a cable car disaster. There was a photograph of him in *The Singapore Monitor* wearing a tracksuit, setting off for a game of squash rackets.

Two days later, at 4.30 in the morning, the *Benavon* arrived at Tanjong Pagar dock. Four cranes immediately commenced loading cargo into her cavernous hold. We sailed for Hong Kong at dusk. The sun was disappearing behind Sentosa Island and the sky was coloured like the lid of a Caran D'Ache paintbox: a frowsty fandango of oranges, purples and indigo. The sea was perfectly flat and alive with sampans and prahdus cutting across our prow to Kusu Island and Pulau Bukum. Before we left harbour it was already dark, and the lights along the port twinkled with all the bonhomie of the marina at Cannes.

I had arrived in Singapore in a state of bleary disrepair. Now, at least, I felt sufficiently revived to tackle the next 15,500 miles in my remaining thirty-eight days.

13 | *In which the* Benavon *crosses the South China Sea. And eyes are kept peeled for Vietnamese boat people.*

The MV *Benavon* was the largest of ten ships on which I deck-hopped around the world: 73,000 tons and the third heaviest container vessel afloat. Her massive grey hull extended halfway to China before we'd even set sail, and you moved between her nine decks by means of a lift. I was signed on board as temporary librarian, which seemed more appropriate than my previous commission on the *Aqaba Crown* as purser-without-portfolio, and undemanding too, since the library had largely been usurped by a video bank. My cabin was normally assigned to an engineer; a narrow corridor of a room with a desk, large bed, armchair and a 16 November 1981 edition of *Punch*, in which several passable shots at the caption contest had been made, by a person or persons unknown, but never posted.

I soon learned the real reason why the *Benavon* was two days behind schedule: she had run aground in the Suez Canal. An Egyptian pilot, negotiating her through the deep-water channel north of Port Said, had steered into a sandbank, blocking the entrance for twenty-four hours and disrupting three convoys. Now, needless to say, the Port of Suez Authority were accepting minimum liability for their error, and a helpless frustration suffused the crew. When I came aboard they were recovering from an extended bout of sleeping sickness. The anxieties of Suez, followed immediately by Jeddah, had permitted little rest for a week, so they had devoted the remainder of the voyage to Singapore to catching up.

Afterwards, whenever I thought of the *Benavon*, it was of linoleum corridors and the clanging of a xylophone summoning us to the poop deck to eat. The forty-four man crew necessitated three dining-rooms: one for the ship's officers (plus the librarian); another for the ratings, who were mostly called Jimmy; a third for the Chinese laundrymen, ship's chippie and Somali fifth engineer.

Meals in the officers' mess, over which presided a reproduction of Anigoni's Coronation portrait of the Queen, were agreeably formal but poorly attended. The logistics of the watches meant that only half the officers could roll up at any one time, so we sat well spaced from each other — our places marked by silver napkin rings — like a succession of jinxed dinner parties to which half the guests had failed to show. The conversation, however, had a reassuring, measured beat to it. The food, which was the responsibility of the steward who sat on my right, was minutely examined by his brother officers as a potential target for wry humour; the relative workload of the First Officer and the Radio Officer ("Sparks") was a long running and well-staked skirmish. Some of the jokes probably had their origin in the age of steam, before the *Benavon* was re-fitted for diesel. We debated, as we traversed the South China Sea, the most convenient ferry crossing to the Isle of Skye: Kyle of Lochalsh versus Mallaig. Scotland featured prominently as a topic: the officers' homes were in Dundee, Glasgow, Stornoway, Kelso and Aberdeen. Everyone, in fact, lived in Scotland apart from the Captain: his address was a box number near Dallas, Texas.

Captain Donald Cowie was a jovial man with thick grey hair and a broad Scots accent. He was the only officer on board to dispense with regulation white shorts and shirt with epaulettes, for fawn trousers and a pullover. This was a trait I met elsewhere: the dogged, professional captain who eschews formality.

The main hazard of the South China Sea, said Captain Cowie, was Vietnamese boat people. "Our sister ship, *The City of Edinburgh*, picked some up last year. It's a blasted nuisance for everybody because you have to stop to take them on board and then complete endless paperwork before handing them over to the authorities in Hong Kong. But really you have no option. You can't leave the poor blighters in the water, though a lot of ships do. It's really only the British and the Americans who'll touch them, and we're fast ships too. I often think of the slower ones, the Chinese and the Russians, who must sail straight past, ignoring them."

The armada of Vietnamese boat people, though less well publicised than the first evacuees, has not abated. Several flotillas put to sea every month, often on impossibly unseaworthy rafts made of rubber tires and car doors. The latest wave of evacuees are professional people: doctors, dentists and surgeons. The government has taken to forcing them into unpaid manual work on ideological grounds, insisting on three months subsistence farming for every nine spent in the surgery. But for the new evacuees the prospect of citizenship elsewhere is remote: the United Nations currently has three million refugees on their books worldwide (Vietnam is the fourth largest source after Ethiopia, Afghanistan and Palestine) and are running short of foster nations.

"Apart from the boat people," said Captain Cowie, "och, this sea is like a blasted motorway. You keep in lane to the Horsburgh Light, then follow the road all the way to China." He scanned the horizon with binoculars and frowned. "Too many small fishing boats cutting across our bow. They try to stay close because we churn up the fish for them, but I don't like it."

Until the installation of tracking satellite, all shipping used to follow the coastal route past Borneo and Kuching to the mouth of the Sulu Sea, before sailing due north to Hong Kong. Now it is possible to plough a direct course "and know exactly where you are to the nearest two hundred yards," while saving a minimum of twenty-seven hours over the Phileas Fogg itinerary.

Captain Cowie was equivocal about the change of route. "Och, it used to be a bit of fun up round Palawan island and Sandakan. We spent several days at anchor outside Sandakan, waiting for a berth in port, and I used to have a lifeboat lowered and fill it with beer and sandwiches and take the men for a picnic on a little island I knew, near the mouth of the harbour. It was a great beach, practically deserted, just a few old people limping past who never bothered us. We went there for years. Then somebody told me it was a blasted leper colony — imagine, man, choosing a blasted leper colony for a picnic. And we'd never even noticed."

Several wives were on board for the express purpose of shopping. Since unloading of the containers is so brisk, they had at most three or four hours to top and tail the markets of Singapore, Hong Kong and Okinawa for bargains. The next couple of days were then spent deciding exactly what it was they had bought.

The *Benavon* cruised past Mangkai Island, then headed north between Paracel Island and Macclesfield Bank. This area of the ocean is pitted with submerged reefs with surprising names: christened after royal children and British colonies by the Victorian admiralty cartographers who first charted them, or after the Dutch and Portuguese ships which ran aground there. Post-satellite, the chance of hitting a reef is negligible, as the Captain of the *Titanic* told the women and children first. Night and day we steamed relentlessly onwards at twenty-three knots, overtaking everything like a nautical juggernaut hogging the fast lane. A north-east monsoon was blowing up from the Philippines, and Captain Cowie wanted to make maximum speed while the going was good.

Modern container ships have such deep holds that you can barely see the sea from the promenade deck: they reminded me of jokes about boarding houses called "Sea View" where the landlady supplies a telescope. They carry more cargo than six of the old ships put together: the four enormous carriages we were delivering for the new Hong Kong underground (MTS) looked like Fisher-Price toys on deck. But the remoteness of the sea was slightly eerie: in the morning it took a few seconds to realise I wasn't staying in some mid-west American motel. Only the engraved navigation charts, amended every four hours with a lethal pair of compasses, verified how rapidly we were nearing Hong Kong.

To both bows of the ship were flying fish; not the giant, flapping Dover sole which wing their way across children's books, but flying sprats. They leapt ten foot out of the sea, then dived into the crest of a wave, a flash of quicksilver against the opaque spray. When cargo ships were lower in the water, I was told, flying sprats used to flop onto the deck during the night, somersault hopelessly, and expire exhausted in the morning as stop press editions to the breakfast menu.

"Do you realise that a Ben Line seaman is in the *Guinness Book of Records?*" The Radio Officer had a knack of locating my areas of ignorance. "A Chinese cook is listed as the longest surviving shipwreck victim afloat in a lifeboat. That was during the war, after his ship was torpedoed. Forty days I think he survived before being picked up. He caught seagulls with fishing tackle and ate them raw."

The approach to Hong Kong by sea is striking; even dyed-in-the-salt seamen with thirty years before the mast leave their cabins to watch. A sequence of small islands, some British, some Chinese, all of them rocky and tangled with undergrowth, loom out of the sea; bleak and mysterious and for the most part deserted: the islands chosen by John Le Carré for springing Chinese agents in hazardous operations involving junks. As we neared Hong Kong itself, and the ports of Stanley and Aberdeen, the coast is dotted with the bizarre homes of Chinese millionaires, invisible from the road: gothic turrets — miniature Windsor Castles — nestling in the shadow of the Peak, and behind them the cardboard shanty towns, clinging precariously to the cliff face, where their houseboys and coolies live in the bodies of rusty cars.

Lined up on the quay, waiting for the ship to dock, were no less than two dozen Hong Kong customs officers in yellow crash helmets. They made a slightly alarming reception committee.

14 | *In which an eventful stopover is made in Hong Kong. And confusion is registered between China and Cheltenham.*

"I know *exactly* who you are. My mother-in-law, Lady Effingham, sends me your cuttings."

A formidable English gossip columnist for the *South China Morning Post* had cornered me between the caviar bar and a perilous dripping ice sculpture of a Chinese dragon. She wore a black taffeta ball gown and deftly brandished three stemmed glasses of champagne and a rolled gold Cartier biro at the same time.

"Mmm," she said, "hot blinis. Two deep spoonfuls of caviar please," she instructed the waiter. "Not that it's likely to run out but it's such utter tedium queueing for more."

The mezzanine floor of the Mandarin Hotel jostled with Europeans in black tie. The men looked prosperous, with the slightly sallow skin of the old China hand; the women took vicarious interest in St Laurent and Calvin Klein.

"Where did you find that pretty frock?"

"This? Oh, only in London. It's just a joke."

"I thought I hadn't seen it out here. You are sly, Jennifer."

After the modulated sobriety of the *Benavon*, the cocktail chatter at the Mandarin was intimidating. I had been hijacked within seven minutes of disembarking by an old friend on the *Far East Economic Review*, and frogmarched into this reception. Everybody else had paid seventy American dollars for their ticket, in aid of the Hong Kong Philharmonic Orchestra, and I felt conspicuous in my tropical suit.

"Don't be ridiculous," laughed the gossip columnist from the *South China Morning Post*. "They're lucky to have us here. Half these people are so bored, they leap at any diversion. I just can't decide whether to use you, Tim Rice or the general manager of Oberoi Hotels as my lead story next week."

The *Hong Kong Tatler* was deploying two paparazzi: Chinese lensmen in white tuxedoes who laboriously consulted their light meters before shooting and then required you to spell your name in block capitals. (Sir Run Run Shaw, His Excellency the Governor Sir Edward Youde, Mr & Mrs Ng Wong.) The pictures, you felt sure, would successfully eliminate any untoward levity from the occasion: Hong Kong society is two decades behind London and New York, and allergic to the warts and all naturalism of party coverage a la mode. The *Hong Kong Tatler* does not run pictures of the tai-pan boogying home by rickshaw after a sake party on the Peak; this is the last frontier of the Madame Tussaud's school of reportage. You can lose anything in Hong Kong — your shirt, your fortune, your marbles, your wife — but not Face.

I had learnt this at first-hand four years earlier. At the time I wrote features for the English *Tatler* (a dissipated step-cousin, twice removed, of the Hong Kong edition) and while in the Far East filed a few thousand words on the expatriate recruits to Jardine Matheson and Swires, the two British trading houses which underpin the island. No doubt the article was facetious — I can remember almost nothing about it beyond someone having a pair of pink satin boxer shorts made up by Mr Sam, the Chinese tailor. In London it passed without comment; it was the type of journalism, concentrating on a single profession such as estate agency, farming, acting, or army ensigns, that is the bedrock of monthly magazines. In Hong Kong, however, it caused a riot. By ill chance the entire sixteen-man holding board of Jardine Matheson was flying out from Gatwick for their annual board meeting. One of the directors bought a *Tatler* at the terminal for his wife, and failed to overlook the emotive coverline "THE JARDINE JOHNNIES: ARE THEY GOING BONKERS IN HONKERS?" Twenty-two hours later, by the time they landed at Kai Tak airport, every single director had studied the piece, and vied with each other in their outrage.

Now, in only a few years, Hong Kong is a much changed place, and many of the directors who had been so affronted had themselves fallen victim to internal power struggles. The Hong Kong share index was shooting up and down like a dying man on a respirator, as each round of talks about the 1997 handback of the island to the Chinese ended in deadlock. A new series of initiatives was beginning the following morning — the British Minister of State for Foreign and Commonwealth Affairs, Richard Luce, had flown in at lunchtime, and the British Ambassador to Beijing, Sir Richard Evans, had arrived under separate cover. He gave a jaunty press conference at the airport, dressed in an impeccable navy blue overcoat, in which he told local reporters that he was delighted to be back in Hong Kong so that he could take the opportunity to visit a decent dentist.

The consensus at the Mandarin was that these prolonged discussions were a triumph of form over content.

"Of course the Chinese could march in any time they wanted," everyone agreed. "Hong Kong isn't the Falklands. Nobody would lift a finger to stop them."

"Except that we're more useful to them as we are. You'll see, they won't make a single change to the way this place is run, not in the first twenty years at any rate."

"Then why the devil are the rich Hong Kong Chinese getting their money out?" That was the only disquieting detail. "They say billions and billions of HK dollars are being transferred to Canada every week."

The sovereignty question has drawn a new species of commentator to Hong Kong: the obituarists. The city was already filling up with writers, predominantly American, researching documentary books about the twilight of the colony.

"If you pirate my title 'The Fall of Hong Kong' I'll sue, you'd better believe it," bawled one cantankerous author across the half-melted ice dragon.

"I've already registered that title," replied the other. "And 'Hong Kong — The Last Thousand Days' and 'The Tai Pan Bequest', so you can litigate all you want."

"This is Saigon all over again," said someone else, a trifle prematurely in the opinion of the fund-raisers for the Hong Kong Philharmonic Orchestra.

An English voice was straining to make himself heard above the roar of voices.

"Ladies and Gentlemen . . . Ladies and Gentlemen . . . quiet for one moment please." The chatter abated a little. "Ladies and Gentlemen, I know that you'll be very pleased to hear that, while we've been enjoying our champagne, a merchant banker has been circulating among us collecting pledges for the Orchestra. I don't know how he's managed it — whether he threatened to call in all our loans if we didn't make a donation — (laughter) — but in less than twenty minutes he's raised in excess of $15,000, and that's US dollars, not Hong Kong dollars." (Applause.)

The gossip columnist for the *South China Morning Post* said, "This really is quite a key event for here, much more important than I'd expected. That's Lydia Dunn, incidentally, the putative first woman governor of Hong Kong."

A paunchy Texan disclosed that his impending book would cover the full spectrum of Hong Kong life, "the big bucks and the tenements". For the purposes of monitoring the big bucks he had rented a suite at the Peninsular Hotel; the Kowloon tenements would be reported at long distance, drawing deeply on his imagination.

My friend from the *Far East Economic Review* suggested we might like to visit some nightclubs.

"Mind how you go, you guys," cautioned the paunchy Texan. "You know what they say about Hong Kong after hours."

We didn't know what they said as it happened, but it was too late, a taxi was drawing up outside the Mandarin.

"1997, please."

Club 1997 is currently the vogue Hong Kong-side cocktail bar, sited halfway down a steep hill behind the governor's residence. The name 1997 is a cocky reference to the lease: the club will close the day the Chinese rumble in. Which will be disappointing for the Chinese, because 1997 is quite a jolly spot. If you closed your eyes you could be in the Members Bar at Newmarket Racecourse. There was a mighty roar of voices: British, public school, confident, rather drunk. The air was thick with squeals of delight and infidelity: the flower of English youth baying for broken promises. I scanned the room for evidence that this was China and not Cheltenham: the only clues were the brown litre bottles of San Miguel and Tsingtao beer lined up on every table. The waiters were English; the pretty girls who lounged on the padded banquettes were English; the boys worked for the English trading companies or the Hong Kong and Shanghai Bank; the records were the eight-week-old British hit parade, recently arrived with the regular shipments of Marmite and *Country Life* by slow boat.

"Christ, Mark," slurred a voice through the smoke. "That's your eighth San Mig on an empty stomach."

"OK, yar," drawled Mark. "Someone had better order me a sweet and sour Miss Piggy."

A big blousy girl was organising a picnic on a junk. "James and Charlotte are on, Alex can't make it, Sarah's confirming tomorrow morning before nine, I've left a message with Simon's armah at the mess to ring me however late or wrecked he is . . ."

Some of the older girls, in their late twenties and early thirties, were members of the notorious Hong Kong fishing fleet, which cruises into the colony trammelling for husbands. Demand for white women always exceeds supply in Hong Kong, despite the growing trend for mixed marriages. The *Hong Kong Tatler* "They Were Married" page is full of criss-cross wedding pictures: "Mr & Mrs Jerry Stapleton held their reception at the Excelsior Hotel. The bride is the former Miss Pinkie Leong." An idiosyncracy of Hong Kong society states that British men should restrain from marriage until the age of 29, but should on no account remain single after their thirtieth birthday. This necessitates a breathless scramble for spouses in the space of a few months, attracting the fishing fleet like seagulls behind the wake of a liner. "But you have to take care where you drop your net," I was warned, "in case you catch a crab — or an old boot."

We moved on next door to a nightclub called Disco-Disco which was packed with Chinese. The wine was less good than the 1997 and was delivered by waiters in satin shorts. The walls at Disco-Disco are covered with mirror, and a hologram made interesting patterns on the ceiling. Quite a lot of Chinese were wearing purple eye-liner and Culture Club T-shirts, and held onto their glasses with purple leather gloves with metal studs on the wrists. I was just being told that there had recently been trouble with punks at the club, when a fight broke out. Glasses were thrown and two men — one Chinese, one Scottish — were dragged struggling into the street.

On the way back to the Mandarin we drove along the narrow lanes behind Queens Road, where the night sky was all but obscured by the strings of Chinese washing that flutters like bunting across the street, then cut back past the governor's residence with its flag pole and limp Union Jack.

When Phileas Fogg undertook his epic journey he was able to make two-thirds of it on British territory and didn't need to bother with a passport. Now Hong Kong is the last remaining pitstop with a British Governor-General. All things considered, however, I wasn't too distressed to quit British soil once again and resume my choppy passage through the Strait of Formosa.

15 | *In which amnesia is experienced in a hotel bedroom. And a hippy recherches à la contre-temps perdu.*

I woke up in a strange hotel bedroom with no idea where I was. Seven weeks of non-stop travelling through fifteen countries was disorientating and I was temporarily at a loss. The room was quite small with whitewashed walls; there were no pictures; a freestanding shower cabinet freestood in the corner; and an anaemic grey light filtered through a chink in the curtains. I drew them back looking for clues: the view was a breathtaking panorama of the central well of the hotel.

Slap, slap, slap. There was a shuffle of slippers in the corridor. I stuck my head out to find a tiny, wrinkled maid sweeping the floor with a brushwood broom. She wore black baggy cotton trousers, a blue jacket with a Mao collar and black felt slippers.

"Would you be so kind as to tell me which country this is?"

She stared at me as though mad, and jabbered in an excitable sing-song dialect which was either Cantonese, Mandarin Chinese, back-street Kowloon or Basque. Then she made good her escape down the service lift in a laundry basket.

On the dressing-table was a mound of foreign money scrumpled up like old Kleenex tissues: Italian lire, Jordanian rhials, Indian rupees, a few Greek drachma, two hundred Singapore and Hong Kong dollars. None the wiser, I dialled the front desk for enlightenment.

"Gleetings sir. You are sitting on the side of the bed in Room 208, Grand New Hotel, Yokohama, Republic of Japan."

So I was. This was day fifty. I had arrived the previous night at midnight, and was boarding the *Charles Lykes*, a cargo vessel bound for Honolulu, this afternoon. Which left me the best part of a day to inspect Yokohama.

Outside on the pavement a crowd of children in earmuffs were building a snowman. It had snowed heavily during the night but wasn't expected to do so again; the sky was cobalt blue, the air crisp and the early morning sun glowed off the white streets. It was half past seven. Opposite the Grand New Hotel was a small garden, Yamashita Park, laid out in the most formal Japanese manner with sunken lily ponds and wicket gates, and beyond that Osanbashi Pier and the south sweep of Yokohama harbour. At one end of the park I could see the red and blue chassis of the Marine Tower with its observation platform, like a delicate version of the Blackpool Tower, and at the other end the terminal of the Shuto Expressway and a plaza of brittle skyscrapers, lightly brushed with snow like dough on pita sticks. Children were walking to school with satchels, dressed in the black winter jerkins with gold buttons that make them resemble crocodiles of French railway porters, and businessmen scuttled by in knee-length overcoats and fur hats.

With shopkeepers sloughing the snow from the pavement with pails of hot water, Old Yokohama put me in mind of Gstaad or St Moritz; the streets are narrow and windy and overhung with wooden houses; and chic expensive boutiques sell French designer labels and designer watches. At any moment I half expected some playboy ski-bum to slalom into view, extruding a spray of powder snow behind him, and curvet inside for a lapis lazuli bracelet. But this was fourteen thousand miles from the Alps. Every third building was a suchi bar with plastic realisations of the dishes displayed in the window: bright pink platters of sachimi and grey bowls of sukiyaki and tempura, disturbingly reminiscent of joke plastic dogs' messes and fried eggs in novelty shops. I drank a pot of green tea, skimmed the *Japan Times* ("All the News Without Fear or Favour") and made my way uptown.

Yokohama was the port where Phileas Fogg and Passepartout had reunited following the debacle in the Hong Kong opium den. The French manservant had meanwhile paced the harbour front, without a yen to his name, wondering at the fiercely oriental scene. "There were bridges half hid in the midst of bamboos and reeds; temples sheltered under the immense melancholy shade of aged cedars; retreats in the depth of which vegetated the priests of Buddhism and the sectaries of the religion of Confucius; guards of the Mikado; and restaurants adorned with streamers and banners." Any similarity between modern Yokohama and the above is purely occidental. Instead there are to be seen bridges half hid in the midst of Hitachi cranes and

Toyota gantries; temples sheltered under the immense and melancholy shade of McDonald's hamburger outlets, retreats in the depths of which vegetate the priests of Sanyo and the sectaries of the religion of microchip; guards of the Mitsubishi company; and sushi restaurants adorned with American Express and Visa stickers. I went into a supermarket to buy provisions for the voyage. A further indication of my escalating travel fever was that I had no idea whether the *Charles Lykes* was an American or a Japanese ship; in the panic to secure a berth I had enquired only about the destination, and paid a bundle of yen without bothering to convert it. I didn't know whether the fare included meals or what status of cabin awaited me, so it seemed wise to expect the worst and be prepared. I bought a half bottle of Suntory whisky for three thousand five hundred yen (about £15), several bags of rice crackers and a six-pack of cold sake. By the time my shopping was completed the sky had turned Kabuki grey and threatened to spew at any moment. So I hastened back downtown through the slush to my hotel.

In my haste to strike out in the morning I had overlooked the jewel on my doorstep. The public rooms of the Grand New Hotel are spectacular: three vast Edwardian drawing-rooms emanating from a lobby that recalls nothing less than the entrance hall of the London Natural History Museum. The walls are decorated above the cornice with an elaborate stucco frieze depicting maritime history: sampans and steamers berthed from floating jetties, and European and Japanese merchants haggling over bales of silk. The sofas and armchairs were highbacked and looked like hand-me-downs from the smoking-room of some Scottish baronial hotel, made all the more incongruous by the low lacquered tables on either side of them. Japanese newspapers were suspended from bamboo poles hung on clothes horses, and the grandfather clock engraved "Manchester, 1897" chimed the hours in a corner. At the end of a long parquet corridor, dotted with roll top desks, was a bar. Of all the bars in all the world I knew I would never walk into a finer one. I had journeyed through three continents to find the Naka-ku bar of the Grand New Hotel, Yamashita-cho, Yokohama, and I felt a profound sense of occasion, of having at last arrived. Generally it is only in retrospect that you can say "Yes, that was what I came all this way to see"; but the Naka-ku bar was like walking into a room that I had always known existed but could hardly have known where. An open fire was burning in the grate while the snow outside the window resumed its swirling. The walls were covered with Argyll tartan plaid like a shooting box, but instead of antlers above the door there were Hiroshige prints of Mount Fuji. The chairs were gilt with petit-point cushions that might once have belonged to Madame de Pompadour, and ranged along the shelves behind the bar were no less than forty-six different brands of whisky: thirty-two of them Scottish, eight Japanese, four Canadian and two special house blends. The most expensive, according to the menu, was Ballantine's thirty-year-old malt at 6,000 yen (£22) for an eighth gill. I ordered a Kirin beer and a plate of sachimi and sat at a table next to the fire and watched passers-by through the window doubled up with cold against the snow.

"You mind if I join your table?" A tall, slightly emaciated man with cropped black hair was towering above me; he wore a grey flannel suit and a blue shirt with contrasting white button-down collar; his nose was very large and flat. His accent was pure New York but I think that even without it or the button-down collar I would have known he was an American; the ready handshake was as firm as a vice. He was saying "Glad to know you, Nick" and the roundness of the greeting seemed to declare "I'm an American and the whole world is swell and when you shake hands with me it's not just as an individual — but with America herself, and New York City, and cable television, and the Johnny Carson Show, and the American Open Golf Championship, and waffles with maple syrup, and all the rest of the bag of tricks that adds up to a great place."

He said: "I'm Bob Ratkai. I don't know if you are familiar with Yonkers but that's where I'm from." Then he said, "Excuse me," and opened his briefcase on the table and fished around among his papers.

I pronged my sachimi.

"It tastes good that stuff — it's raw fish," said Bob Ratkai, a shade gratuitously since I had all but finished it. "Some people can't eat it, makes them sick."

Then he ordered a whisky. "The price of bourbon out here is crazy but you've gotta keep on truckin', that's what I say, yessir, keep on truckin'."

He spread his papers on the table until they covered almost the whole surface, and the remains of my sachimi were buried under a fretwork of business cards. "Now who am I meeting with this afternoon, uh-huh?" He ticked various names on a list. "I sell watches by the way — imported," said Bob Ratkai.

I said, "Isn't that rather an uphill struggle? I thought Japan was the top watch exporter."

"Uh-huh," said Bob Ratkai. "I think you could say that, but it's business."

Then he added, apropos nothing at all, "I used to be a hippy you know that."

He said it challengingly as though I might contradict him.

I said, "How interesting. How long ago was that?"

"Maybe ten years. Then I chucked it. You could say I outgrew it I guess."

"Really."

I didn't particularly want Bob Ratkai to elaborate on this theme. There is always something tiresomely obsessive about people who claim to have tried and "seen through" a particular creed, as though their own change of heart somehow discredited the whole philosophy. This is true of liberalism ("I used to be a Liberal"), censorship ("I was bitterly opposed to it in any form until . . ."), communism, catholicism, the lot. Bob Ratkai had all the ugly characteristics of a born-again capitalist.

"Sure I was a hippy," said Bob Ratkai. "You wouldn't think so to look at me now, but sure I was. Uh-huh."

It was one o'clock, I didn't need to be at immigration until half past three and had no particular place to go. My carpet bag was packed and waiting in the cloakroom, so I swallowed my misgivings and submitted to the inevitable.

"You ever read *Village Voice* magazine? Then you've seen the want-ads section at the back. Well they have a category for bums looking for travelling partners, and when I used to read the *Voice* there were four whole columns of just that. This was in '71, '72, when you could still make a trip all the way to India without taking a plane — before the Russians screwed up Afghanistan, and Iran (he pronounced it Eye-ran) went down the john.

"Anyhow I was living in New York City at that time, though my folks were in Yonkers, and it seemed like a good idea to do some travelling so I answered several of these want-ads for people heading East. What you did was mail a photograph of yourself and some details about where you were heading for, and if this fitted in with the others then you made a plan to meet up. I got a reply from two chicks heading for Nepal — Rebecca and Sarah — and we met in a coffee shop in

SoHo and I guess we must have hit it off okay because the following month we flew together to Amsterdam to begin the journey.

"I guess you could say we dressed pretty weird by today's standards, not that it looked that way at the time. Rebecca and Sarah were both from upstate New Jersey, which is as straight as they come, but already they had all the right gear before we set off; muslin scarves with bronze discs tied round their hair and Nepalese jewellery and beads. And we all of us wore denim dungarees because the zip-bibs were neat for passports and money.

"So we stayed in Amsterdam for maybe a week, which was a spacy place to hang out in '72, and then we took a bus from there all the way to Istanbul. By the time we arrived we just wanted to crash out. Those bus journeys take it out of you. They were ridiculously cheap, maybe twenty dollars one way, and the drivers never seemed to have the right papers so there were delays at every border. And the customs — uh-huh — they were bastards, and if they found a trace of dope they would throw you in jail just like that, especially the Greek customs. And then the bus kept breaking down, so what should have been seventy-two hours became more than a hundred before we got there. So we rented a room in some cheap hotel close to the Blue Mosque and slept it off.

"We had a week in Istanbul before the next bus left for Teheran. Istanbul was full of overlanders; we hung out at a place called The Pudding Shop where they sold Western food: lamb chops and crinkle cut fries; and saw the covered bazaar and Topkapi Palace and all that jazz. Becky — that's Rebecca — and Sarah were tight with their money so we didn't spend much, and we all shared one bedroom with three beds at the hotel because it worked out cheaper that way. We weren't very enterprising, we never went more than half a mile from the hotel, but there was a lot of cheap dope about and we spent time tripping in the room.

"Then we went on to Teheran, which is much the same as Istanbul, and then on to Meshed. As I say, you could get dope everywhere then — good quality too, not cut with anything — and the first thing we did whenever we arrived was buy some. Usually we were offered it at the hotel. Our only rule was not smuggling it across the frontier because it just isn't worth the hassle if you're picked up.

"Anyhow, we had bought some at Meshed off an Iranian, a student, and were smoking on the flat roof of the hotel because the food was inedible and it took your mind off it. We'd been up there maybe two, three hours, when there was a lot of commotion and three big guys came onto the roof in leather jackets, and said they were police. They took away the joints and confiscated our passports, and suddenly we realised it was pretty heavy. I shouted something, I was fairly well out of my head, and one of the policemen booted me in the stomach. Then they told the girls to strip, right there on the roof, claiming they were searching for more dope, and all the hotel staff were leering and it was pretty unpleasant. I didn't know what was going to happen next, I thought maybe they'd rape the girls, nothing would have surprised me, but they didn't. They told us to report to the police station the next morning, where they made a big deal of Meshed being a holy city and all that, and then they fined us seven hundred and fifty dollars. I hadn't even got that much money but Sarah had an American Express card. There's no Amex office in Meshed but in the end we persuaded the hotel to advance us the cash for a big commission, and we got the hell out of Iran the same day.

"Did I mention that Becky was now my girlfriend? That had started in Istanbul. So I slept with her, and Sarah had a bed in the same room.

"After Meshed nobody felt much like dawdling in that area so we kept on jumping buses through Afghanistan and Pakistan until we reached India. India was much better, we really liked India. We headed north to Kashmir, staying first in a hotel in Kathmandu, then took a long lease on a room overlooking the spice market. This was kind of fun and we wandered about the town talking to the other travellers (there were always several hundred passing through) and buying food in the market; they have great fresh bread and water melon in Kathmandu. Uh-huh, and then Becky and Sarah wanted to get into yoga and meditation, so we started attending classes at some local ashram — not a very good ashram I'm afraid, not a famous one." Bob Ratkai looked a bit resentful about this.

(How interesting, I thought, a minor-ashram hippy with a chip on his shoulder.)

"The classes didn't do much for me. In fact they were a load of bullshit; the swami could say anything at all and they'd say it was profound, but half the time it was something quite ordinary like money being a stumbling block to faith. But Becky said it helped relax her, and she sure was relaxed, so I left them to get on with it and wandered about on my own. That was the mornings, and then at about three o'clock we'd eat, and then rest, and then get up again in the evening and then eat and smoke.

"We'd been in Kathmandu about four months when I had an idea. Becky had been trying to buy henna for her hair and had problems explaining what she wanted in the market, and other travellers said they'd had the same experience. And suddenly I thought, why not start a shop selling that kind of thing and cold beers for the overlanders? I figured it wouldn't cost much to get going, and it would solve my other problem too which was that I was running short of money. So I asked around and quite soon I found a site near the bus station, which is a good place to be, and went into partnership with Becky and Sarah. I reckoned we were ripped off on the rent but it still wasn't expensive and a few weeks later we opened up.

"At first there wasn't much stock, not nearly enough to fill the shelves, just toothpaste and razor blades and so on, plus maps and Lonely Planet guide books. But every morning I searched the market and bought stuff in bulk and put it in the shop with a mark up, and pretty soon it started to shift, especially souvenirs like brass boxes and joss sticks. Then we got into batteries and film which always go well, and had some crates of denims and cheesecloth sent up from Delhi, and afterwards shoulder-bags and slippers. We kept stamps for postcards and let people leave their luggage with us for a few days while they went climbing, and had a message board which travellers could use as a postal address. All those kinds of facilities really helped business, because when people came to collect their bag or post a letter they'd stay on for a meal and a beer.

"After a year we had quite a reputation and were doing great business. The thing about overlanders is they all want to get some place remote, but they don't want to get ill. It's kinda comforting to have a base camp where you can eat safe food and get information, which was what we provided. And all the time we were diversifying. For instance Becky and I went up to the villages and got the women to make us up some skirts, and I started a small travel agency as a sideline: nothing fancy, just bus tickets and charter flights leaving once a fortnight to Delhi, but quite profitable.

"Now one thing you've gotta understand is that this was '72, and although I ran the place as a business it couldn't look that way. We were very into being straight with the travellers, and we wouldn't rip them off or add more than thirty percent markup to anything we sold. Nor was there any systematic stock taking. We just kept a list of what went out and then replaced it, and when we needed money we took it from the till. Not that we needed much money since we ate at the shop and the room was only three hundred rupees a month.

"But as the turnover went up and up I thought, what the hell, maybe I could make some real money if I got it together. Becky and Sarah still played hookey every morning with the swami, leaving me to open the shop, and if it hadn't been for me nothing would have been reordered and the shelves would have been empty in six weeks. Whenever I mentioned this to Becky she smiled and said I was a crypto-capitalist, and the shop was only a means to an end, to pay for our stay in Kathmandu, and that attitude made me mad. A few more months of this and I wanted out.

"I began looking round for potential buyers and started a dialogue with some Indians who owned a hotel. They were keen to buy us out and offered a good price on the understanding we'd leave Kathmandu and promise not to start a rival outfit. This seemed fair enough and I told them to go ahead and draw up some proposals.

"Then I told Becky and Sarah and they were crazy. They said I had no right to sell the shop behind their backs, and they wouldn't play ball. They had no intention of leaving Kathmandu, they were studying under the swami, and I should tell the Indians the deal was off.

"Jeez that pissed me off! I told Becky that everything was over between her and me, and I moved out of our room into the Indians' hotel. I was still determined to sell the shop, and I consulted several local attorneys about my rights. They said it might be possible to assess my cut on an effort-put-in basis and I told them to go right ahead. I was sick of Kathmandu by now, the place stinks. I kind of began to despise the overlanders too, they are so gullible and tight at the same time, and I doubled all the prices out of spite to screw them. I made them pay to leave their filthy rucksacks in our store, and pay to post messages on the board, and I stocked magazines like *Fortune* and *Forbes* which was guaranteed to get on their tits. Becky and Sarah didn't say anything about this — I thought maybe they hadn't even noticed — they ignored me when we saw each other, or stared at me in a pitying way which was infuriating.

"Then one afternoon I'd been in a meeting with my attorney in his office and was walking back to the store when I saw a long line of people outside the door. There were two or three hundred of them, overlanders, Indians, beggars, you name it, all shoving their way to the front. Well, I elbowed my way right through and what I saw there damn near made me faint. Becky and Sarah and the swami were handing out free clothes and food, and people were fighting to get their hands on them, and leaving with armfuls of books and toothpaste and the bronze Buddhas and Vishnu calendars I'd collected from all over. Then I really let fly. I lashed out at the swami and might have floored him too if I hadn't been restrained. Becky came up to me and explained in a soft voice that they'd already sold enough stock at half price to make back what we'd started out with, and now they were giving the rest away. She said it had been the swami's solution when they had consulted him about what to do. 'I think it was very wise of him, don't you?'

"Later that evening I was given my one third share which was three hundred and fifty dollars. I sold my camera and some odds and ends I'd picked up on my travels and made it up to five hundred. That was just enough dollars on the black market to buy me an air ticket back to the States; it didn't even leave enough for drinks on the plane.

"God knows what became of Becky. I never heard from her or Sarah again. I guess they held me in contempt after that. But I must admit I'm kinda curious; they might still be out there for all I know, living in our old room. I hear not so many people pass through that way now, but whenever I run into anybody who has, I always ask. It's getting sort of difficult to describe the girls properly: weird really to think they're both thirty-six."

Bob Ratkai pleaded a pressing engagement to see a man about a watch at the Isezakicho Shopping Centre, and left me to my statistics. The New Grand Hotel seemed as good a place as any to make a no-crosses-counted appraisal of the itinerary. Ever since Singapore I'd been in-creasingly reluctant to face the fact that I was dangerously behind schedule. Phileas Fogg had made Yokohama in forty-two days; I'd arrived at the same point on my fiftieth. Delay by delay, an hour here and an hour there, time had slipped through my fingers until it had turned into eight whole days. I could see perfectly well how it had happened, each wasted day was quite distinct: the unanticipated stop-over in Piraeus due to the muddled timetable; the twenty-six hours spent bobbing offshore in Aqaba; the extra day frittered in Bombay when Mr & Mrs J Adams had reserved the last sleeper on the Madras Mail; the unexpected hiatus in Singapore after the *Benavon* ran aground at Port Said. Altogether I was languishing a hundred and ninety-two hours behind schedule. It seemed most unjust. It wasn't as though I had lingered at any stage; I hadn't taken up with a sing-song cabaret star in Singapore, or a yum-yum girl in Wanchai. I was simply the victim of circumstances beyond my control: storms in the Aegean, Egyptian bureaucracy, Sudanese hubbubs, Indian train timetables, unmarked sandbanks . . .

On the wall of the Naka-ku bar was a map of the world: not the perspective that Europeans are accustomed to, with Great Britain slap-bang in the middle, America to the left, and Japan on the extreme right; but a Japanese world view, with Tokyo in the centre, America to the right and Britain clinging like a limpet to the margin. The change of perspective made the Pacific Ocean daunting, an enormous light blue chasm that divided the map in half: the width of India fitted comfortably inside it eight times. I wasn't anywhere near half way round the world and already I'd used up fifty of my eighty days. Yokohama was only ten hours ahead of Greenwich on the GMT international clock, and I had to work my way right round to nil again. Granted, it now takes less time to cross the Pacific than in the last century, but the deficit seemed far too great to make up. From that moment I began to detest the conceited Phileas Fogg, with his maddening phlegmatic temperament, and racked my brains for scapegoats who had got me into this predicament in the first place.

16 | *In which three and a half thousand miles of South Pacific is crossed by freighter at the rate of five hundred calories per mile.*

Twenty-four hours after leaving Japan we ran into the first rough weather since the Mediterranean: a stomach churning mongrel of hurricane and tornado.

The *Charles Lykes* was an American freighter, flagship of the New Orleans Lykes Line, and her full hold of cargo meant maximum discomfort from swaying for her eight Stateroom passengers. Approximately every fifteen seconds the ship rose with the force of the Yellowstone National Park geyser, wavered perilously, and lurched steeply forward into the trough. As she reached the bottom of the wave there was a tinkling of broken glass as toothmugs smashed on the cabin floor, suitcases slid out of lockers, cameras toppled from cupboards and bottles of Thousand Island dressing slalomed across the galley.

The moment the ship began her ascent, the process was reversed: Thousand Island dressing was reunited with tuna sandwiches, suitcases slid back into lockers, and the deck was awash with slivers of zoom lens and toothglass.

Safety bars were erected around the beds where the passengers languished unhappily: our complexions spanned the full spectrum of popular soups, from old-fashioned green pea to raffish avocado and clam chowder. The cabins, as it happened, were the most comfortable on the journey, with giant picture windows which afforded dramatic perspectives of the raging sea. Curtains were kept tightly drawn.

Through the cabin walls drifted shirty voices in dialogue with their god: "OK, OK, you've made your point — now switch it off will you."

The Captain of the *Charles Lykes* was heroically unsympathetic.

He was a wiry Californian in a blue anorak who could have under-studied Captain Bligh in *The Mutiny on the Bounty*.

"Hell you bunch of canaries," he chided the passengers in one of his folksy addresses from the bridge. "You just haven't found your sea-legs yet. When you've been at sea for twenty, twenty-five years — then give me tornadoes."

As the storm intensified, the Captain's speech became incoherent and he took pains to avoid the society of his passengers. Cornered in the wheelhouse, he muttered enigmatically in a tone that, once un-scrambled, could only be interpreted as caustic. After forty-eight hours of battened down hatches, however, he relented a little and took a straw poll. Who was in favour of heading south into calmer waters, which would add half a day to the voyage?

Everybody was except me — at this stage in the Phileas Fogg chal-lenge I couldn't afford the extra day.

"Let's ride the squall out, Captain," I told him, confident that we'd already been out-voted seven to two.

The other passengers gawped incredulously. "Ride it out? Fry me for an oyster, are you serious?"

(Of course I wasn't. I merely said it for effect.)

The Captain paced the deck for a few minutes, then reached a wily compromise. We'd continue on virtually the same course. But tell the passengers we were striking south.

If a week is a long time in politics, then a week on the Pacific is a lifetime. Especially when you are marooned three thousand miles from anywhere with the Flintstones. Not that my fellow American passen-gers kept pet dinosaurs, but they shared Fred and Barney's round-the-clock obsession with junk food. Travelling by freighter there is little to do except anticipate the next meal, and these high calorie orgies followed each other with barely an hour's respite in between. Some of the passengers were so obese that they couldn't sit down in the ship's armchairs, only on the sofas; still they thought of nothing beyond their enormous appetites and the means of satiating them. Four times a day they scrutinised the small type of the menu, debating how much food they could reasonably order before the chef closed the kitchen.

"Hey, steward, get me a short beef with spaghetti, and a side order of Mexican enchiladas, burritos and tamales. And a plate of corn fritters with fried rice. And if you've got any of that blueberry pie a la mode fetch me out a slice of that. No, make that two slices — with topping, for sure. And bag me up a turkey club sandwich in foil to carry out."

There seemed a very real danger of our running out of food before reaching the International Dateline and I began to hoard Saltine crackers and cubes of Jell-O in my cabin as hostages to fortune.

Four nights out of the eight-day voyage we put our clocks forward one hour. These twenty-three hour days made the constant eating even more oppressive, since the meals were crammed into truncated timetables. The storm made it impossible to sleep at night, so the passengers dozed by day, rendering it ever more difficult to tell whether it was breakfast, lunch, dinner or supper we were awaiting. Certainly the menu held no clues.

The voyage took on the quality of an existentialist play in which the characters baffle the audience with an obscure parable of life in purgatory, set in the saloon of a steamship. Only the spontaneous orders to the steward proved the performance was unscripted.

"Hey steward, got any more of that coconut cake?"

"Hey steward, how come I don't get any eggs with my hash browns?"

Conversations carried over from one meal to the next, with no acknowledgement of passing time. A question posed on the hundred and fifty degree latitude could be answered fifteen hundred miles further on, on the hundred and sixty-fifth degree. Our observations became diffuse and unrelated.

"Jimmy makes his own barbecue sauce, it's so tasty with corn fritters."

"When we have guests turn up unexpectedly, do you know what I make for them? Trifle! That's right, a trifle. I guess I use up all Erwin's Grand Marnier that way."

"This meat makes me kind of nostalgic for Pebbles."

"Pebbles?"

"Our dawg. His dawg mix reminds me of this oxtail."

"They're featuring pastrami on rye for dinner with potato salad."

"Do you know something, Nicholas, I was disappointed with Japanese food. Somehow, I don't know, I expected it to be more different."

"Pebbles used to like pastrami, remember?"

"Japanese food isn't *different*?" This was Erwin speaking. "Have you tried kochee — you can smell it four blocks away."

"Tell me, Nicholas. Is it true you still have hot water radiators in London?"

"So my best Grand Marnier goes into your goddam trifle, does it?"

On the evening of the third day the wind dropped and the sea became calm. Deck chairs were lashed to the rail and the passengers limped outside into the fresh air. Of all the legs on Phileas Fogg's journey the Pacific scenery can have changed the least: deep blue water stretching for miles into the distance and not a sign of life or traffic. The emptiness was awesome. For hours we stared over the rail looking for evidence of progress. Did the sea become less black as we steamed further from Japan, or was this an early warning of sea blindness? On the afternoon of the fourth day we passed another ship, a Russian trawler, and elbowed each other out of the way in our haste to take a look.

The following morning we saw a seagull — a black-beaked Goony Bird from Midway Island — and it monopolised conversation for the day. You would be surprised how much mileage you can wring out of a seagull, by the time you've discussed its wingspan, feeding habits, migration, danger from oil slicks and a dozen other aspects besides.

We passengers were ingenious in our efforts to occupy ourselves. No avenue was left unexplored in making our own entertainment. Some days we played golf on the deck with imaginary balls and clubs. "Great shot Erwin, straight into the bunker."

One Californian stood on the fo'c'sle completing a cyclorama of photographs of the view through 360°. He was confident it would be endlessly diverting for his neighbours back home in Oakland to see thirty-six frames of the blue horizon.

After dinner we curled up in the saloon like boa constrictors digesting a bellyful of cholesterol. At a card table in the corner, illuminated by a low wattage overhead light, a gentle game of picquet was in progress. On a sofa a fluffy-haired matron appliqued a pin-cushion with the legend "Louise will make a House a Home". In all probability this was Miss Jane Marple, taking time out from an Agatha Christie thriller.

There can't have been a person on board who didn't contemplate murder just to break the routine. Motive: cold-blooded boredom. All we needed was the victim. There were eight candidates, each one of them spoiling for a fatal dash of spiked tabasco in their Bloody Mary.

VICTIM A: Marcie, 56, a widow from San Diego. Collects Chinese carpets and Tiffany stained glass. Recently retired from her job as senior vice-president for personnel in a major insurance corporation. Spent several months in Nasser's Egypt in 1957. Latent Islamic sympathies.

VICTIM B: Bob, 62, from Los Angeles. Works on the management side of an aerospace company. Served at Arnheim in the Second World War, later spending some time as a prisoner of war. Firm fan of the Syndicated Columnist Andy Rooney.

VICTIM C: Bob's wife Mary, 60ish. Drinks Budweiser lager and favours electric blue trouser suits. On a previous cruise was once invited to a cocktail party by an English Duke and Duchess. Claims not to recall their names and to have found them snooty.

VICTIM D: Mary's sister May, 58. White-haired and kittenish. Innocuous personality masks ruthless hand at picquet.

VICTIM E: May's corpulent husband Bill, 61. Works in same aerospace outfit as his brother-in-law. Brooding and silent. Possibly hot-tempered when roused. Never seen without his baseball cap.

VICTIM F: Charlotte, 45, married to the ship's radio officer. Once spent a week in London on an American Express package tour and found herself sitting next to her son's orthodontist at the Shaftesbury Theatre. Has since been convinced of the smallness of the world.

VICTIM G: Japanese student, 21, with unpronounceable name. Embarking on a round the world tour with $6,500 in travellers cheques to last him a year. Shaky English. Points at items on the menu at random. Often eats tinned pears with dill pickles off the same plate.

VICTIM H: Subversive English writer in panama hat. Sometimes scribbles a snatch of conversation on the cuff of his shirt. Otherwise immersed for long periods in the *National Geographic*, perusing fascinating articles on Canadian wheat farming.

During the fifth night of the voyage we crossed the International Dateline and had the benefit of two consecutive Tuesdays. Everyone agreed that if you were going to gain an extra day somewhere, right out of the blue, it couldn't have happened in a more interesting place, right out in the blue.

On the sixth day we spotted a dolphin on the starboard side, though it might have been a floating car tire, no one could say for certain. Maybe the three rolls of film would clear up the enigma once they were developed.

On the seventh day, halfway through dinner, though it might have been breakfast (who could tell?) I remembered it was my birthday: my twenty-seventh. I had earmarked this year for broadening my horizons, so took a long hard stare out of the porthole.

On the afternoon of the eighth day we passed the Island of Niihau and by the evening reached Honolulu. We docked at Berth No 1 shortly before nine o'clock. Frankly I was rather disappointed to find no reception committee of Hawaiian maidens waiting on the quay, doling out garlands of flowers and wishing us a saucy "Aloha". Apparently they earn better money posing for tourists brochures and taking cameo roles in *Hawaii 5–0*.

The late edition of the *Hawaii Star Bulletin* was on sale at the customs house. "KILAUEA VOLCANO ERUPTS", bawled the headline, a trifle emotively as it turned out: boiling lava had spurted a full six inches from the mouth of the crater. The date on the paper, however, was reassuring; it confirmed my own estimate of our progress. Despite the storm we had crossed three thousand five hundred and twenty miles of the Pacific in a hundred and ninety-two hours, clawing back four whole days on my eight-day overdraft on the Fogg scale.

17 | *In which a yacht is sought in the marinas of Honolulu. And a visit is paid to The South Pacific Man.*

Honolulu, capital of the Island of Oahu, itself the second largest of the eight Hawaiian Islands, the fiftieth state of the American Union. Two thousand miles from the mainland it is a superannuated holiday resort with some of the priciest real estate anywhere in the world. Half an acre of inland scrub with a two-bedroom bungalow retails at a quarter of a million dollars. The coast is fringed with high-rise holiday hotels and marinas. Hawaii is the ultimate manifestation of the All-American vacation: exactly the sort of place, in fact, that the Americans do so badly.

In all probability I would be trapped in Honolulu for weeks, perhaps for ever. No passenger ships ply between the islands and the mainland; cargo vessels head south-east for Los Angeles or the Panama Canal; the only scheduled route to San Francisco is by cruise liner, and these neither pick up stray passengers nor call at Oahu in early March. My only hope of leaving Honolulu by sea was to cadge a lift on a private yacht, several thousand of which were moored around the island. At this time of year the marinas are thick with West Coast holidaymakers cruising across the North Pacific for a fortnight's shark fishing. My plan was to scour the waterfront, cap in hand, ready to submit to almost any humiliation in return for a long-distance hitch-hike to the Golden Gate.

Meanwhile I looked around for a hotel room to use as base camp, thus further aggravating an already strained accommodation situation. Honolulu in the first week of March bursts at the seams. The Hilton Hawaiian Village was offering guests $250 as an incentive to check out. Condominiums were packed like Kowloon tenements. Sidewalks teemed with people, average age seventy, in swirling Aloha shirts with garlands draped around knotted chicken necks. Old women with hollow faces, filled out with false teeth like wire coathangers inside hot water bottles, hobbled about on crutches wearing grass hula skirts and muumuu kaftans. The focus of life on Honolulu is Waikiki Beach, a two mile margin of gritty sand before a corniche of gimcrack hotels. By day the beach is packed with surfers, banking four deep on the crest of every wave. After seven o'clock it becomes a collecting ring for prostitutes — several hundred of them on a balmy night — who commute between the uptown motels near Diamond Head. The day I arrived in Honolulu the American aircraft carrier *Kitty Hawk* had put into Pearl Harbour, disgorging seven thousand ratings onto the flesh market. You could find a vacant motel room for love and money, but not for bona fide travellers cheques.

"Aloha!" A peaky ginger-haired girl was sprawled on a sofa outside the lift on the ninth floor of the Miramar Hotel.

"Good morning." I assumed she was a floor maid and hurried past to my room. I was relieved to have at last found a bed so close to Waikiki, and looked forward to taking a shower.

When I re-emerged forty minutes later the ginger-haired girl was still there.

"Aloha!"

"Good afternoon." I waited for the lift to arrive. I noticed she was wearing a pink T-shirt with a stencil of the Hawaiian Islands across her chest. She looked pinched and consumptive; her face was heavily freckled.

I wandered along Kalakaua Avenue, Honolulu's main drag. The weather was clammy and I felt sluggish. I ought to have made a start frisking the marinas, but deferred making the effort. I searched for something to eat. Every shop was an amusement arcade, a carry-out restaurant or a souvenir boutique. I was by now a connoisseur of tawdry souvenirs, and could price the world's tourist junk to the nearest five cents, but I was out of my depth in Honolulu. South Pacific knick-knacks bring a new dimension to the word ephemeral: plastic leis (garlands of flowers) imported from Okinawa; plastic grass hula skirts; hideous plastic trolls in Hawaiian costume, with disturbing button-down eyelids; plastic pineapples to suspend from the trees back home to remind you of your vacation. From every arcade came the ratatattat of Pacman and Space Invader machines. "All our games purely for fun." Gambling is illegal in Hawaii: it is Las-Vegas-on-Sea but without the payouts. The hotels have large, rather grubby lobbies lined with vending machines: postage stamp machines, hot drink machines, machines dispensing cigarettes and newspapers and sachets of popcorn and suntan lotion. All of them require complicated combinations of coins, and none of the hotels issue change. The machines were in any case mostly out of order. The hotels have outward-bound names like Tradewinds, The Driftwood, and The Outrigger Surf. In their shade are restaurants "with reputations for fine dining". The Hawaiian speciality is the teriburger — a tasteless half-caste of Japanese teriyaki and American hamburger — which is washed down the throat with soapy Hawaiian cocktails called "Diamond Head Dynamite", "Kilauea Killer" and "Heleikada Hellfire". In the street, students hand out advertisements for barbecue buffets: "All you can eat for $6.95"; "guaranteed no limit — it's you who decide when you've had enough — not the chef"; "Open salad bar from 4 p.m. to 9 p.m. Pay once and eat your heart out."

I paid once and ate my heart out on a few mouthfuls of teriburger. Then I returned to the Miramar Hotel.

"Aloha, Nine-Two-Oh!" 920 was my room number. The ginger-haired girl was still sprawled outside the lift. She smiled in the goody-two-shoes way they smile in soap serials. Clearly she wasn't a maid. I wondered why she chose to spend her holiday in the passage, if she was staying at the hotel.

My map of Honolulu marked two major yacht marinas: the Alawai, outside the Hilton Hawaiian Village, and Fisherman's Wharf at Kawalo Basin, half a mile short of the Aloha Tower. I decided to try Fisherman's Wharf first, then work my way back via the Alawai. I set off to find a taxi.

"Aloha, Nine-Two-Oh!" said the ginger-haired girl. "You Australian?"

"No, English actually. From London."

Then the lift doors opened.

"I'm Carrie-Anne," she shouted as the doors closed behind me. "Be sure to have a nice day."

The Fisherman's Wharf is the older of the two marinas and rents boats by the hour. There are cardboard cut-outs of sharks and red snapper, and for a dollar you can be photographed next to them holding a fishing rod. Six or seven hundred yachts bobbed from buoys in the harbour, and sunshine glistened off their white decks. At the far end of the wharf is a restaurant clubhouse, and I made enquiries upstairs in The Captain's Bridge Saloon. A dozen Americans were quaffing bourbon or a syrupy cocktail made with one part guava-juice to three parts orchid petal and paper parasol.

I explained my mission and, considering its impudence, they took it well. A man named Grady bought me a guava cocktail. They were all most friendly but in agreement that I was barking up the wrong marina. The Fisherman's Wharf was used by locals, there was very little holiday mooring. The buoys were rented on long leases, and few of them belonged to mainlanders. They knew of nobody about to sail for San Francisco. I would have a much better chance at the Alawai marina.

The Alawai is several times the size of Fisherman's Wharf. More than three thousand dinghies and yachts are moored there in a permanent state of flux. Twelve narrow quays extend from a concrete terminus, and an arcade of glitzy boutiques and chandlers stores sells provisions and sawn-off jeans. Californian girls were sunning themselves on deck, and Mexicans with Castro moustaches hoisted cartons of Budweiser lager on board. Music blared from every deck. This week was the twentieth anniversary of the Beatles' first tour of America, and on this spurious pretext all three Hawaiian radio stations were celebrating with a non-stop "Merseython" tribute.

I began buttonholing people at random on the quay.

"Excuse me, are you by any chance sailing to San Francisco within the next twenty-four hours, and would you possibly have room for an extra passenger? I know this sounds crazy but did you ever see a film called *Around the World in Eighty Days* . . . you didn't? . . . well, it's about this Englishman called Phileas Fogg . . . that's right, David Niven . . . No, I'm not him . . . I see, your boat is going to stay moored here for another month? . . . Ah, never mind."

There was something cumulatively absurd in repeating the story. With each telling it sounded more implausible and more like a stunt for *Candid Camera* or *Game For a Laugh*. People started looking nervously round for the concealed film crew. I felt like a salesman peddling life insurance: a foot-in-the-quay merchant who has to compress the salient points of his message into three sentences before losing the element of surprise. Even then you couldn't get away in under fifteen minutes. I wanted a quick answer: Yes or No. Instead I became a wharfside entertainer. If people believed my story they wanted their friends to hear it too. They wanted an itinerary of the whole route. Atlases were produced, addresses exchanged. If ever I was in the San Antonio area I was to be sure to give them a call. What a shame Jerome wasn't here right now; he took a vacation in London last fall. Did I possess a Burberry raincoat, not that I needed one here in Oahu, ha ha. Perhaps if they gave me their measurements I could mail them a raincoat on my return.

All of which was very diverting but brought me no closer to San Francisco.

After a couple of hours canvassing, I learnt short cuts. There was no point approaching yachts with names like Pauhana, Paiko, Kauila, Ke-Au-Hou or Mauka; these were Hawaiian and weren't going anywhere. Instead I concentrated on Wagon Trail, Misty Blue, Windsong, Rocky Mountain and Stone Crab, which invariably belonged to mainlanders. Also anything less than 140 foot long and with an engine smaller than a chest of drawers was incapable of making the crossing rapidly enough.

Paul and Tricia Koeppe were smothering a bowl of tinned button mushrooms under a blanket of Roquefort cheese dressing when I approached their table. It was set up on the quay, next to their yacht *Ka Lae*; a Hawaiian name as it transpired, christened after the southernmost point in the United States. Paul Koeppe was a man in his late forties with a tidemark of black curly hair around his ears and the back of his otherwise bald head, and a heavy jowl. He looked mildly belligerent. His wife was at least a decade his junior and was wearing a yellow one-piece bathing costume which matched her corn-coloured hair. She had slightly leathery sunworshipper's skin and two full hands of gold rings, arranged like knuckle-dusters. She seemed amused by my story.

"I'm sure we can take you," she said. "There's only Paul and me and three crew; Paul likes to do his share of the sailing himself. There's enough room."

Paul Koeppe was less enthused. He said, "We're not particularly fast, you know. We take six days to make San Francisco. You could find quicker yachts."

"But not sailing tomorrow honey, he won't," said Tricia Koeppe. "Anyway we are fast, or so you're always telling everyone."

She escorted me around the *Ka Lae*: a moderate sized yacht with engines more powerful than its frame really warranted. The guest cabin was evidently designed with a hunchback in mind.

"It will be fun having a passenger," said Tricia Koeppe. "We've been away for five weeks already and Paul doesn't like partying in port."

"So long as you're not going to delay us with customs declarations," said Paul Koeppe. "I don't want to get involved with customs."

I said I'd already cleared customs and immigration on the *Charles Lykes*.

"OK," he said. "If that's what Tricia wants, I'll take you. We sail tomorrow at five in the evening. Be here 4.30."

"Aloha, Nine-Two-Oh!" The ginger-haired girl — Carrie-Anne — persisted with her lift-side vigil. I would have been disappointed if she hadn't been there, and double-checked the floor number. "How are you finding Hawaii?"

"Fine, thank you." I was heartened by discovering the Koeppes and felt more favourably disposed towards the place.

"You want to see Al Harrington?"

"Who's he?"

"You don't know Al Harrington? How long did you say you've been here?"

"A day, but I still haven't a clue."

"Then for sure you've got to come along. Ah've got two reservations. Meet you in the lobby at five o'clock. Aloha!"

Then, just as the lift doors began to close, she sprang up from the sofa and dived inside. I was so surprised to find she could walk, and wasn't rooted by her thighs to the cushion, that she had disappeared before I could side-step the invitation.

Nightlife in Honolulu is held in the thrall of two rival cabaret entertainers: Don Ho and Al Harrington. Each of them fronts a different "Polynesian Extravaganza" with claims to being the most exciting on the island. In appearance they respectively resemble Engelbert Humperdinck and Tom Jones, and their shows aspire to a homespun razzamatazz in the Las Vegas tradition.

"They're both equally good," said Carrie-Anne obstrusely, "but ah think Al Harrington has the edge."

I said, "Are you sure you can spare the ticket? Did somebody drop out?"

"Ah buy two tickets each night," said Carrie-Anne. "Either for this show or for Don Ho. Then see who turns up."

"You mean you wait by the lift every single day?"

"Not always," said Carrie-Anne. "Sometimes ah lay by the swimming pool."

We were milling outside the Polynesian Palace waiting to be let in. The early performance hadn't yet finished and music wafted from inside: snare drums, bass guitar and coconut castanets. A poster in a glass case told us more about the impending cabaret.

"You may remember him from a decade ago in the old *Hawaii 5–0* television series but today visitors and residents alike know him as 'The South Pacific Man'. Samoa-born and Hawaii-raised, Al Harrington deserves that title.

"Your evening in this plush showroom begins with a lavish buffet, which includes roast beef carved to your liking. Then the dishes are cleared away and Al appears on stage and announces he will pose for pictures before and after the show. This is just one example of Al's 'Aloha Spirit' for his fans. He is renowned for his philanthropy as well as for his philosophies. This big, gentle man is as relaxed and congenial up on stage as if you were in his living-room. One of the most outstanding things about this show is the man's love for his heritage and for his country. He makes some interesting comments on Hawaii and ends the show with a rousing rendition of *America The Beautiful*."

A publicity photograph of the South Pacific Man showed him in a striped bandeau, presenting a garland of orchids to a fat woman on stage. I began to harbour misgivings about Al Harrington. But these were as nothing compared with my misgivings about Carrie-Anne.

It is a shortcoming of mine that, outside people of roughly my own background, I am hopeless at guessing ages. Americans are particularly trying: appearing either much older than they really are, puffy-faced and world-weary at thirty; or recklessly young at forty-five. Carrie-Anne, I estimated, could be anything between twenty and thirty-eight. Her clothes were bubble-gum but her neck was as broadly grooved as an old 78 rpm record.

"You see that line there?" Carrie-Anne was showing me her palm. "Three months ago it ended parallel with the knuckle. Now it stretches right down to mah wrist."

"Is it a scar?"

"No it's not a scar, it's mah luck line. Every day it grows longer. Let me see yours."

I held out my palm for inspection, though with reluctance.

"That's OK, that's OK, Nine-Two-Oh, no problems there." She ran her little finger along the luck line in a way that managed to be salacious without being the slightest bit erotic.

The seating at Al Harrington's Polynesian Extravaganza is organised along a series of refectory tables, each table holding fifty couples. As soon as the doors opened Carrie-Anne led me to her "lucky" place, which happened to be the two end seats closest to the stage. It might have been my imagination, but I was fairly sure the waiter caught her eye as we walked past and nodded conspiratorially.

"Be a big boy Nine-Two-Oh and fetch me some lean beef and potato salad."

I said, "You don't have to address me by my room number you know."

Carrie-Anne said, "Ah think it's kinda neat and keeps things easy. That way ah can remember everything about you at one time."

Al Harrington, true to his word, appeared early on stage and posed for photographs. Most of the audience immediately took up their option and ran to the front. Authentic as he undoubtedly is as an example of Hawaiian nightlife, I felt no great urge to lay out thirty pence on having Al Harrington's picture developed, so applied myself instead to a slice of coconut cake.

"Aren't you going to take his photograph?"

"I don't think I'll want to see him again once the prints come back."

"Is that why you haven't photographed *me*?"

"No, of course not."

Carrie-Anne looked petulant so I took the camera out of its case and peered through the viewfinder. Suddenly, I can't think why, Carrie-Anne's nose looked like the little nub of cucumber in cling-film which always gets left to shrivel at the back of the fridge.

"No, this background's no good," I said with a view to conserving film. "I'll take you later."

"So you think there's going to be a 'later' do you, Nine-Two-Oh? Naughty, naughty, Nine-Two-Oh!"

The show traced the history and culture of Hawaii through singing and dancing. A troupe of Polynesian girls in hula skirts aped the six wives of King Kauhumanua and hairless young men, naked from the waist up, beat on the hollow trunks of banana trees. As evidence either of his philosophy or his philanthropy, Al Harrington told us the three legacies of Captain Cook to Hawaii: iron nails, measles and venereal disease. All this immorality had an unfortunate effect on Carrie-Anne, and it soon became obvious that her strategically placed knee had not butted the waistband of my Crolla tropical suit altogether by accident.

After the final chorus of *America The Beautiful*, which was not a decibel less rousing than the programme had promised, and which the audience in its delight insisted on having twice repeated, we left to find a drink. It had been my intention at the earliest opportunity to slope off and watch an episode of *Hart to Hart* on Hawaii Channel 15 but I was reckoning without the dogged determination of Carrie-Anne. As soon as we hit the pavement she said, "You like Hawaiian Blues, Nine-Two-Oh?"

I shrugged.

"Because they build them lovely at Moose McGillycuddy's across Kuhio."

Moose McGillycuddy's cocktail bar ("Get Loose with a Moose") was pitch black, but once your eyes accustomed to the dark, it seemed to have a Wild West theme. Saddles and wagon wheels were nailed to the wall, along with Navajo rugs and the skulls of long-horn steers. Bottles of Coors beer kept cool in a trough of iced water, and the pump on the fresh orange juice dispenser was functionally disguised as the handle of a Cherokee tomahawk.

We drank Hawaiian Blues, a drink consisting mostly of crushed ice, and ate teriburgers. I told her about my journey and how I was only in Hawaii for one night.

"You got two single beds in your room?" asked Carrie-Anne.

"Yes, I believe I have."

"Ah thought so. All the rooms on the lobby side have two beds. In fact ah knew you had two beds when ah said Aloha."

Carrie-Anne was sitting beneath a spotlight which made her ginger hair blaze sinisterly. "You know this town's full-bursting with people. Well doesn't it seem kinda dumb for us to have two rooms? If ah only came to sleep in yours, well, ah could ask the desk to rent mah room out. Ah keep all mah things packed ready in the suitcase."

She leant back and, in the glare of the light, I saw she couldn't be a day less than thirty-five. Her expression was lascivious and ugly, and I knew there was nothing in the world I wanted less than a caprice with this person.

"I'm sorry Carrie-Anne, but it's late and anyway," I added lamely, "my luggage is spread out on the other bed."

Suddenly she was furious. Her eyes narrowed and her lips pouted viciously. "Wah, you clever cool bastard. You cool bastard. Do you realise you've just cost meh sixty-five bucks?"

"Surely not sixty-five?"

"Yes, sixty-five, dumbhead. Twenty bucks for the two tickets, plus forty-five room charge."

"I can hardly be held responsible for the sub-let of your room."

"Wah can't you? This is only the second time someone's done this on me this whole vacation, and ah've been stopping here three weeks. Ah'll even with you yet, Nine-Two-Oh."

Carrie-Anne had raised her voice and the other tables began staring at us through the gloom.

"Well I'm going," I said. "Here's thirty dollars for my ticket. I'm sorry if you feel let down." Then I beat a dignified retreat in the direction of my hotel.

Twenty minutes later I was in bed watching television and reading the *Hawaii Star Bulletin*. Candace Charlot, the paper's top columnist, was reporting on her special brief — celebrities.

"The stars have certainly been out in force recently. Latest luminaries to visit Hawaii include *Dynasty* star Linda Evans who was spotted at Trappers in the Hyatt. Also enjoying the Aloha welcome was cartoonist Walter Lantz, creator of that crazy woodpecker Woody, in town to soak up that good old Maui sun."

Just as I was absorbing this astringent commentary on Hawaiian lifestyle, I noticed that a green light had come on by the door which meant that a message was waiting for me at reception. I leapt out of bed, then crept back. Maybe it was a trick and Carrie-Anne was behind the door with a slop razor or, worse, her suitcase. I dialled the front desk.

"Sure, there's an envelope in your locker. Hand delivery. Want someone to bring it on up?"

The envelope said simply "Nine-Two-Oh."

Inside was a torn scrap of a Moose McGillycuddy menu, on which a vacillating hand had scrawled this heartwarming message. "I don't know whether all that gammon you talked about your journey round the world was real or not, but if it was, I hope you fail real bad."

18 | *In which a voyage is undertaken from Hono-*
lulu to the Golden Gate. And an insight
gained into a particular state of matrimony.

It struck me as extraordinary, in retrospect, that Tricia Koeppe had pleaded my case for a lift before her husband. Her timidity in his presence, and her fear of doing anything that might upset him, was pathetic, and I could only suppose that the diversion she hoped to find in me would offset the displeasure of Paul Koeppe. Tricia met me on the quay when I came on board, and seemed relieved by the lightness of my luggage: her husband had threatened to refuse large suitcases. She hustled me into my cabin, urging me to unpack, and I heard her hurrying to report my arrival.

"Nicholas is here, Paul, nice and punctual. He's only got two small bags."

Paul Koeppe grunted and said nothing.

I put on bathing trunks and a shirt and went up on deck. Paul Koeppe was relaying instructions to his crew, who looked fit and competent and were less casually dressed than most Americans. Tricia Koeppe was busying herself in the galley. She had changed her bathing suit, since greeting me, from a green polka dot to a pink one: she seemed to have an inexhaustible supply of them, for I do not remember that I ever saw her in the same one twice. All her bathing suits were one-piece. Later she said that her husband disapproved of her wearing bikinis in front of the crew.

I joined her in the galley and she cracked open a can of beer. "Get your unpacking done all right?"

"Yes, fine." I made some complimentary remark about the yacht and what fun it must be to cruise for six weeks at a time.

"I suppose it is fun," said Tricia. She sounded dubious. "Yes, it's what I wanted and I suppose it is fun."

"Doesn't the captain get a beer?" Paul Koeppe was staring surlily into the galley. "Or is this party for two?"

"Of course not, honey. We were just talking. I'll get you a beer right away. One Budweiser coming right up, captain. Nicholas was just complimenting us on the yacht."

"You're an expert on yachts are you?" He looked at me for an answer.

"I'm afraid I'm not really. I meant how comfortable it is."

"So it could be purely cosmetic for all you know. We might capsize as soon as we cast off, and you'll be none the wiser." This, though I didn't appreciate it at the time, was a first-class joke by Paul Koeppe's standards. He rocked with mirth. His belly vibrated with laughter. He slapped his sides and then his bare knees, which drew attention to their hairiness. Tricia Koeppe, anxious to ride his good humour to the full, laughed too. The tiny galley shook with merriment.

Then, as suddenly as it had begun, the joke was over.

"I'm off to pay the harbour dues," said Paul Koeppe, all passion spent. "We'll sail as soon as I get back. Make sure you're all on board unless you want to be left behind."

We sailed at five o'clock and were still in sight of Oahu when we ate dinner. Tricia Koeppe was a good cook; her speciality was stuffed tomatoes and aubergines. Before her marriage, she had lived in Manhattan and eaten out all the time. She had been to every first-class restaurant between Greenwich Village and the Upper West Side. Now you could put her down in New York and she wouldn't have a clue where to go. Her husband wasn't interested in food so any trouble she took over the cooking went unnoticed. But she would always run a clove of garlic around the inside of the salad bowl, and make her own Italian dressing, because it pleased her to know things had been done properly.

Dinner was eaten in the open air at a table outside the galley. It was a foible of Paul Koeppe's to treat mealtimes with flexibility; sometimes lingering in the wheelhouse for an hour after dinner had been announced, and sometimes appearing on the very stroke of six, impatient for his food. As a result, by half past five, Tricia was always in a state of high anxiety. Despite the smallness of the yacht she was reluctant to summon him more than once, and since it was inconceivable that we should make a start on our own, a terrible apprehension gripped us as we listened for his tread on the poop deck and watched the food turn stone cold.

If I have given the reader the impression that Paul Koeppe was a stupid man, then I have done him an injustice. Far from being stupid, he was actually very sharp. His business as a freelance realtor had flourished; he had speculated on certain areas south of Los Angeles becoming valuable and they duly had; his understanding of property prices around the world was astute; his hypothesis on real estate in London — a city he hadn't visited for ten years — was far-sighted; he had made his own fortune and was now pleased to spend three months a year on his own yacht; Tricia was his second wife, she had claimed to love the sea as much as he, and he could see no reason why she shouldn't be content.

As a conversationalist he was unpredictable and argumentative. His English was rather poor, and my American is far from fluent, so we communicated with each other mostly with the aid of hand signals. Nevertheless, he was fond of telling anecdotes which featured himself in a good light, and I took pains to encourage him. His stories were remarkably one-tracked: Paul Koeppe, acting on a hunch, buys a parade of old warehouses for a song. Six months later, guess what, property developers are falling over each other for those warehouses. But Paul Koeppe keeps his head. He knows that all the time his site is becoming more valuable, and the longer he keeps everyone hanging on, the more plans they have made for development, and the more architects' fees they have laid out, so up and up soars the price. Result: Paul Koeppe clears another half million bucks.

His prejudices were numberless. Among the more prominent were women who trapped men into marriage through pregnancy (something Tricia, at least, had never done since they were childless); people who expected annual raises as of right; Americans who balked at strong government in El Salvador; and the slovenly habits of foreigners. The British, I soon discovered, were by no means exempt from the last category.

"About fifteen years ago I stayed in a hotel overlooking your Hyde Park, and, would you believe it, the john in the bathroom wasn't even sanitised and sealed?"

He stared me full in the face to see the stupefaction with which he expected this information to fill me.

I said it didn't surprise me in the least. Covering the loo with a polythene wrapping is not the custom in London. Often I thought Americans sealed their plumbing at the expense of proper cleaning.

After this bigoted exchange we steered clear of each other for a couple of days, and concentrated instead on the speedometer. This was more elevating. Paul Koeppe was a restless man and couldn't bear his yacht to stand idle for a minute. No sooner had he arrived in a marina somewhere than he wanted to be off again; he kept the engines running night and day because he couldn't abide the notion of drifting. For the first forty-eight hours out of port we passed a fair amount of traffic, but the sky was overcast and we mostly stayed indoors. I helped Tricia Koeppe in the kitchen or frowsted in my cabin reading a book. On the third afternoon, however, it became quite warm and we sunbathed on towels spread out on the roof.

The swell was not very great and the closeness of the yacht to the water reduced listing. The days were long and idle. We made jugs of strawberry daiquiri and nibbled tacos. I read my book or skimmed American *Vogue* and *Cosmopolitan*. Tricia Koeppe painted her toenails. We discussed film stars. We played Beggar-my-Neighbour and Snap. We squeezed lemon juice onto our hair. Occasionally Paul Koeppe joined us for an hour, but sunbathing bored him to distraction. He preferred to sit on the side of the yacht, his stubby legs dangling overboard, potholing with his thumb in the depths of his nostrils.

"You know, Nicholas," he said, "when you've done loafing around the world you should buy real estate in Edinburgh and Glasgow. Borrow the money from the bank if necessary. Prices are going to soar for small conversions. That's my advice to you. Leave it another six months and it will be too late and you'll get snafooed."

On the morning of the fifth day, for reasons I never discovered, the Koeppes had had an argument. Paul Koeppe had been drunk the night before, and I supposed it had developed from that. Whatever the cause, they weren't speaking to each other, and whenever they passed on deck they glared. Breakfast was impossible. Paul Koeppe, usually morose until after lunch, went out of his way to be agreeable to me in order to irritate his wife.

"Would you like to take a turn at the wheel this morning? If you come up after breakfast, I'll give you a lesson, it's perfectly straightforward."

"I'd enjoy that. Thank you."

Tricia Koeppe scowled.

"Quite a coincidence," she said sarcastically. "Four days at sea and you choose this morning to give a lesson."

"Well, honey, I didn't suggest it before because I thought you were enjoying this young man's attentions. That's how it looked to me. I didn't want to interrupt your cosy chats. Of course if you don't want Nicholas to take a turn at the wheel, you only need to say so."

"Christ! You know that's not what I mean," said Tricia Koeppe, scraping back the table and storming into her cabin. She slammed the door and, seconds later, terrible choking sobs emitted from inside.

"Women!" said Paul Koeppe. "I reckon we better get the hell outta here, don't you?"

When my lesson was over I searched for Tricia. She was sunbathing at our usual place on the prow but looked, to borrow her own phrase, uptight. It is embarrassing for a guest to be caught between a warring couple, and I was anxious not to take sides. I was worried she might interpret my hour at the wheel with Paul as disloyalty; it was, after all, Tricia who had wangled my passage.

But I need not have worried. She was full of remorse and her only object now was to make peace with her husband. She said that unless this was quickly done, he would become moody, and once that happened it could take days to lift. She would do anything to placate him. For dinner she would make beefburgers, which he particularly enjoyed and she detested.

She explained that she had met Paul Koeppe at a dinner party in New York. She was twenty-five at the time and he was thirty-nine; that was six years ago. They had married almost immediately, after a whirlwind romance, and spent their honeymoon on a yacht; not this yacht, but her predecessor. Paul had kept an apartment in New York in those days, but soon after their marriage he had moved his operation to the West Coast. Tricia had few friends in California and found it difficult to hold onto those that they had. Paul didn't seem to need friends and was indifferent to their opinions of him; he almost seemed to relish losing them. Several times when Tricia had planned a dinner party weeks in advance, and prepared an array of special food, Paul would announce on the eve of the party, "Sorry Tricia. The party's off. We're sailing for Acapulco tonight." Then she'd have to ring everybody up, having invented some lame excuse, and know perfectly well that they didn't believe a word of it.

Matters, she believed, could only become worse. She detested the yacht. What had promised to be a vehicle for freedom, lazily cruising the Caribbean, had become a prison ship, racing from one port to the next, until she hardly knew where she was or what the date was. Her only option was to jump ship and leave Paul, but what would she do? She didn't even have her own credit cards so how could she subsist? Even if she returned to New York, which she would dearly love to do, she had no job and no apartment. Before her marriage she had shared an apartment on 76th Street, but her room-mates had dispersed long ago and she didn't fancy cooking for a living which was her only accomplishment. Somebody, a long time ago, had suggested she might model, but now it was too late and her hands were wrinkled from sunbathing.

I had not looked forward to dinner that evening, but in the event it passed off well. Generally we drank lager, but in honour of our progress (Paul expected to reach San Francisco by late the next day) we had wine which raised everyone's spirits somewhat. Paul was less abrupt with his wife than usual, and she in turn was sweetness itself. He ate his beefburgers with gusto. Tricia was pleased. He gave a long and verbose account of the difficulties he had surmounted over a property deal in San Diego, and we listened with every appearance of lively interest. After the pudding, Tricia sat on her husband's knee.

We toasted each other. A third bottle was opened. The stars above the West Coast glimmered like an Oscar ceremony. Paul Koeppe peed over the side into the sea.

The following afternoon we approached San Francisco, sailed beneath the Golden Gate, past the prison island of Alcatraz, and put into pier number 39 on Crowley Plaza.

The Koeppes made their way to a cash-and-carry for provisions; they would sail for Los Angeles in the morning. I made a beeline for a hotel with a telephone; I was anxious to plot the fastest journey across the width of America.

In less than a fortnight I must be in London.

19 | *In which an unexpected change of plan necessitates a diversion. And mention is made of telephone sex and shoeshine boys.*

Devastating news caught up with me in San Francisco. The ship I had been hoping to take from the port of New York for the final leg of the journey across the Atlantic to England had been delayed by engine trouble, and would no longer be useful for my itinerary. Furthermore, no ship of any nature — passenger or cargo — was scheduled to sail from New York for the next ten days. Failure loomed sickeningly at the final hurdle.

Up until now I had planned each leg of the route myself. The Atlantic, however, was too far in the future to make a firm booking before leaving England, and too awkward to arrange by telephone from Asia, so I had sought help from Lloyds of London, the international insurance market. It was the cleverness of one of their marine syndicates, who have access to the world's cargo movements, which tracked down the solitary vessel leaving the East Coast that week for Britain. This was a Canadian cargo ship, the *Dart Europe*, which was scheduled to sail not from America but from Montreal at 6 a.m. in four days' time. This was twenty-seven hours earlier than the elusive New York ship and meant covering an additional seven hundred miles as well as a further set of customs and immigration. Did I think I could make Montreal in time? I said "Of course" and hot-footed it to Amtrak, the Trans America Railroad Company.

Amtrak's Transbay Terminal on 1st Street and Mission, downtown San Francisco, has one of the most efficient computerised ticket routing systems in the world. Press a button and the computer displays the shortest distance between two points, as well as availability and foibles of connections. A Creole woman clerk in the ticket office tapped out a series of digits on her keyboard.

"When did you say you wanted to arrive Montreal?"

"Not later than 8 a.m. on the 17th."

"I'm sorry, but the earliest we can get you there is 9.30 a.m. on the 18th."

"That's no good at all. My ship will have sailed. Are you sure there's no quicker way? What if I changed at Chicago for Detroit or Port Huron, crossed the Great Lakes by ferry and headed north via Toronto? Is that possible?"

"No can do." The Creole clerk consulted her screen. "The Port Huron train leaves from Chicago every afternoon at 1.40 p.m. You don't arrive Chicago until 3.50 p.m in two days' time."

I sat down on a bench and studied the map. There are twelve states between San Francisco and Montreal, including the interminable prairie heartland of Wyoming and Nebraska, and the smallest of them is 270 miles across. I considered hiring a car, but even averaging sixty miles an hour for sixteen hours a day there still didn't seem much prospect of covering the 4,280 miles in time. The train would drive nights as well as during the day, and if that couldn't make it then the position must be hopeless.

On Transbay Central Terminal I sat down and wept, or at any rate cursed my bad luck. Not that one was liable to attract much sympathy on 1st Street and Mission. It is a desolate spot. A drunk was hectoring a lone woman traveller, and bag ladies had made nests out of old newspapers underneath a bench. Several acid-heads were loitering with intent to vandalise a telephone kiosk, and signs everywhere cautioned you that San Francisco is the pickpocket capital of the world.

I hadn't noticed, in my brown study, that the bench I was sitting on was a shoe-shine pew, until a spritely old man began daubing my toe cap with polish. Having your shoes cleaned is one of the most consoling pursuits imaginable, so I kept my best foot forward. Round and round he went, sloughing the heels first with a rag, then a wire brush, before sealing the patina with transparent wax until my walking shoes shone like a pair of conkers. He was completing his seventh and final lap of the sole when the Creole ticket clerk stuck her head out of the window and said, "If you don't mind a real tight connection in Chicago, I think you might still make it."

"Heavens, why didn't you say so before?"

"Well we don't recommend it as a rule. If the San Francisco train is late you'll surely miss it and then passengers complain. That's why we route them on the later train to New York Grand Central Stat:on. But if you're prepared to take the risk you can route direct to New York Pennsylvania Station, which is also the terminus for Montreal. That way you could do it."

"Do I leave tonight?"

"No, the California Zephyr is a morning train. It departs here 10.55 a.m., arriving Chicago approximately fifty-three hours later at 3.50 p.m. Then you take the 4.50 p.m. Broadway Limited Express to New York arriving late afternoon on the 15th, and connect with the Montrealer later that evening. You arrive Montreal at 9.35 a.m. on the 17th."

This would allow me a three-hour margin before boarding the *Dart Europe*.

Phileas Fogg and party, as it happens, also gained an additional day in San Francisco for precisely the same reason. Allergic to sightseeing ("He looked without seeing anything"), Fogg wisely decided to take a three-dollar carriage to the International Hotel and there spend the day eating oyster soup and dried beef. On the way, however, he could not help but notice "the broad streets, low evenly ranged houses, the Anglo-Saxon gothic churches and temples, the immense docks, the palatial warehouses, the numerous vehicles in the streets, and on the crowded sidewalks not only Americans but also Chinese and Indians."

All these characteristics are still part and parcel of San Francisco, except that the Chinese enjoy full American citizenship, with green cards, and Indiatown has been superseded by Japantown. Today, however, Fogg would also have noticed (or rather not noticed) another, seedier side to San Francisco; the oriental massage parlours on every street corner, the packs of macho homosexuals who roam the city after dark in leather trousers and lumberjack shirts, the dope addicts who crash out in Union Square or against the shop windows of Macy's department store, and the superannuated hippies jangling tambourines and smelling of joss sticks. The day I arrived in San Francisco the hippies seemed to be suffering a reverse: the Berkeley Psychedelic Cab Rank — for twenty-three years the flower people's own taxi service in East Bay — announced its liquidation. A spokesman for the rank, Buffalo, aka Grateful Dead freak Bill Miller, blamed "Reaganomics, preppies and the recession."

"People seem to prefer bow ties and blow drys to our service," he lamented.

No city in the world distributes more brochures or handbills to its tourists than San Francisco. In the course of the day my pockets were stuffed with them: discount vouchers for crab suppers, invitations to jazz festivals, offers to buy real estate on easy terms, and the magazine *Pleasure*. I did not bother looking at *Pleasure* ("the journal for gentlemen alone on the Bay") until I was soaking in a warm bath at the Bedford Hotel off Union Square.

Only San Francisco could support a magazine for people who prefer sex on their own. *Pleasure* is the contact paper for the city's sixty telephone sex exchanges. The procedure is simple: you dial a switchboard, quote your American Express or Visa credit card number, wait for it to be cleared, then talk dirty. Teams of girls (and men) hang on the line ready to interview your most sinister fantasies out of you. All you need to do is indicate your preference and leave the stimulating probing to them.

"Why risk infection?" asks Linda from a half-page advertisement in which she is wrapped in a passionate embrace with a telephone receiver. "When you can have me come whisper in your ear?"

"Our service registers on your monthly statement as a cocktail bar," reassures another. "Don't worry, Vice-President, your secretary will never know. Confidentiality and satisfaction guaranteed."

"Special introductory first time offer. Twenty dollars for initial fifteen minutes. Thereafter one dollar per minute or part thereof."

Since the scare of sexual disease hit San Francisco two years ago, prostitutes have seen their business evaporate. Telephone sex is infection-proof and approved by hotels, who levy a hefty service charge on local calls and are spared the nuisance of whores in the bedrooms.

After bathing I dialled a few of the numbers at random. I do not know whether 6.30 p.m. — the cocktail hour — is peak rate, but all the sex lines were permanently engaged. From my bedroom window at the top of Post Hill I had a panoramic view of San Francisco, from the brownstones of Sacramento Square to the Trans America Pyramid and back across the tiled pagodas of Chinatown. It was strange to think that, in hundreds of apartments all over the city, people were lolling alone on beds and preening their hang-ups to invisible confessors.

20 | *In which certain incidents are related, only to be met with on the San Francisco to Chicago railroad.*

The San Francisco to Chicago Express ("The California Zephyr") leaves not, as you might suppose, from San Francisco but from the West Coast suburb of Oakland. In every other respect, however, the Zephyr is an utterly logical locomotive.

The Amtrak carriages are all double-decker, with short-term passengers travelling in the lower compartment, and lifers billeted upstairs with a high-security observation car of their own. I found my seat, hung up my jacket, took off my walking shoes: there were fifty-three hours until we were scheduled to arrive at Chicago Union Station. The sun beat down onto Oakland goods yard and the rusty Central Pacific cattle trucks and Cotton-Belt box-cars. A steel foundry beyond the perimeter fence looked picturesque in the dancing sunlight. Despite anxiety over my tight itinerary, I felt oddly light-headed. I knew by now that I preferred travelling by rail to ship in a crisis: your options remain open. If we ran into a herd of buffalo on the prairie, I could always detrain and dial a minicab.

At 11.25 a.m. the Zephyr rolled out of Oakland and began its journey north along the Pacific coast: Richmond, Martinez, Suisun-Fairfield, Sacramento. There are thirty-five stations between San Francisco and Chicago, and seven of them fall in the first two hours. We started out like a local train, picking up shoppers, and only gradually — somewhere after Colfax, but before Truckee — achieved the status of a Grand Trunk Express. The scenery between the Californian provincial towns was delightful: clapboard houses with rickety jetties tottering across the mud flats which unite American river with San Pablo

Bay; and on the inland side of the track, mustard fields which stretch like miles of gold teflon carpet into the distance. We were crawling along so slowly that you could watch people on their verandahs — a man was gutting fish, a woman knitting on a rocking chair — and when we passed the pink McClellan Air Force Base there was time to see a rookie in a jeep sink a whole can of Coors lager.

"I wonder if we're going to go any faster," I asked a man with orange quiffed hair.

"We'll gather a bit of speed in Nevada, but not much. We won't touch seventy between here and Chicago; these trains can't take it. Or at least the track can't. The gauge is designed for freight not passenger trains, and they frequently topple over."

I looked surprised at this.

"Sure they do, I'm not kidding. Almost every month there's an Amtrak derailment. Then they take you by coach to the nearest station until they can shunt up a new train. It's nothing like the European system."

He asked me where I was from and where I had been staying.

"San Francisco? Me also, I've got a girlfriend at college there. Were you in town last week for the International Hookers Convention? You should have been, it was incredible: a big parade of hookers from all over the world followed by a five-day seminar on conditions of work."

Mike was heading home to Wisconsin. He said he was an abstract photographer and sold his work to a gallery in Chicago. Chicagoans, he believed, were just about ready for abstract photography.

"Two years ago they still had a cowhand's mentality: now matters are improving." As a measure of his confidence, Mike was refining his style. Previously he had made fifteen prints of each photograph and asked one hundred dollars each; from now on he was going to limit the edition to one print and ask five hundred dollars.

"But won't you lose a thousand dollars on each negative?" I objected.

"Could be," said Mike. "I suppose you could look at it that way."

You can tell you've left California and entered Nevada when the palm trees stop; they are a much more reliable indication than the state line which is half buried under sand. We had reached the lowlands of the Sierra Nevadas — Carson Valley — and the land was scarred with sandpits like bunkers on a fantastic overgrown golf course. During the gold rush the population had exceeded seven thousand; now it is barely a hundred. The prospectors stripped away the top soil hydraulically, exposing the gold seams and leaving the earth as barren as a war zone. When the government banned hydraulic mining, the pits were abandoned as too expensive. Now only the occasional foundation of a log cabin in the forest marks the site of the boom towns.

From Carson Valley we began to climb. The track followed the gradients, sometimes circling the same peak three times to gain height, before plunging into narrow gorges from which there seemed to be no exit. The curves of the line were so bold and the precipices so extreme, that the engine and front six carriages often steamed below us in the opposite direction as though part of a different train.

"Good afternoon ladies and gentlemen, this is your guard speaking." The intercom crackled through the observation car. "Well I sure hope you folks are sitting next to someone you like, because we're going through a two-mile tunnel here. After that we will arrive at Reno. Reno in five minutes, ladies and gentlemen, for anyone disembarking at sin city."

Reno is the Las Vegas of the Sierra Nevadas: a one-tracked casino town said to combine the sleaziest aspects of the Casbah in Tangiers and the Cannebiere in Marseilles. When Phileas Fogg stopped in Reno it was for breakfast. Nowadays breakfast is just about the one thing you can't get in Reno.

You saw the town coming for a mile: the Sunset Motel, the El Taho Motel, Rancho Novalto ("Sleep it off on a waterbed"), the Comstock Casino. It would be hard to invent a place which announced, with the brevity of a few downtown hotels, such a manifesto of frisky sex. The place reeked of brassy blondes who would slit your wallet while they picked your throat; mid-west Jezebels who would love you and leave you, or leave and love you, whichever cut up the roughest; and one-gallon-spivs in ten-gallon-hats who shot from the groin. All the lowlife on the Zephyr disembarked at Reno, wearing slit dresses inappropriate to rail travel. As we gathered steam again, we saw them sloping uptown in twos and threes, making for the Golden Nugget Saloon, the Six Gun Motel, the Pink Pussycat Bar or the high kicking cabaret of Frederic Apcar's Top Streak.

A moonfaced man approached me in the bar car. He said he had heard I was English and could I perhaps do him a favour. His thirteen-year-old daughter liked all things English. "I buy her English shirts,

English shorts, I'd buy her English shoes except the sizes are different. Her two favourite people in the world are both English: Princess Diana and Boy George." The moonfaced man poured me a glass of Napa Valley sherry. "Now," he went on, "I know fathers aren't supposed to interfere, but I *approve* of Kate's taste and I want to encourage her. I mean, Princess Diana makes a great job of being Princess, and Boy George makes a great job of his songs. And neither of them are into drugs that I've heard of; they're neither of them Reds. They're *healthy* heroes. So if I give you Kate's address, could you send her a postcard from England and write it 'To Katie. Love Princess Diana.' Or 'To Katie. Love Boy George.'? Could you do that for me?"

(Weeks later, in London, I came across the address tucked inside a book and mailed a card of a British policeman to Trenton, Pennsylvania. I inscribed it "To Katie. Love Princess Diana. And Boy George." In two different coloured biros.)

I drank Napa Valley with the moonfaced man as far as Winnemucca. He said he was a chef and was travelling all the way to New York for his eldest daughter's second marriage. The reception was to be a silver service lunch in a fancy hotel. Afterwards, for some reason not connected with the nuptials, the whole party planned to take a limousine to Trump Tower and stare up at Johnny Carson's apartment from the pavement.

I found it difficult to sleep on the California Zephyr. Owing to the urgency of my departure I had been unable to secure a couchette until Chicago, so was travelling "coach class". This involved wide-bodied seats which reclined to an angle of forty-five degrees and are promoted by Amtrak as "easier to get a good night's rest than on a jumbo jet". I find it difficult to sleep on aeroplanes too, so this was no great endorsement. For half the night I wrestled with a puny pin-cushion sized pillow. Sometime after Carlin, Nebraska, however, I must have dropped off, because when I awoke with a cricked neck it was 5 a.m., the state was Utah and we were approaching Salt Lake City.

If you want to make friends and influence people on the Grand Trunk Express, make a joke about Mormons. The observation car filled up at 5.45 a.m. with spectators spoiling to poke fun. We were scheduled to spend an hour at Salt Lake City (while carriages from Seattle and Los Angeles were hitched behind our locomotive), and there was a creepy fascination at staring out at this innocuous station platform which bears the name of the headquarters of the Church of the Latter Day Saints. I have only twice known the same feeling: staring up at the windowless interrogation floor of Lubianka prison in Moscow; and leering across the fence into a nudist beach in the South of France.

"I spent an evening in Salt Lake City on the journey out," said Mike, the abstract photographer. "The whole place is dead by nine o'clock. I walked all the way to the tabernacle and couldn't find a bar that would serve me."

"That's because you're not a Mormon," said a knowing man with a furled copy of the *Salt Lake Tribune*. "If a Mormon wanted a beer he could have got one all right. They can tell at a glance who is and who isn't."

"How? By a secret sign?"

"Intuition. Vibes. Call it what you like. Maybe they sniff each other's arses. One thing I do know, it wouldn't take two Mormons five minutes to find one another, not if they were the only two Mormons in a baseball stadium."

"Not that they would be," said someone else. "In a baseball stadium. Mormons aren't permitted to play sports."

"That's only on the Sabbath."

"But is the Mormon Sabbath the same length as everybody else's Sabbath, that's what I'm asking."

When Phileas Fogg and party passed this way, the Mormons were already raw material for slapstick comedy; a century later they draw abuse that would be criminal if it were racist. Their doctrine is certainly potholed with potential for great gags.

In 1827, a preacher named Joseph Smith was walking up a gentle slope near Palmyra (now crossed by New York Highway 21) when the Angel Morom son of the prophet Mormon, appeared before him in a pillar of smoke. The angel instructed Joseph Smith to dig a hole in the ground and there he found two tablets of stone carved with Egyptian hieroglyphs, and a pair of optical instruments, the Urim and Thummim, with which to decode them. Smith carried the tablets back home where he arranged them behind a screen, and dictated his translation to a bevy of scribes, who were not allowed to look upon the tablets because they were too holy. In due course the translation was found to be written by the prophet Abraham, and revealed that the seventh "missing" tribe of Israel had in fact made it to America, discovering the continent several thousand years before Christopher Columbus. There they had flourished with a large Christian community until their blasphemy had obliged God to strike them from the face of the earth, removing all traces of their residence with them.

(This rider about removing all traces was only discovered on the tablets at a later date, after concerted rounds of scepticism from archaeologists.)

Joseph Smith, meanwhile, had been chosen by God to assume the mantle of the Seventh Tribe, which would henceforth be called the Mormons. To temper their good luck, and to prevent them drifting into complacent blasphemy, the Mormons would be persecuted as never before and roundly mocked. In order to get the mocking off to a good start and to sow the deepest possible seeds of suspicion in the minds of their detractors, Joseph Smith allowed only a handful of senior Mormons ever to see the tablets, which were later destroyed.

Three characteristics distinguish the Latter Day Saints from the common run of off-limits churches: their passion for genealogy (ancestors, if publicly named in the tabernacle, may be elevated retrospectively to heaven, which is otherwise closed to non-Mormons), their strong singing voices (the Osmond Brothers were Mormons, if corroboration is required), and the fact that they may take more than one wife.

Shortly before we left Salt Lake City, a sombre party of men in brown suits boarded the train and were widely taken to be Mormons. However since they neither prattled about their ancestors, sang loudly, nor angled polygamically for fresh spouses, they might just as easily have been Jehovah's Witnesses.

It had snowed in Utah during the night and the Great Salt Lake, a corner of which we were now skirting, was encrusted with an alloy of salt and powder snow, rippled, trisulcated, like the icing on a Christmas cake. Seventy miles long and thirty-five wide, the consistency of salt to water is greater than the Dead Sea and as emetic; no fish can survive. A few Mormons still pan their own salt from the bank, deeming it wasteful to buy from the supermarket what the Lord in his mercy has supplied for free. I wondered what the Djibouteans, and the tribes of Eritrea and Southern Sudan, would make of the Great Salt Lake; the deposits you could gather in one morning would make you a saline millionaire in East Africa. With wealth of that sort you could afford a permanent suite at the Hotel Sahara in Tukar.

"Ladies and gentlemen, this is your cabin steward speaking, I just want to spend a few minutes with you folks telling you about our lunchtime menu in the restaurant car." Frszeeeeeekshz. "Sorry about that folks, having a little problem there with the mike. Well, ladies and gentlemen, as I was saying before the gremlins took over, we are featuring three lunchtime selections today which I know you're going to enjoy very much, so stay tuned. We've got Fisherman's Catch, which is trout stuffed with crab meat in the chef's own style. And we've got a grilled New York steak, cooked as you like it. And finally, in addition to our regular burger, we're featuring a Zephyrburger. Our chef, Wilson, is going to do a little more garnishing than is customary, so if you want a burger today make sure you put a big Zee next to it for the full works."

Q: What do American cuisine and American scenery have in common?
A: Enough is never as good as a feast.
   It was an Englishman who told me that one. It isn't very funny so I took it for philosophy; except that Brian was a scientist with a literal turn of mind. He was reading *Blue Highways: A Journey into America* by William Least Heat Moon, an Indian writer who made a pilgrimage down the blue highways — back roads — of the United States. Most of Moon's observations are cerebral, but Brian was reading the book as a guide, noting the names of steak diners and motels worth visiting.
   Three ticket collectors made a sweep of the carriage looking for hobos.
   "Here come the Gestapo," said Brian. Like most scientists there was an anarchic streak in him. But he produced his ticket quietly enough.
   Brian was researching horseshoe crabs at a laboratory near Cape Cod. This was his third year with horseshoe crabs. Previously he had studied other types of crabs in Australia and at Cambridge. He was thirty and had just completed his first major paper. He unlocked it from his briefcase and gave it to me to read. It was typed up on a word processor and ran to fewer words than this short description of Brian. He harboured ambitions of eventually having his paper published in

the letters page of *Nature* magazine. But that depended on the reaction of his peers. I read it twice but it meant nothing to me.

"I'm sure it's brilliant, Brian, but I'm afraid it's beyond me."

"I thought it might be," said Brian. "Only sixteen people in the world understand it and they're mostly in Japan."

In retrospect, whenever I thought of California Zephyr, it was of a string of steel cabins grinding their way up a mountain range, whimpering with the exertion, before thundering down on the other side — the carriages seeming to overtake the wheels — clattering over the points and yawing back upon the engine like a jackknife. As we approached each summit the whole train rattled — it was a species of death rattle — and I was reminded of that moment on the Big Dipper at the fun fair when the car has completed its ascent and is trundling around the plateau towards the switchback. For fifteen hours we never left the mountains. Each range was steeper than the last: the Sierra Nevadas, the Humboldts, the Wasatches, the Rockies. The constant swaying made it impossible to write; my notes from this part of the journey look like a seismograph. Coffee was served in plastic cups with spouts — the sort babies drink liquid food from — and the altitude made beer explode from the can into your face.

The rivers we crossed on cast-iron suspension bridges were frozen solid, and peaks higher than six thousand feet were above the snow line. There were tracks of animals in the snow and traces of old camp fires. A baldheaded eagle swooped with bared talons onto a rift in the ice and carried off a 2lb salmon to its eyrie. Sixty miles south of Provo, Utah, we passed a log cabin with a fluted stove chimney buried up to its eaves by snow drifts; a ladder had been leant against the wall and the only entrance was a trap door in the roof.

A man wearing a suit and brown leather cowboy boots joined me in the observation car. He was slim and rather distinguished with short black hair; he looked about forty-five and was an expert on all kinds of field sports. His name was Ward. He said he had recently returned from a hunting trip to New Hampshire, where his sixteen-year-old son had taken his first stag with a bow and arrow. "We were so proud we got a lot of our friends over and ate that deer in one sitting."

For the next two hundred and thirty-eight miles the train followed the course of the Colorado river. The surface of the river had begun to thaw, and hummocks of grey ice had broken away from the bank and were drifting downstream. The railway track is the only transport along the valley which was lined with white-tailed deer and elk drinking the icy water.

"Holy Smoke, look at those elk!"

A herd of about two hundred stared complacently up at the train.

"I've just seen more deer in that one mile than in ten years of hunting in New Hampshire."

Ward's hobby was collecting guns. "I must have a hundred now, mostly British brought out of India. I use a dealer in London to find them, though they're getting to be expensive; when I started you could pick up an early Rhodda for five hundred bucks, now they're ten, fifteen thousand. Since Sotheby's and Christie's started their gun departments it's rather taken the fun out of it. The only thing I insist on is that all the guns in my collection are in working order; I like to take them hunting. Sometimes I work on a nineteenth-century Purdey or Westley-Richards for six months before I use it; they don't make the cartridges any more so you have to adjust the calibre. But they're first-rate guns. I have Holland & Hollands and Reillys that are twice as accurate as anything being made today. I store them all in a walk-in vault, they're getting to be too valuable to leave lying around in the gun-room. My rarest rifle belonged to the Maharajah of Patiala; came out of India of course. I was so excited when I got that gun I went to meet it off the plane at the freight terminal."

His subsidiary hobby was collecting sporting manuals.

"Especially British big game hunting in Africa and India. There's a guy called Baker who wrote a lot about Ceylon. *Wild Beasts and Their Ways* is his most famous book. He made all his expeditions with his wife but only mentions her once. That was in the jungle in Kenya. Savages had surrounded them in a hut in a clearing and the bearers had fled during the night. The savages were moving in for the kill. 'At this crucial juncture,' writes Baker, 'Lady Baker released a firework from the verandah scattering the natives.' That is the one and only occasion we hear about Lady Baker. She must have been quite a lady."

I asked Ward whether he'd shot in Britain. I thought he would enjoy Scotland.

"No," he said. "I never have. I don't know any Scottish lairds and I'm not the kind of person who's interested in paying five thousand bucks to pretend you're a weekend guest. So I guess I never will. One place I *would* like to visit though is the Caucasus. I hear they've got some real testy taur out there above the tree line."

On the afternoon of the second day we began our descent towards the plains. First, however, we had to negotiate Dead Man's Curve: the sheerest of the Rocky Mountain ranges and the scariest. The railway winds along a narrow ledge five hundred feet above a breakneck canyon, and a thousand feet above the track is a road. Local youths use it for roadster racing, overtaking each other on the hairiest bends at night so as to avoid the police. In the last five years sixteen cars have skidded over the edge and the rocks above the canyon are littered with the rusty, dented carcasses of Ford Mustangs and Lincolns.

At six o'clock we stopped for ten minutes at Grand Junction Station. Guards collected the brown rubbish bags from the rubber booths between the couplings and tossed them onto the platform. The nickname of Grand Junction Station is Trashville, Utah. A party of rednecks joined the train at Trashville: gross, puffy-faced cowpokes with beer guts, string ties and stetsons. They staked out a corner of the bar and managed, in the space of only ninety minutes, to drink the train dry of Miller lager before disembarking at Glenwood Springs.

I woke up in Nebraska. My clock showed 6.40 a.m. Good. Another half hour and we would arrive in Omaha.

The country on both sides of the tracks stretched into the middle distance without a sign of life. There were no fields, no farm houses, no homesteads, just a massive, desolate tract of prairie, sterile with cacti, thistles and dust. It was twenty minutes before we passed a water trough and another twenty before we saw a farm. A wooden wind pump marked the extent of someone's property and bison were penned into a corral. At last we arrived at a station, but it looked too small to be Omaha. I pulled back the curtain to check the name: the board above the ticket office said "Lincoln".

I got up and found a guard.

"I'm afraid we're running a little behind schedule; we lost time during the night around Fort Morgan."

"How much time?"

"Oh, nothing serious. About an hour and ten minutes."

"But I've got a connection this afternoon in Chicago. For New York. The 4.50 Broadway Limited Express."

"You still won't be too late, sir, even if you do miss the 4.50. There's another train to New York via Cleveland at 6.20 p.m."

It didn't seem worth pointing out that the Cleveland train ("The Lake Shore Limited") arrived at Grand Central Station too late to cross New York to Pennsylvania Station to catch the Montrealer to Canada.

We wondered what they did with themselves, the people who lived in the prairie. The train had crossed the state line into Iowa, and was midway between Creston and Osceola, but the scenery hadn't altered in five hours. The farms were forty minutes apart and the towns parochial to a fault; to call them one-horse is to libel horses. Creston, Iowa, has two shops: a general store and a burglar alarm emporium.

Twice, in the middle of nowhere, a display of dead rattlesnakes had been nailed to a telegraph pole.

A countrywoman, who was riding the train from Omaha, stared mesmerised out of the window. "Looking out there you'd think this state was flat broke," she said at last. "And that's just the way the farmers like it." She glanced round to see if anyone was listening. "They're simply rolling in the stuff; not that they spread it about. Take a look at their houses — square little boxes and ninety-nine percent of them painted white. If the harvest's good and they make another million bucks, maybe they add a porch. If the harvest fails, or is flattened by a typhoon, the government compensates them anyway. That's Iowa."

The train was becoming sordid after two days of travel; the wash-rooms were blocked and the bar had run out of fresh limes. The abstract photographer, crab scientist, hunter and I drank beer and read whatever newspapers local travellers had left behind. These we divided into several sections so that everyone could have a page. The heat outside on the prairie touched the low nineties, the atmosphere was sluggish and I skimmed the *Salt Lake Tribune*.

"Carrots have been named vegetable of the year by the National Garden Bureau. They are easy to grow and delicious to eat," writes *Tribune* garden editor Genevieve H. Folsom. "You can plant carrots in rows in single file or broadcast or scatter them in broad areas up to twelve inches wide. Both methods will work . . ."

Suddenly the carriage was suffused with the most appalling stench. We had run over a skunk and its noxious broom had been sucked up through the air-conditioning unit.

Burlington, Iowa. An industrial town on the banks of the Mississippi. Four shops visible from the train: a drive-in supermarket, Venus Adult Books, a video warehouse and a pawnbroker.

I went downstairs to find the bar steward; he had told me he collected foreign coins and I had promised to pan my carpet bag. I found him some Italian lire and Sudanese and Egyptian piastres. He appeared delighted.

"Suedarn? I don't reckon I've heard of that one before. Where is it?"

"Africa."

"And Eggyipt?"

"Also Africa."

"Then why don't they just put Africa on the back, like we put the United States?"

"Because Africa has more than one country. They're not states."

"Sure, but they're still Africa."

"Ladies and Gentlemen, we will be arriving at Chicago Union Station in five minutes; that's five minutes Chicago Union. The local time is 4.30 p.m. Amtrak apologises for the forty minute delay owing to adverse weather conditions around Fort Morgan."

Only forty minutes late! That left me twenty minutes to catch the Broadway Limited.

The matt black silhouette of the Sears Building loomed briefly between a break in the warehouses.

"This is Chicago, left side and trading; left side trading, Chicago Union Station."

21 | *In which the East Coast of the Americas is traversed with great haste, and an excursion made into Canada.*

I had harboured ambitions, while in Chicago, of seeing a man who danced with his wife, but this was a pipe dream; the Broadway Limited was already boarding passengers and the barrier would close in less than five minutes. I found my couchette — my "Slumbercoach" — and crawled inside. It was like sleeping in an igloo: a moulded plastic bubble, ingeniously constructed to enable an armchair to convert into a full-length bed at the turn of a piston. The train left Chicago Union Station and already it was dark and chilly outside; we had made the transition from West to Central time and climate.

I made my way through three carriages to the dining car, bruising my elbows at every coupling and wrestling with obstinate metal doors. Four black stewards, all Southerners, were playing poker but they threw in their hand and gave me a table. Soon the other tables filled up. Outside, lights twinkled in the parlours of suburban Illinois and Indiana. Few houses had bothered to close their drapes, and teenagers were jiving to records in rumpus rooms and fathers cowering upstairs in their dens.

"You mind sharing?" A steward ushered a tall, rather prosaic man to my table.

"By all means." I moved my newspaper to make room.

The man nodded but didn't speak. His hair was thin on top but long over the ears. He displayed a tired condescension peculiar to the owners of cashmere overcoats.

I resumed my perusal of the *Chicago Sun-Times*.

The man withdrew from his pocket a copy of *The New York Review of Books* which he proceeded to read with baleful attention.

Every so often he coughed quizzically, as though his sensibilities had been affronted by a particularly intemperate review.

Once he burbled "Ha! Ha!"

I could not help noticing that, every few minutes, he gravitated to the inside back cover of the paper, and scanned those columns with a fastidiousness that made me suspect him of being either the author or the subject of some review.

I was drinking California burgundy, and when I ordered a second "split" (only quarter bottles are available on Amtrak) I asked the steward not to pour the new wine on top of the old, since they had run out of my original choice and the substitute bottle was quite different. The steward seemed amazed by this pedantry and hurried away to tell his friends.

"You were correct to say something," said the man in the cashmere overcoat. "If you don't cavil, what hope for standards?"

His voice was high-pitched and nasal.

I said I had noticed he was engrossed in *The New York Review of Books*.

"Yes indeed. Do you take it?"

I said that sometimes I saw it but could hardly describe myself as an addict.

"Ha! Ha! I suppose it is an addiction of sorts. Ha!" He snuffled merrily.

I asked what had taken him to Chicago and whether he was enjoying the train.

"Always I travel by train. Once a month I deliver a lecture at the Institute and couldn't think of flying. I value the opportunity too much for studying my fellow creatures. The facility to analyse one's countrymen is the most absorbing vice in the world."

I didn't know what his subject was but I would have bet anything that it was nineteenth-century English literature. I had the sudden sensation of sharing the buffet car with some refugee from *Mansfield Park*. My own speech became correspondingly formal. I wanted another split of burgundy, and was tempted to say "It is a truth universally acknowledged that a single man in possession of two dollars must be in need of a bottle."

He put down *The New York Review of Books*. I asked to look at it. I was curious to see which review it was he had been studying. Subtly I worked my way forwards, pausing for a few moments to scan a notice about George Sand, until reaching the inside back flap. The page was covered with classified advertisements for literary lonely hearts. "Cultured woman, mid-forties, enjoys Dickens, Thackeray, Montaigne, wishes to meet gentleman for friendship/marriage." The man in the cashmere coat had underlined several box numbers and put question marks alongside several more.

The train lurched, the brakes squealed, we had stopped at Fort Wayne.

Far more than the California Zephyr, the Broadway Limited is full of design references to the railroads of the Wild West. The corridor of the sleeping car has curtains in place of doors, and there is a games saloon at the disposal of passengers with a booth selling decks of cards. Several of the coach class travellers sat up all night engaged in a raucous poker tournament which they were only completing when I surfaced for breakfast.

The snow outside the window, and the full moon, made it light enough to read with the lights off. The drifts in Ohio were quite deep, and the snow on the steeples of the wooden churches made them look like a display of Christmas cards. We whistled past estates of middle-class houses, with their large yards sweeping down to the railway line, double garages, french windows and a swing hanging beneath every tree. In each home a light had been left switched on in the hall and sometimes, upstairs in a bedroom nestling beneath the eaves, a glimmer through the curtain indicated that somebody was reading late.

During the night we neither gained nor lost time and by morning we were in Pennsylvania, between Lancaster and Philadelphia, and men in fur hats were shovelling snow from their doorsteps and children setting off for school. Outside every suburban station was an enormous car park, for the benefit of commuters, who shivered and stamped their feet on platforms awaiting the local train.

I returned to the restaurant car in search of breakfast and talked to a man who said he had been in Iran a month before the Shah flew out. He regarded the experience as his closest call with death. He was a hotel manager in Baltimore and had happened to be on vacation in Teheran with his family, staying with some American friends. One morning, out of the blue, the Iranian Minister for the Environment had rung him up at the friend's house. Nobody knew how the Minister could possibly have heard of him.

"I understand you are a top hotel manager," the Minister had said.

"Would you be at all interested in managing the Shahabas Hotel in Isfahan? We will triple your present salary and provide you with a house, a car and a driver."

Almost before he knew what was happening, he was on the next plane to Isfahan to inspect the place.

"The hotel was amazing, beautiful lobby, five-star fitments from top to bottom. The only thing that concerned me was that there seemed to be almost no staff. I asked the Minister about it. 'That's why I sent for you,' he replied. 'I stayed here last week myself, and the service was so shocking that I sacked the whole lot, from General Manager down to boot boy. You can pick your own team from scratch.'

"I must admit I was tempted. The salary was astronomical, I could have afforded to retire in five years. But my wife didn't like the idea nor did the kids, so in the end I turned it down. Three weeks later they started evacuating American residents."

From Pennsylvania onwards the scenery is urban and industrial: paint factories, cold storage plants, foundries and warehouses. Many were boarded up, evidence of America's inner city malaise. Passengers who had hitherto languished in their slumbercoaches like foetuses in the womb, clambered out, stretched, and stood on the metal coupling between the carriages, staring out of the window. By my watch we were running on time to the very minute.

The putative manager of the Shahabas Hotel said goodbye; he was getting off at Newark.

"Take care you don't attract the Penn sniper."

"The Penn sniper?"

"Yeh, he's potted eight so far. Must be a nut. Has this thing about railway passengers. But he's clever, you've got to hand it to him. Cops can't seem to catch him. Sometimes shoots point blank on a platform, sometimes from the roof. But always Pennsylvania Station, knows the place inside out."

Rather to my relief, I had the minimum time to dodge death at Penn Station. I bought a copy of *Time* magazine ("Michael Jackson — why he's a Thriller"), symbolically toasted the Big Apple with a cocktail at the station buffet, and boarded the Montrealer for Canada.

A symptom of the accelerating tenor of the trip was that I knew next to nothing about Canada. I didn't give the place a moment's thought until we crossed the frontier. In the early part of the expedition, up as far as Singapore, I had read guide books and assiduously followed the route in Fodor. Hong Kong I knew already. But from Japan onwards I was travelling blind. Phileas Fogg crossed America with the curtains drawn; I crossed it with my head stuck out of the window, impatient for the next station and picking up what information I could. Canada, as a late addition to the itinerary, could hardly expect thoroughness.

In any case it was difficult to see outside. The window of the observation car was plastered with ice, as diaphanous as frosted glass, and the glimpses I had were of frozen lakes, rushes frigid with hoarfrost and perished snow. Canada in March is still a country in hibernation: houses were shored up against the snow, windows made draught-proof with tape, and the main roads salted. Fences dividing back gardens protruded only six inches above drifts of rime, and the faces of the few people waiting at the stations were plethoric with cold.

Waterbury, Essex Junction, St Albans, Cantic. Now we were rumbling through an avalanche shelter, now emerging again into a perfectly flat expanse of white like a photographer's cyclorama backdrop. The ice on the pane thawed a little and a chunk slid down the side of the coach, leaving a smear large enough to peer through. I peered through. A woman in a fur hat and sheepskin jacket was walking her dog, and shook her stick at the passing train.

To pass the time, I made a list of all the things I know about Canada.

1. Pierre Trudeau, President or Prime Minister (or had he recently resigned?). Womaniser in the Gallic tradition. Wife is Margaret Trudeau and unreliable: once had a crush on either Prince Charles or Mick Jagger or both.

2. Wellingtonia trees wide enough to drive through.

3. Grizzly bears in the north.

4. The Royal Canadian Mounted Police ("The Mounties").

5. Women novelists. But I couldn't name any.

The only fact I was certain about Canada is that they speak French in Quebec and English in Montreal.

At 9.42 a.m. — seven minutes late — we arrived at Montreal Central Station. I changed money and flagged a taxi.

"Racine Terminal please. Dock No 59."

"Comment? Pardon Monsieur. Ici nous parlons seulement le français."

22 | *In which a voyage is undertaken in Arctic conditions. And the author expresses concern for his own sanity.*

The thermometer in Montreal showed twenty degrees below zero. In less than two days, since leaving the prairie, the temperature had dropped by 110°F, and the tropical suit was becoming a liability. I will not publicly embarrass by naming the person who counselled against taking an overcoat, but I muttered his name often as the voyage progressed past Newfoundland (which is on the same parallel as Siberia) and along the icebound St Lawrence Seaway. The *Dart Europe* was moored to a jetty four miles south of Montreal; she would clear immigration in three hours and in the meantime I took shelter in a hut. Outside, a bitter north-east wind was blowing from Greenland and the seaway was alive with hummocks of ice, like miniature icebergs, bobbing their way north in the current towards the Atlantic.

The *Dart Europe* is a Belgian vessel of the Compagnie Maritime Belge, affiliated to the Canada Line; she was expected to take ten days to cross the North Atlantic, arriving at Felixstowe in Suffolk on the evening of my seventy-seventh day. I found my cabin and took a bath. The bath was deep and the water scalding. Over the next ten days I spent hours immersing myself in hot water after a brisk refrigeration on deck, like the steam bath treatment for purging the soul at a Japanese ski resort.

As soon as we sailed, the grinding began. It sounded like the noise that a branch makes when it's caught in the tire of a car, turning over and dragging across tarmac. The ship was breaking through ice and the noise of displaced floes was deafening on the lower deck. Sometimes, where the ice was thin, it abated slightly; but where the ice was thick it could have been a gravel pit that we were sailing through at a steady fifteen knots.

A notice in my cabin explained the terminology of ice:

Bergy bit — a large piece of floating glacier ice generally showing less than five metres above sea level but more than one metre.

Brash ice — accumulation of floating ice made out of fragments of not more than two metres, across the wreckage of other forms of ice.

Close pack ice — pack ice in which the concentration is six-eighths composed of floes mostly in contact.

Consolidated pack ice — as above, but in which the floes are frozen together.

Fast ice — forms and remains fast along the coast, where it is attached to the shore to an ice wall, between the shoals or grounded icebergs.

First year ice — sea ice of not more than one winter's growth, developing from young ice.

Floe lead — a passageway between pack ice and fast ice which is navigable by surface vessels.

Floeberg — a massive piece of sea ice composed of a hummock or group of hummocks frozen together.

Glacierberg — an irregularly shaped iceberg.

Grey ice — ten to fifteen centimetres thick, breaks on contact.

Growler — smaller piece of ice than a floeberg, often transparent, that appears green or almost black in colour.

Hummocked ice — sea ice piled haphazardly. When weathered has appearance of small hummocks. Also known as screwing ice.

Iceberg — a massive piece of ice of greatly varying shape, which has broken away from the glacier, and which may be afloat or aground.

Ice blink — a whitish flare on low clouds above an accumulation of distant ice.

The list ended at "I"; the second sheet was missing. But I had an idea that, in the alphabet of ice, the first nine letters are the decisive ones, so it was no real loss. I made sallies on deck to identify ice, but ten seconds was enough to induce nausea. Gusts of wind howled up the seaway, draining the blood from the face, and leaving it raw. We were approaching Quebec and the steps of the St Lawrence were dotted with wooden churches and bungalows half buried behind ice walls.

In the summer the view must be spectacular; but from November to April it conjures Dostoevskian spectres of suicide. Two hundred miles from Montreal we dropped the pilot at Escoumins, then headed through the Gaspé Passage, past the Anticosti Islands and along the desolate coast of Newfoundland. Seventy miles to the south were the Magdalen Islands, annually blockaded by a Greenpeace flotilla at the start of the seal-culling season; a hundred miles to the east was Cabot Strait.

Captain Marien lent me *The Mariner's Handbook*, published by the Hydrographer of the Admiralty, and I read the chapters on Arctic survival. The Hydrographer, whoever he may be, is evidently a man of great initiative.

"Large animals, such as polar bears and sea lions, may be taken with club or spear. A carefully whittled club can be a deadly weapon in the hands of a patient stalker. A spear, for throwing or hand use, may be fashioned by lashing a knife to a stick or pole. Polar bear liver should be avoided since it contains considerable excess of Vitamin A which will cause illness.

"Rabbit should not be eaten exclusively, although the rabbit is probably the easiest of any game to obtain in Arctic regions. A continued diet of rabbit meat only will cause severe diarrhoea within ten days, and death within a few weeks. Even after a few days the survivor will find discomfort and no hunger satisfaction despite increased intake."

The moment we passed the Cabot Strait, and were no longer in sight of land, I collapsed. Seventy days of non-stop travel had finally caught up with me and now, with three thousand miles of ocean between the *Dart Europe* and England, my only object was sleep. In the morning I wrote up my notes; in the afternoon I dozed. Every day I achieved less and slept more. Composing a paragraph became an insuperable task which must be rewarded with a nap. My sentences became shorter. And shorter. In the early chapters of this book (I flicked back with disbelief) I had launched elaborate clauses, flirted with semi-colons and ablative absolutes. Now I wrote like an Arctic explorer whose sledge and corgi dogs have plunged into a deep crevasse, and who is making a dispassionate record of his demise in a log book. Three times a day I ate. The crew of the *Dart Europe* ate well, and effervesced about French restaurants in the Guide Michelin within easy drive of Brussels. After lunch I dozed. The temptation to start drinking was overwhelming; a fridge in my cabin contained a crate of Stella Artois. But one bottle served only to make further work impossible, and was not enough to stay guilt. So the first bottle became two and from there it was no distance to oblivion. I put on three shirts and walked on deck, teeth chattering and chilblains breaking beneath my knuckles. Sailors in fur-lined anoraks were scraping ice from the companionways. Shafts of arctic light — the aurora borealis — invested the grey sea with the aspect of an engraving by Gustave Dore. A storm, said the Chief Mate, lay ahead of us and a low depression behind; rough weather could overtake us from either side.

"Monsieur, we have sighted an iceberg, you will come directly to the wheelhouse, please."

Captain Marien's kindly tip-off sounded, through the distortion of an intercom, like the first step of a mandate to abandon ship.

But the iceberg was nine miles away, as massive as an aircraft carrier, cruising south-west in the direction of the Bahamas where it would eventually melt over coral reefs.

After five days at sea, with two thousand miles of Atlantic behind us, we had neither gained nor lost a single mile on our schedule.

"Alors, le bateau contemporaire c'est l'autobus," philosophised the Chief Engineer. "Si c'est dimanche c'est necessaire Felixstowe."

A swell was blowing up in the mid-Atlantic, and the table-cloths were sprinkled with water to make them adhesive. I embarked upon a novel from the ship's library, *The Well of Loneliness* by Radclyffe Hall, a peculiar choice of book for a merchant vessel but with the advantage of being 590 pages long. After dinner we watched horror videos and drank brandy. At night I was tormented by dreams of eating polar bear liver, lightly grilled with bacon, and being slowly poisoned by a surfeit of Vitamin A.

I had returned to London; my journey was almost over. The *Dart Europe* had sailed all the way up the Thames, past Greenwich Hospital, Rotherhithe and Wapping Old Steps, and was moored alongside Westminster Pier. A large crowd of well-wishers, dressed as for Derby Day, had assembled on the embankment and were belaying messages of encouragement.

"Good luck to you, squire. We knew you'd make it."

"I had my doubts to tell you straight, but the missus she said, 'He'll be here come the eightieth morning, you mark my words, John Bull'."

A prominent Pearly King and Queen were pressing me to accept the freedom of Aldgate East.

Suddenly I was back at the Reform Club and the mosaic hall with its twenty ionic columns of red porphyry. Aged members were waving top hats, to the consternation of their nurses, and the band had struck up the opening chords of *The Symphony in Blue*.

A dais had been erected at the foot of the stairs, on which was presiding Princess Michael of Kent, flanked by the Chinese Ambassador to the Court of St James (who bore an unmistakable resemblance to the doorman at the Kwai-Phor Club in Singapore) and the Director of the Ecole des Beaux Arts.

"Jolly well done," the Princess was saying, "the success of your expedition will benefit mankind for years to come."

"She's right you know," nodded an eminent neurologist from the Paddington Hospital for Tropical Diseases. "Some of those cholera smears from the Sudan will keep our chaps busy for months."

I was proceeding to the dais to accept my silver globe, when a scuffle broke out at the back of the hall. Three men in astrakhan overcoats were elbowing their way through the crowds.

"Thank God we're not yet too late," cried the first, who I recognised as the Chairman of the Arts Council.

"Another five seconds and the scoundrel would have taken the prize!" exclaimed the second, who was no less a personage than the secretary of a National Book Club.

"And without a twinge of remorse, confound him!" echoed the third, whose book reviews in a distinguished newspaper are invariably instructive.

"Your Royal Highness, I think an explanation is owed," said the Chairman of the Arts Council, addressing himself to the chair. "The gentleman standing before you is an Imposter. Far from going around the world, his travels in fact extend no further than the Isle of Eriskay in the Outer Hebrides!"

A gasp of astonishment rose from the hall, followed by a rumble of indignation.

"Scarcely credible gentlemen, I know, but nonetheless true. And if you will only bear with us, we will shortly expose the full extent of his chicanery."

"I think it is fair to say," said the Secretary of the National Book Club, taking up the tale, "that we had our suspicions from the start. The Imposter, having spent the previous five years vegetating in several leading restaurants, was frankly unfit to make a long journey abroad. So we decided to put a tail on him. It is not generally known that the

Arts Council maintains a unit of actors for this express purpose, able to transform themselves into sherpas or coolies as required, to verify the orthodoxy of every expedition."

"Though in this case," put in the third man, "he came as near as dammit to outwitting us."

"It was a brilliant bluff of yours, leaving the train at South Croydon and then jumping back on board as it pulled out of the station. By then our man, who was carrying a harpoon by the way, had passed the ticket barrier and you had shaken him off."

"Oh yes, gentlemen, he took the boat-train from Victoria all right, but he never reached Folkestone. Somewhere after Croydon he left the carriage and, by means of a brilliant cross-country route, made his way north to Oban. During the night he assumed the disguise of a Scottish matron, with red wig and shawl, and by the time he passed Carlisle was travelling under the pseudonym 'Maudie McKechron'."

"From Oban he caught the Castlebay Ferry to the Island of Barra, and there booked a three-month holiday-let on a farmhouse on neighbouring Eriskay. He knew he was unlikely to be disturbed since the island is inaccessible except by rowing boat, and he took the further precaution of notifying the boatman that he was in quarantine for the measles."

"Had he sat tight, writing his book, he might have got away with it too," said the distinguished critic. "But conmen can never resist going one step too far."

"In a way it was his insistence on accuracy that was his undoing," noted the Chairman of the Arts Council. "If he hadn't borrowed so many maps and guide books from the Barra mobile library, we'd never have located him. I think it was the street plan of Honolulu that finally gave the game away. The librarian became suspicious and quite properly informed the relevant authorities."

At this point a terrible booing and cries of "Shame! Shame!" rose from every part of the building, and next door in the Travellers Club several portraits of famous explorers crumpled in their frames. At the end of a long corridor a bell began tolling — as sonorous as the Lutine Bell on the floor of Lloyds of London, which attends a great shipping tragedy — boom! Boom! BOOM! There was a hammering of heels on metal stairtreads and the smell of frying bacon. Boom! Boom! BOOM! First watch was over. It was breakfast time on the *Dart Europe*. In four days we would arrive at Felixstowe.

———

"I have received a cable from Felixstowe," remarked the Captain one evening at dinner. "Our berth at port will not be vacated until four hours after we're scheduled to arrive, which means we'll miss high tide. So we cannot dock until the following evening."

The evening of the seventy-eighth day!

I thought that I had put all anxiety about the schedule behind me, but now it came rushing back, nagging my sub-conscious and spoiling my naps. Foolishly I had omitted to pack a British Rail timetable into my carpet bag, so was vague about the service between Suffolk and London. It might conceivably take forty-eight hours to undertake this cross-country journey, and only the slightest delay would nudge me back into extra time. Now that the outcome was largely out of my hands (we were sailing at full speed and I could hardly swim ahead of a ship) it mattered more than ever that I arrived on time. Although speed was always the *sine qua non* of the expedition, there had been times when it hadn't bothered me much: I took the fastest trains, the most direct ships, and treated the challenge as a game of logic played with timetables, with the world as the board. "Ship runs into sand-bank — go back three spaces"; "Sudanese Consulate refuses to issue visa — miss a throw". For three months I had been making every move on the premise that it is better to arrive than to travel hopefully; to arrive late — even by one day — would rob the whole expedition of coherence.

The *Dart Europe* was still seven hundred miles from Felixstowe and we hadn't seen another vessel for five days: our route was three hundred miles more northerly than the New York traffic, and the waves which broke over the prow were slate grey. With each day that passed I felt more sluggish. I had been struck down by Channel Fever: a listlessness that makes you sleep fifteen hours a day, like a convalescent from hepatitis. I had lost track of which day it was and had to refer to the menu: le samedi; three more days until Felixstowe.

And then, on the tenth morning, we were passing the Scilly Isles and by the same evening were fifteen miles off the coast of Devon. Plymouth, the Isle of Wight, Folkestone, Dover; we cut north-west across the Channel, past the Thames estuary, and by the following dawn were riding at anchor less than twelve miles from Felixstowe.

23 | *In which a rescue is effected in the nick of time. And the Reform Club at last revisited.*

Although Felixstowe is the most efficient port in Britain, it is far too small, and more than thirty cargo ships were queuing for berths in the harbour. From where we were anchored, the Suffolk coast was nothing more than a black smudge on the horizon, and there was no early prospect of docking. Some vessels had already been waiting for thirty-six hours; it was indescribably frustrating to languish so close to land as the clock ticked towards zero hour. Unless the *Dart Europe* was allocated a berth by the following afternoon, low tide would prevent me from landing until the eightieth morning.

"Telephone call for you." The steward was tapping on my door.

Telephone? Surely this must be a practical joke. But no, we were now within range of ship-to-shore radio.

The Harwich coastguard was on the line. "Arrangements have been made to have you sprung from the ship by launch. The harbourmaster will be with you in an hour."

Fifty minutes later a black speck appeared out of the mist, which grew, as it got nearer, into a speedboat. Two harbourmasters in navy blue jerseys semaphored instructions for my carpet bag and swordstick to be lashed together and dangled over the rail. The sea was too rough to lower the passenger gangway, so I was in turn secured to a pulley and winched into the launch. Then we set off with all possible speed towards the blur that was England.

It is impossible to return to your native country after a long journey without a sense of foreboding. Suffolk in March, with its shingle beaches and ploughed fields, looked bleaker than Montreal. I thought of all the things that are forever England, which were beckoning me from the haze: the Indian restaurants, the Chinese take-aways, the Italian pizzeria I go to on Sunday night and the Filipino check-out girls at the supermarket. It felt good to be arriving home.

A customs officer was waiting on the quay.

"Which countries have you visited on this journey?"

I named nineteen in no particular order.

"That sounds reasonable enough." He chalked my bags without opening them.

The train from Ipswich to Liverpool Street was almost empty; a handful of theatregoers were heading for Shaftesbury Avenue. The station news kiosk was closed, so once again I was reduced to foraging for abandoned newspapers, this time the *East Anglian Daily Times.*

Liverpool Street bustled with commuters. If they saw anything strange about a man in a panama hat on Platform 7, they did not show it; most were in any case cocooned inside their evening newspapers.

A rank of black taxis was ticking over by the exit.

"The Reform Club please."

It made a pleasant change not having to direct the driver street by street. I put my feet up on the tip-up seat as we cruised down the Strand towards Trafalgar Square. London seemed oddly empty after the rest of the world. In Cairo, a journey of this scope would have taken a day.

A small group of well-wishers were waiting on the steps of the Reform Club; they might, for all I know, have been standing there the whole time I was away.

"I couldn't take any money from you guv'nor," said my cab driver, but when pressed accepted his fare plus a hefty tip.

"Magnificent!" said a perfect stranger, walking past with a furled umbrella like an extra from Michael Todd's *Around the World in Eighty Days* film.

Inside the Reform Club all was serenity. A couple of members blew dust off their crossword and hailed a glass of port; the telex machine in the hall reported a minuscule movement in the price of gold; the cloakroom reeked of bay rum hair lotion; the swipes of mango chutney, diesel oil and sweet and sour sauce on my tropical suit were studiously ignored by the club's inscrutable porters.

The Ormolu clock above the fireplace showed 9.50 p.m. on my 78th day.

I had circumnavigated the globe in a little under one thousand eight hundred and eighty-two hours, and had returned to the Reform Club with thirty-eight hours and ten minutes to spare.

24

In which it is proved that the author has gained nothing by this tour of the world, unless it be Contentment.

It suited my cyclical temperament to have expended so much energy on reaching the very same place that I started out from. Altogether I had covered just under thirty thousand miles at an average speed of 375 miles per day. I had passed through thirty-eight different customs posts, crossed eleven seas and oceans, taken nine trains, ten ships, three rickshaws, one elephant, forty taxis and as many false turns.

In the course of the journey I had distributed more small coins as baksheesh than you would find at the bottom of an average wishing well; washed my teeth in more bottles of mineral water than are procurable in any Bavarian spa; been the target for more misinformation from passers-by than is freely available on the sidewalks of the New York Bowery; experienced more extremes of heat and cold than at a well equipped Surrey health hydro; paced the streets of more Chinatowns than there are Chinese in China; and seen more poor, emaciated loafers than you could hope to locate even in the depths of a Leicester Square amusement arcade.

Of the seventy-seven nights away from London, fifty-seven of them had been spent on moving vehicles, either train, ship or taxi. And now I was back at Square One.

No doubt it is possible to make the circuit still faster, if your schedule were devised by an international panel of statisticians from NATO, OPEC, NASA and the SAS. I imagine them monitoring the route on a huge relief map, of the type seen in films about the Battle of Britain, with wooden chocks representing Arab dhows and gale warnings chattering through on a telex. The Madras Mail's progress across India would have been tracked by satellite, and when the California Zephyr ran late a dozen branch lines would light up on a screen, indicating alternative connections by box-car. But if there is a small plastic man on the board — and a human being is required to realise his progress around the world — I hope above hope that the victim won't be me. Because I shall be altogether elsewhere: somewhere where visas are superfluous and water can be drunk straight from the jug; where exotic foreign vegetables are plumper and fresher than in the market at Port Sudan, and where a bottle of Stella Artois isn't simply a solution for washing down malaria tablets. And when I arrive at this place (having taken the precaution of booking a table first), I shall stay put. Because no wisdom from travel is quite so great as this certain knowledge: that you are holed up in the best of all possible places, in the best of all possible worlds.